YEADON'S REGISTER

of

L N E R

LOCOMOTIVES

Volume Thirty-Four

**Class NE 38, D17/1, D17/2, D18, D19, D20,
D21, D22, D23 & D24**

YEADON'S REGISTER OF L.N.E.R. LOCOMOTIVES - VOLUME 34.

EDITOR'S NOTE & ACKNOWLEDGEMENTS

It may have been noticed that with each sucessive volume of *Yeadon's Register* we are trying to keep each group of company locomotive types together. Where only one or perhaps two of a type exist in a certain company then they are included with other similar types from other companies. Of course it is not always possible to keep the same types or classifications together in one volume but sometimes we manage it and the result, sometimes, is a larger than normal volume. No.34 is one such tome as we have managed to keep all the North Eastern 4-4-0 tender engines together and, include also the Hull & Barnsley 4-4-0 tender engines, which were NER property for a short period before they became LNER Class D24

So, we present here ten classes of locomotive, including the two D17 sub classes or Parts thereof. The singleton NE 38 class engine No.281 has its repair history, and its only portrait, included within the Introduction section of the book. All the others, D17/1, D17/2, D18, D19, D20, D21, D22, D23, and D24 all have their own usual 'chapters', with well captioned illustrations. Some of the engines presented here worked far beyond their expected economic life and in many cases served three different owners over a long period in two separate centuries. Hence, the long histories of some and the copius illustrations showing each and virtually every change, major and minor, in their long lives.

Eric Fry continues to support the *Register* with his knowledge, enthusiasm and determined proof reading which weeds out typographical errors and expands some of the more obscure facts.

Typesetting numbers is one of the more difficult tasks of that particular branch of printing and we must thank Mike and Roy for their accuracy and persistence.

The Archive of the University of Hull is one of the more welcoming archives in the UK and the staff there, comprising Heather, Helen and Judy are always helpful, friendly and very patient. For those of you interested in the Yeadon section of the archive it is well worth a visit.

So, another volume is completed and hopefully the Registrar will be looking down on us with approving eyes. Having got thus far with the *Register* we are sure that some satisfaction and pride will be felt by Jean and Simon Taylor. Thanks to both of you for your continued support. Once again you the reader's keep us going and for that we convey our thanks. Without doubt we know that a certain Yorkshireman would be extremely happy knowing that so many of you get so much pleasure from this long running series.

The next *Yeadon's Register of LNER Locomotives*, Volume 35, contains the repair history of the Great Eastern J14 and J15 0-6-0 tender engines.

Material contained within this volume has the following catalogue references:
DYE/1/24; DYE/1/25; DYE/1/92.

> *The Yeadon Collection is available for inspection and anyone who wishes to*
> *inspect it should contact:-*
> The Archivist
> Brynmor Jones Library
> University of Hull
> Hull
> HU6 7RX
> Tel: 01482-465265
> A catalogue of the Yeadon collection is available.

First published in the United Kingdom by
BOOK LAW PUBLICATIONS 2004 in association with CHALLENGER
382 Carlton Hill, Nottingham, NG4 1JA.
Printed and bound by The Amadeus Press, Cleckheaton, West Yorkshire.

INTRODUCTION

NE 38

Originally this class consisted of twenty-eight engines built during 1884 and 1885. By Grouping only one engine, No.281, remained and its life as an LNER engine was measured in weeks as it was withdrawn on 16th February 1923, albeit nearly forty years old.

The class had been built in three batches, two batches of eight each from Gateshead works during 1884 and a batch of twelve from outside contractor R.& W. Hawthorn & Co. which were delivered towards the end of 1884 and into 1885. There was also to be a third batch from Gateshead but during construction the design was changed to an 0-6-0 side tank and no further '38' class engines were built.

Alexander McDonnell was responsible for the design of the North Eastern '38' class and the fact that his tenure of less than two years as the NER Chief Mechanical Engineer was evidence that these 4-4-0 engines were not what the Company required or indeed needed. There are many circumstances surrounding McDonnell's resignation and the reader is referred to a fuller story to be found within *Part 3C* of the RCTS publication *Locomotives of the LNER*. What the NER got was a 4-4-0 tender engine which was ideal for secondary duties when what they wanted was a 4-4-0 tender engine for hauling the heavy express passenger trains of the period.

No.281 was the only one of the twenty-eight Class '38' which the LNER took over and it was withdrawn as early as 16th February 1923. The class was built in 1884/1885 to McDonnell design and No.281 is substantially as taken over except that the small wing-plates at the base of the smokebox front had been removed.

281

Gateshead.

To traffic 12/1884.

REPAIRS:
Dar. ?/?—?/1/97.**G.**
Dar. ?/?—?/12/06.**G.**
Dar. ?/?—?/7/18.**G.**

BOILERS:
No boiler no. known.
D1282 *(new)* ?/1/97.
D1690 *(ex364)* ?/12/06.
 D754 *(new)* ?/7/18.

SHED:
York.

CONDEMNED: 16/2/23.

All the class were reboilered between 1895 and 1900 with the then standard Worsdell boilers which dimensionally were similar to the original boilers but had slightly more tubes.

Westinghouse brakes were fitted as standard but four of the engines allocated to York shed were also fitted with vacuum brakes; No.281, also a York engine, was not one of those so fitted and never did get a vacuum ejector.

Being relegated to secondary duties from the start, the class was used on all parts of the NER, most eventually finding their way to the Southern Division where the terrain was somewhat kinder.

D17/1 and D17/2

The tables within this volume concerning the D17/1 engines are separated from the D17/2 engines. Photographic coverage is separate but the introduction to the two parts is combined.

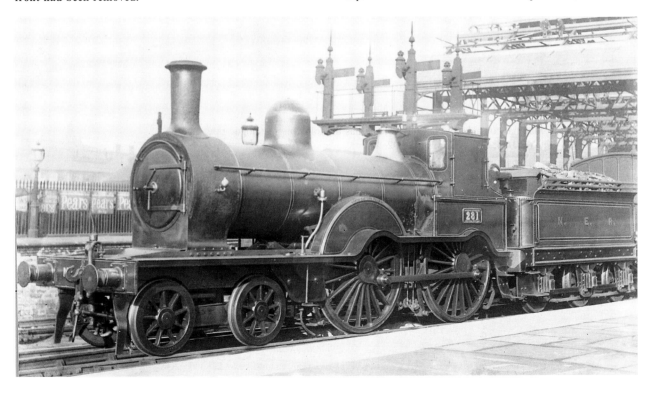

By Grouping, the engines consisting NER Class M, which went on to become LNER Class D17/1, numbered twenty engines, Nos.1620 to 1639, built at Gateshead between December 1892 and March 1894. The thirty engines of NER Class Q which, after 1923 became LNER Class D17/2, had also been erected at Gateshead in three separate batches of ten - Nos.1871 to 1880 in 1896, Nos.1901 to 1910 in 1897 and Nos.1921 to 1930 also in 1897.

Although of similar size, with 7ft 1¼ in. coupled wheels, the Class M and Q engines originally differed in a number of ways, Class M being unconventional in having the valves to their inside cylinders positioned on the outside of the engine frames (although driven by inside motion), whereas the Class Q engines had their valves inside. The boilers, using saturated steam, used on the two classes were not identical. An unimportant but very visible difference was that Class M had normal plain cab roofs, but Class Q were provided with an elegant clerestory section complete with side ventilation.

All but the last engine of the M class, No.1639, had flat valves for the cylinders whereas the last engine came out new with piston valves. From 1903 until 1908 these flat valves were gradually replaced by piston valves of an improved pattern, now inside the frames instead of outside. No.1639 was also brought into line during this period.

The next stage in the evolution of this class was superheating but that did not occur until March 1914 when No.1633 became the first of three engines to gain a superheated boiler that year. Most of the class were superheated by the NER but four of them were done by the LNER, the last three in 1929 some two years after the first withdrawal had occurred.

The thirty engines making up Class Q were all built with slide valves and these were replaced by new cylinders with piston valves of the same pattern as latterly fitted to Class M. Many of them were superheated at the same time as they were fitted with piston valves although the first ones to get piston valves fitted did not receive them until 1913 when Nos.1873 and 1924 both got piston valves and superheated boilers in October. Altogether twenty-three of the Q's got piston valves and superheating at the same shopping though not all of those were done by the NER. The other seven received them on separate occasions with the last superheating taking place in June 1931 when No.1929 was shopped; it had got its piston valves in August 1924. Long before Grouping the two classes shared the same boiler design which, in its superheated form, became LNER Diagram No.65.

All the engines were equipped with both Westinghouse and vacuum braking gear and were withdrawn in that condition.

The twenty Class M engines were built with tenders having a 3,940 gallon water capacity and able to carry five tons of coal, however these tenders were not equipped with water pick-up scoops at first whereas the thirty engines in Q class (except No.1871) had tenders fitted with such from new. On the other hand the tenders behind engines Nos.1872 to 1880 had a greatly reduced water capacity as they were not fitted with the 565 gallon well tank. Because of the important work carried out by the two classes in NER days the tenders were all brought up to the maximum capacity and fitted with water scoops. In the late 1930's instructions were issued for the removal of w.p.u. gear from this class as by then the work undertaken by the surviving engines had greatly diminished the need to top up tender tanks at high speed and besides, tender exchanges between classes had started in 1929.

From new, these engines were engaged on working the prestige trains of the ECML partnership with the class allocated to Gateshead and York sheds in England and outstationed to St

Margarets in Scotland. The twenty engines of Class M took a leading part in the 1895 'races' with No.1620 probably getting star billing, albeit with scant concern for safety at the time.

When the Class Q engines started to come into traffic in 1896 they took over many of the top jobs from the M class engines and so the latter started to be allocated to sheds where they had previously never been. Botanic Gardens at Hull was one shed where they were an immediate hit, being used on the fastest trains to Doncaster and Leeds. As locomotive development proceeded further on the ECML the Q class engines were in turn replaced on the top jobs and so the whole class of fifty engines were now working secondary, semi-fasts and main line services on all parts of the North Eastern system. By Grouping the D17/1's were dispersed to Hull, Gateshead, Tweedmouth and Alnmouth. The D17/2 engines could be found at Carlisle, West Hartlepool, Scarborough, Neville Hill, Gateshead and Starbeck. During the LNER years the engines were moved around again and sheds having them for the first time included Bridlington, Darlington, Middlesbrough, Newport, Northallerton, Selby, West Auckland. During the early part of 1927 No.1880 went for a three month stint at Cambridge whilst Nos.1927 and 1929 were hosted by Stratford during a motive power shortage on the GE Section. York shed housed the last two working engines using them on local services or on Inspection Saloon duties before their withdrawal.

Withdrawals had started as a whole in 1931 when three went for scrap although in 1927 No.1628 had been withdrawn because of accident damage at Hull. From 1932 up to the start of WW2 a total of thirty-seven D17's were condemned with seven more going during the conflict, amongst them was the last of the Part One engines, No.1629 which was withdrawn in September 1945. However, No.1621, which would have become LNER No.2108, was chosen for preservation in 1945 so that LNER Class D17 is now represented in the National Collection albeit in its North Eastern guise.

The two Part Two engines which survived the war miraculously lasted long enough to become BR engines, however, neither of the pair, Nos.2111 and 2112 (ex1873 and 1902), got BR numbers being withdrawn just weeks after nationalisation.

D18

Another class which appeared from Gateshead in 1896 was the Q1 class which consisted of just two engines, Nos.1869 and 1870. They had been equipped, for the sole purpose of taking part in the 'races' of the period, with the largest diameter coupled wheels, 7ft 7¼in., ever fitted to a locomotive running in Britain. But, as things turned out, the races of 1888 and 1895 were never to take place again - common sense had prevailed and the Victorian lust for biggest, fastest, longest, etc., had tempered. It might seem to us, in this day and age, that the building of two locomotives purely for racing along sections of the ECML on a daily basis was something of an extravagance on the part of the NER Directors but the glory involved in having the fastest trains between two points was at that time about as prestigious as it could get. The railways had yet to reach their heyday and they were still the fastest form of transport on the earth.

However, the big wheeled 4-4-0's would never be tested either in racing conditions nor, apparently, in test conditions which is a shame really as that coveted 100 m.p.h. figure might easily have been won by an LNER constituent long before the claims of that rambling line in the west of England.

Like the D17 class, this class also underwent change from slide to piston valves and superheating, No.1869 getting both at

Twenty engines, which formed LNER Class D17 Part 1, were built from December 1892 to March 1894. Numbered from 1620 to 1639, they were rebuilt between 1903 and 1908 with new cylinders which had piston valves above them. Superheating of the class began in 1914 but four were still saturated when they became LNER engines.

The thirty engines which made up LNER Class D17 Part 2 were built from June 1896 to November 1897 and numbered 1871 to 1880, 1901 to 1910 and 1921 to 1930. All differed from the Part 1 engines in having slide valves until October 1913 when the rebuilding to piston valves and superheating began.

The two engines which comprised LNER Class D18, Nos.1869 and 1870, were built in May and June 1896. By Grouping both had the same boiler as the D17 engines, No.1869 being superheated in March 1920 and No.1870 in March 1915. In September 1911 No.1870 had been rebuilt with piston valves and No.1869 got them in March 1920 but with 19in. cylinders whereas No.1870 got and kept, 20in. diameter cylinders. Both had, and retained the Ramsbottom safety valves, also NER design mechanical lubricator. They were fitted with Raven fog signalling apparatus, the striker being just behind the front edge of the leading coupled wheel. They differed however in their whistles, No.1869 keeping the normal bell-shaped pair.

the same shopping in 1920 whilst No.1870 had a four year interval between getting piston valves then superheating in March 1915.

When built these two engines had what might be termed non-standard boilers which no other engine could use, therefore when the time came to replace them it was decided to equip both engines with boilers fitted on the Q class engines. These were similar but had a firebox 3 inches shorter in length. No.1869 got a new saturated boiler in 1910 and in the following year No.1870 got a second hand saturated boiler whilst its slide valves were changed to piston valves. No.1870 was superheated in 1915 and No.1869 in 1920 when it too was given piston valve cylinders. When both engines were withdrawn in 1930, their Diagram 65 boilers went on to do further service with engines of both parts of Class D17.

The tenders built for these engines were the same as those built for the Class M 4-4-0's with a capacity of 3,940 gallons and five tons of coal, however, they differed in the fact that they were fitted with water scoops, the first such tenders attached to any North Eastern locomotive. Both tenders survived the engines at withdrawal (see also Appendix volume).

From new these two engines were allocated to Gateshead shed from where they worked the ECML express passenger services in both directions. However, by 1910 they were resident in Leeds where Neville Hill shed used them on trains to Hull, Scarborough and York and also northwards via the Harrogate route to Northallerton and Stockton.

Condemnation came to both engines in October 1930.

D19

This singular member of NER Class M was built by Wilson Worsdell in 1893 as a one-off two cylinder compound example of the North Eastern's simple Class M1 (LNER D17). Numbered 1619, the engine was put into traffic from Gateshead works at the same time as the Class M1 engines were also being turned out. Apparently it was successful enough to show a saving in coal consumption but Worsdell, who was instructed by the NER Board to build No.1619 in the first place, was not a great believer in compound traction. However, he did agree to further development of the compound system when the NER's Chief Draughtsman, W.M.Smith designed a three cylinder version which could be and was eventually applied to No.1619.

In August 1898 the engine left Gateshead works having been rebuilt with three cylinder compounding which comprised one high pressure cylinder inside the frames with two low pressure cylinders on the outside. To compliment the front end rebuilding, a new and larger boiler was installed. Even though the compounding did show savings in traffic, this 4-4-0 was the only one of its kind on the NER. Although two Atlantic types (see Volume 31) had been built as four cylinder compounds in 1906, Smith's death shortly afterwards allowed Worsdell to bury the further development of compounding ideas, at least on his railway and No.1619 carried on working in compound form for the North Eastern, and later the LNER, until its withdrawal in 1930.

The M classification of this engine was changed in 1914 to the self explanatory 3CC so that the M1 class 4-4-0's could become simply Class M.

Throughout its life No.1619 was in the passenger green livery of its owners, its 1930 demise enabling it to go for scrap in LNER green.

When new, No.1619 was stationed at Gateshead shed working the important Anglo-Scottish expresses in both

directions from Newcastle. At about the turn of the century it moved to Leeds from where it worked regularly on the expresses to Newcastle, then by 1907 it was at Botanic Gardens to work the secondary though important residential services between Hull and Bridlington. For its last four years of life it was resident at Bridlington shed working the same services to Hull besides those to Leeds and Selby.

D20

In its quest to handle successfully the increasingly heavier express passenger trains of the East Coast Main Line partnership between York and Edinburgh, the North Eastern Railway, through Wilson Worsdell, developed the Class R 4-4-0. At the time it had the largest diameter boiler of any previous NER design but most of the other dimensions involved were taken from existing classes although the coupled wheels were 6ft 10 ins. in diameter. Piston valves were fitted from new and this combination made for a good hard working locomotive capable of handling the heaviest expresses of the time.

Between August 1899 and May 1901 the North Eastern turned out thirty Class R 4-4-0s from Gateshead works. These thirty appeared in three batches of ten and the first twenty came out in strict numerical order: Nos.2011 to 2020, August to December 1899; Nos.2021 to 2030, August to December 1900. The last ten, which immediately followed the previous batch came out between December 1900 and May 1901 but their numbers, 2101 to 2110 broke the sequence.

From September to December 1906 ten more Class R engines appeared and these had a more random theme to their numbering: 476, 592, 707, 708, 711, 712, 713, 723, 724, 725. The final twenty engines, although turned out from Gateshead in a continuous sequence during 1907, were ordered in two batches of ten each. Their running numbers were allotted, and carried, accordingly as follows:

To Traffic	Works Nos.	Running Nos.
Feb. - June 1907	63 - 72	1026, 1042, 1147, 1206, 1209, 1217, 1232, 1234, 1236, 1260.
June - Sept. 1907	73 - 82	1051, 1078, 1184, 1207, 1210, 1223, 1235, 1258, 1665, 1672.

Note: No.1184 was wrongly shown in the printed North Eastern records as being put to traffic in January 1907 but the original entry in the NER Engine Register is hand written and shows June 1907 as the building date. The boiler put onto No.1184 when it was built was constructed in May 1907 and finally the works number also supports June. Therefore the table relating to No.1184 shows June 1907 as 'to traffic' date.

Superheating of sorts was fitted and tried to one of the class in 1907 when No.1235 appeared new with a longer smokebox than was normally fitted to the engines. The header fitted to this engine was a Sisterton type which after trials had proved it to be too small, a larger model was tried in 1909 only to be removed after a few months and until 1911 No.1235 kept the extended smokebox. In 1912 superheating of the class started in earnest but was not quite completed by Grouping and two engines had to be superheated by the LNER. For the superheating, the smokebox of all the engines in the class was extended. Both Robinson and Schmidt type superheaters were employed with the latter type being the favoured model during the NER period and early LNER years. However, from 1932 the Robinson type was employed on all the new Diagram 59 boilers carried by this

Built in 1893 as a two-cylinder compound, in 1898 it was used by chief draughtsman W.M. Smith for his patented 3-cylinder compound design of one high pressure cylinder between the frames and two outside low pressure cylinders. It remained the sole example on the North Eastern, but at Grouping there were four Atlantics on the Great Central and no less than forty-five compounds of the 4-4-0 type on the Midland Railway.

The first thirty engines which were to become LNER Class D20 were built between August 1899 and May 1901 numbered 2011 to 2030 and 2101 to 2110. Note they were non-superheated and neither were they fitted with the extra rail around coal space as this shows 1903 appearance.

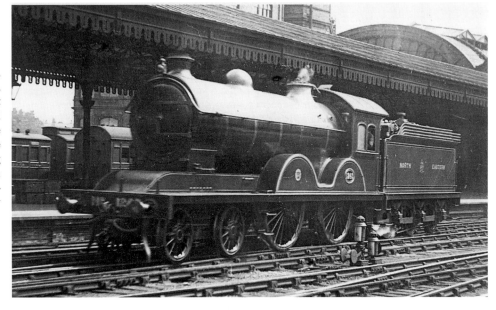

Ten engines, Nos.1237, 1238, 1239, 1240, 1241, 1242, 1243, 1244, 1245 and 1246 were built between November 1908 and August 1909. They were without superheaters so the smokebox was only 3ft 1in. long and they did not have steps on the front plate. All had four-column Ramsbottom safety valves. York.

class. All sixty of the original boilers were built at Gateshead with two spares made in 1903/4 and five more spares in 1910. Of these sixty-seven boilers, twenty-six subsequently had superheaters put in them. All had been cut up by 1929. Further boilers were constructed at Darlington, ten in 1911 (the first three were saturated but had Schmidt superheaters put in between 1916 and 1921, whilst the remaining seven had Robinson superheaters when new), five in 1913, ten during 1915 and 1916, eight in 1919, ten in 1923, and twenty-six more by February 1930. All had Schmidt superheaters except for the seven in 1911. Finally, eleven new boilers were made in the period 1932 to 1934 with Robinson superheaters. Darlington had constructed a total of eighty Diagram 59 boilers between 1911 and 1934. Thereafter the design was changed to the 59A pattern.

When the redesigned Diagram 59A boiler was introduced in November 1935, Robinson superheaters were used in all thirty-eight of those built up to June 1949. When boiler redesign began at Darlington in 1935, the D20 class was the first to be tackled. A single plate barrel was used but the position of the dome was unchanged. There was a very minor change in the position of the 'pop' safety valves, which were mounted directly on the firebox so that no cover was needed around the base. Both Diagram 59 and 59A boilers could be easily interchanged within the D20 class but no other class could accommodate them. Altogether forty-five D20's carried a 59A boiler at one time or another. Some engines reverted to the Diagram 59 type. The first eight Diag.59A boilers had the same size dome as Diag.59, but from September 1943 further 59A boilers had dome covers of larger diameter but not so tall.

In October 1936, at a time when Edward Thompson was Mechanical Engineer at Darlington, No.2020 appeared rebuilt with new cylinders incorporating long travel piston valves. The engines was then thirty-seven years old and in addition to a Diagram 59A boiler it was given new frames. Its appearance was changed by raising the running plate over the coupled wheels and doing away with the large combined splasher. A new cab was fitted and many other parts were also renewed, even the entire body of the tender. It was also converted to left hand drive. Although it became a more efficient machine, to most eyes No.2020's appearance was not improved.

No more D20's were similarly altered until after Gresley died in April 1941 and Thompson succeeded him. Almost immediately Thompson issued instructions to Darlington works to convert the rest of the class, but as it was wartime only the cylinders and motion were replaced (plus a change to left hand drive), the outward appearance to remain unaltered. Nos.592 and 2101 were so converted in October and December 1942 respectively and at the same time these two and No.2020 were given the classification D20/2. Due to war such conversion was then halted. However, material was in hand and No.62375 (ex 712) joined D20/2 in October 1948, but the Railway Executive stopped any further conversions of these then elderly engines.

The D20 tenders were all of similar pattern and carried five tons of coal. The water capacity was 3537 gallons for the first twenty constructed. A larger well tank for the remainder increased this figure to 3940 gallons and some of the earlier tenders were altered to correspond. Only two coal rails were at first provided on the first examples, but this became three with a fourth around the coal space, with backing plates.

When No.2020's tender was rebuilt in October 1936 its new body held five tons of coal and 3600 gallons of water. It uniquely had a solid coping with stepped out sides and back. this tender remained attached to No.2020 until withdrawal as No.62349 in February 1956.

Between May 1949 and June 1950 ten of the tenders running with Class D20 engines were given completely new bodies. They had flush sides with an upper profile not unlike LNER Group Standard designs and held $6\frac{1}{4}$ tons of coal and 3900 gallons of water. No water pick up gear was fitted, this feature having been removed from all D20 tenders between 1937 and 1945.

Westinghouse braking for the engine and train was supplemented with a vacuum ejector for alternative train braking. Only one engine, No.2020 when rebuilt in 1936, lost its Westinghouse brake and was converted to vacuum for engine and train. The other D20/2 rebuilds were not thus altered. All the class eventually lost the Westinghouse connection at the front end, but the short standpipe on the tender remained fitted to most of them until withdrawal, even on the ten rebuilt tenders.

These locomotives, the North Eastern's most famous class of 4-4-0, fell victim to the LNER 1928 economy campaign and lost their green livery thereafter. Black became their garb, unlined from 1941 onwards, none received lining in BR days.

When the LNER 1946 renumbering scheme had been formulated in July 1943 two of the 1907 built D20's had already been withdrawn. The remaining fifty-eight were allotted new numbers 2340 to 2397 in order of construction. However, the eighteen survivors of the two 1907 built batches were given new numbers 2380 to 2397 in numerical order (rather than in order of construction) as if they had been built as a single series. Therefore this Register presents the engines in that LNER order; hence the works numbers and dates to traffic are not shown in a chronological sequence.

As mentioned earlier, these engines were built to power the heavy express passenger trains on the ECML. Their lifetime mileage's are testament to their reliability and virtually up to Grouping they had charge of most of the important passenger trains on or passing over the NER. Gateshead and York sheds had the largest allocations of the class with about fifteen each whilst others were found at Heaton, Haymarket and Neville Hill. At the start of the LNER period Gateshead and York still had the lion's share of the D20's but the class had by now been more widely distributed, having lost a lot of their main line work to the growing fleet of Pacifics and the large number of Atlantics. The appearance of the D49's in the mid 1920's brought a further reduction in main line work and an increasing number of sheds began to take the D20's onto their books. Whereas in 1920 only about half a dozen sheds shared them, by 1935 this number had risen to a dozen and this remained virtually the norm for the class until withdrawal. Although most of their LNER work was on secondary services, they remained reliable engines and still capable of both speed and strength. By 1957, after an illustrious fifty year working life, the D20 class became extinct with the withdrawal of the last six engines (all survivors of the 1906 and 1907 batches) from Alnmouth shed.

D21

The largest of the North Eastern 4-4-0 tender engines, the ten members of NER Class R1 (Nos.1237 to 1246) had been built at Darlington between November 1908 and August 1909. Worsdell built this class to supplement his Atlantics (LNER C6 and C8) on the heavier ECML passenger expresses.

The new engines were scaled up versions of Class R but had the same size cylinders and coupled wheels of that class with a boiler similar to the Atlantic design. The boiler type (LNER Diag. 60) was not used by any other class and so these engines did not enjoy as long a life as most other NER 4-4-0's.

6

Superheating began in August 1912 and was completed by July 1915 by fitting the ten original boiler with Schmidt superheaters and constructing two new boilers fitted with Robinson superheaters. When the time came in 1920 and 1921 to build new boilers for the class, Schmidt superheaters were used throughout; even the two boilers fitted with the Robinson type were superseded in 1930 by two new boilers fitted with Schmidt superheaters. These were the last Diag. 60 boilers built.

After June 1928 when the class ceased to be painted green, they still presented an imposing appearance in red-lined black livery, especially when kept clean.

During 1941 all the class changed their large 4,125 gallon North Eastern tenders which were fitted with water scoops, for former Great Northern tenders. However, this exercise involved more than just coupling up a different tender because the GNR type were equipped for vacuum braking so the Westinghouse equipment was removed from the engines and the vacuum brake was substituted. Because of a shortage of steel, the D21's NER tenders were needed by Darlington works to put behind newly built J39's.

The D21's spent much of their pre-Group existence allocated to York and Neville Hill sheds from where they performed mostly on the heavy slower timed expresses. By Grouping the situation was much the same but within a couple of years, and with the introduction of Gresley's Pacifics on the ECML, these engines were redistributed so that by early 1926 Neville Hill had four, Starbeck had two and the shed where everything not needed on the ECML seemed to end up, Hull Botanic Gardens, also had four. The latter shed used them on the heavier Liverpool expresses as far as Sheffield, also on the Leeds trains and even as far as Nottingham. Within five years the D21's were concentrated at Neville Hill (8) and Starbeck (2) and for the rest of their lives they worked only from these two sheds.

Three of the ten engines were withdrawn before they could be listed in the 1943 renumbering scheme and the seven survivors were allocated numbers 2217 to 2223 in order of building. But, in the event none of them lasted long enough to have the new LNER numbers applied and so they were cut-up as they were built with North Eastern numbers.

Relegated to secondary duties from the early 1930's, the class soldiered on into WW2 before withdrawals took place, the first of which occurred in December 1942. Two engines lasted until 1946 but when No.1245 was condemned in February, D21 class was extinct. In 1943 after withdrawal during the war of No.1241 undertook one last duty for its country when it was given a coat of white paint, towed all the way to Pembrokeshire where it was used for target practice by the RAF. Full of holes, it was returned to Darlington to be scrapped.

D22

The thirty-seven engines which made up LNER Class D22 had been built between 1886 and 1891 in both 2-4-0 and 4-4-0 wheel arrangements, also as simple and compound engines embraced by three separate North Eastern Railway classifications - D, F and F1. All had 6ft 8in. coupled wheels and were of the same general dimensions.

T.W.Worsdell was responsible for their design and all were constructed at Gateshead works. The first engine to appear was Class D 2-4-0 No.1324 in late 1886. It was a two-cylinder compound with the cylinders between the frames, driven by Joy valve gear and proved to be unsteady at speed due to the dissimilar size of its cylinders. Ten more compound engines were turned out in 1887, classified F, and these had a leading bogie. Later

that year, for comparison, another ten 4-4-0's, classified F1, were built and these used simple expansion. Then, at the end of 1888, a second Class D 2-4-0, No.340, was built. This was like the pioneer engine but had an experimental set of piston valves. Finally, during 1890-91 fifteen more Class F compound 4-4-0's were turned out. Construction is summarised as follows:-

Class	Type	Built	Running Nos.
D	compound 2-4-0	1886	1324.
F	compound 4-4-0	1887	18, 42, 115, 117, 355, 514, 779, 663, 356*, 684.
F1	simple 4-4-0	1887	230, 673, 777, 803, 808, 96, 1137, 85, 154, 194.
D	compound 2-4-0	1888	340.
F	compound 4-4-0	1890/91	1532 to 1546.

No.356 was numbered 1 prior to 1st January 1914.

Wilson Worsdell took over as Chief Mechanical Engineer of the NER in 1890. Six years later he began the rebuilding of his brother's class D, F and F1 engines into a single class based on the F1 4-4-0 simple expansion design, but with piston valves and Stephenson link motion. The first to be rebuilt were the two Class D 2-4-0's, converted to 4-4-0 in 1896. The main period of rebuilding was 1900-11 for the Class F and F1 engines, the compounds being changed to simple and all getting the new cylinder layout with piston valves. Thus by 1911 all thirty-seven engines were to one homogeneous design and from 1914 were known simply as Class F.

The next stage in the life of this class was superheating which took place from September 1913 to June 1920, no doubt the advent of war slowing the process somewhat.

Westinghouse brake for engine and train was provided throughout their career, Nos.1532-46 being additionally fitted with vacuum ejectors for alternative train braking when new. Four more engines, Nos.340, 777, 808 and 1324, were given vacuum ejectors before Grouping. During the LNER period, and to comply with the Unification of Brakes requirement, nine more of the class were fitted with vacuum ejectors whilst nine others never got them, being scrapped before fitting.

The capacity of the tenders attached to the engines built during 1886-88 was quoted as four tons of coal and 2651 gallons of water. The tenders built in 1890-91 held five tons of coal and 3038 gallons of water, the latter obtained by fitting well tanks. The earlier tenders were later rebuilt to correspond. Two coal rails were at first provided, a third with a fourth around the coal space being added later to some of the tenders although eight never carried these additions.

Lined passenger green was the livery at Grouping but this class became victims of the LNER painting economies and those that survived long enough were turned out in lined black livery.

The majority of the class spent most of their working lives in Yorkshire, particularly East Yorkshire. Hull Botanic Gardens shed, from where many D22's worked all their lives, had a large allocation of the class throughout the LNER period. Carlisle had three of the class prior to Grouping which it kept until their withdrawal. Only a few examples worked from Tyneside sheds and north thereof. No.777 spent the first four months of 1927 in East Anglia working from both Ipswich and Norwich sheds, whilst No.1540 had a similar 'holiday' at Cambridge shed. Both returned to Botanic Gardens from whence they came. However, the 'pathfinder' for these sojourns onto former Great Eastern territory was Selby's No.1544 which moved to Ipswich in December 1926 and returned home via Norwich in April 1927.

The first withdrawal was due to an accident in 1927 but two years later condemnations started in earnest when eight of the class were withdrawn; eleven more went for scrap in 1930 and by November 1935 the last of the class, No.1537, had arrived at Darlington for scrapping.

D23

Twenty 6ft 1¼ in. engines which made up NER Class G1 (Class G from 1914), were built at Darlington during 1887 and 1888 to the design of T.W.Worsdell for secondary services on the railway. Typically, the engines took up the random vacant NER numbers and these consisted the following, in order of building: 557, 678, 675, 23, 274, 676, 677, 679, 258, 328, 222, 223, 337, 521, 1120, 214, 217, 372, 472 and 1107.

Initially 2-4-0's, all the class were rebuilt to 4-4-0 standard between 1900 and 1904. At the same time piston valves and Stephenson motion replaced the original Joy motion and slide valves. 18in. cylinders took the place of the 17in. diameter cylinders they had been built with. Later, from 1913 to 1916 all the class were superheated, the final major change before Grouping when they became LNER Class D23. Both Robinson and Schmidt headers were used in superheating the class, roughly on a 50/50 proportion. These boilers were now compatible with the boilers used on the 0-6-0's which became LNER Class J24 but few exchanges, if any, were made until 1929 when a couple transferred between the two classes. As the engines were condemned from 1929 onwards, their boilers were cut up with them and none were put aside as spares for the J24's.

During 1928 and 1929, all but three of the class (23, 214 and 676) had vacuum ejectors fitted to complement the Westinghouse equipment.

This class retained their original tenders from building, through rebuilding and on to withdrawal and except for the addition of a well tank, to increase their water capacity to just over 3,000 gallons, the tenders were subject to detail changes only, such as extra coal rails and then plating around the coal space.

During North Eastern days, both before and after rebuilding, the class was mainly concentrated in Yorkshire with Hull Botanic Gardens shed having the lion's share of them. However, immediately after Grouping some transferred to the Darlington area and a few years later a couple migrated even further north to Duns and Tweedmouth. In 1928 Botanic Gardens had only two of the class compared with sixteen prior to 1923 and the single examples at Bradford Manningham and Malton completed the Yorkshire complement; by the end of the following year Hull had none. On the other hand Darlington had eight of them in 1928. Withdrawals started in 1929 and in 1935 the last of the class, No.1120, was condemned but it was allocated to what was by then an LMS shed - Bradford Manningham.

At Grouping the whole class were running in full NER lined green livery but under the LNER the small size of their coupled wheels ruled out express passenger livery and they all changed to black by 1925.

D24

In December 1910 five new 4-4-0 passenger tender engines were delivered by Kitson & Co. to the Hull & Barnsley Railway which classified them 'J'. These engines took the numbers of the five smaller 2-4-0 engines they were replacing: 33, 35, 38, 41 and 42. The earlier engines then went on the Duplicate List but did not survive to Grouping. The coupled wheels of the new 4-4-0's were 6ft 6in. diameter and the domeless boiler, which was unsuperheated, was compatible with the Company's 0-6-0 tender engines and had the same LNER Diagram number, 58A.

Twenty years after they were built, new saturated domed boilers, to Diagram 58B, were made and fitted at Darlington to all five engines. These boilers too were compatible with Class J28 and in fact had been designed specifically for the 0-6-0's. At withdrawal of the D24's, these boilers found further use as stationery boilers although one of them went to Class J28 for four years before joining the others 'on the ground'.

Although becoming North Eastern engines in 1922, none were fitted with Westinghouse pumps and kept their original vacuum brakes until withdrawal.

When they became LNER property four of the five retained their H&BR green livery for a short time before they got the LNER passenger green livery. Prior to Grouping No.3038 (2427) had been painted in NER green and it kept that paint until late 1925 when it too was painted in the LNER green. When the 1928 painting economies took effect, this class were designated to become black painted engines with single red lining.

The usual work for this class during H&BR days up to 1917 consisted the haulage of the express passenger services from Hull (Cannon Street) to Sheffield (Midland). However, this service was cut back during WW1 to Cudworth and then in 1924 it started from Paragon station in Hull as the H&BR station was closed to passenger traffic. Later the service was cut back still further to terminate at South Howden - hardly a decent job for a large 4-4-0 passenger engine still in its prime. As no reasonable work could be found for them, the D24's went into store at the old H&BR works at Springhead. During the previous twenty years prior to being laid off, the D24's had also been used for long and medium distance excursion work, some reaching the west coast at such places as Blackpool, Morecambe and even Llandudno. During LNER days Botanic Gardens shed used them on regular service trains to Doncaster, Scarborough and York.

Never the most handsome of engines, the D24's were not amongst the most numerous either and so when the world-wide economic downturn took a grip of the United Kingdom in the early 1930's it was inevitable that the five ex H&BR 4-4-0's would be amongst those engines whose services were no longer needed. After a period in store, mainly inside Springhead works, the first of the class (2425) was withdrawn in August 1933, two more (2426 and 2428) followed in December and right behind them went No.2427 in January 1934. No.2429, by some miracle, clung on until the following September when it was scrapped and D24 class became extinct.

Of the thirty-seven engines in the D22 class, twenty-seven had been built as 2-cylinder compounds of North Eastern classes D and F. The other ten were simples - Class F1. Between October 1896 and June 1911 all were given new cylinders with piston valves, the compounds being converted to simple expansion in the process and all thirty-seven were then substantially alike. From June 1914 all were classified as F.

Twenty engines which became LNER Class D23 were built from November 1887 to November 1888 as 2-4-0 type but were all rebuilt to 4-4-0 between December 1900 and August 1904.

Five engines, Hull & Barnsley Railway Nos.33, 35, 38, 41 and 42 were built by Kitson & Co., Leeds, in 1910 and taken over by North Eastern Railway from 1st April 1922.

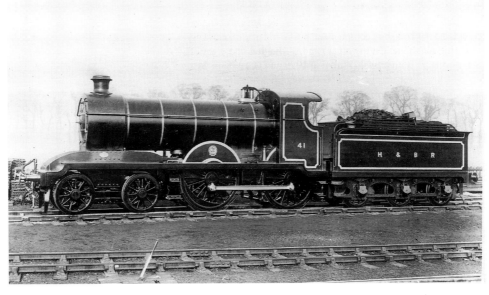

At Grouping, Nos.1624, 1631, 1634 and 1638 were still without superheater and although No.1638 got one in May 1924, the other three were not so fitted until as late as 1929 - No.1631 in January, 1634 in August and 1624 in November. No.1631 kept the original style chimney without a windjabber until 1928.

(above) Engines with a superheater, which were all of Schmidt type, had an extended smokebox and a steam circulating control valve on its left hand side for element protection. The boiler feed was normally by a live steam injector on each side to a clack box below the dome. Goswick 1927.

(left) On some of the boilers an exhaust steam injector on the left hand side took the place of the live steam type, no feed pipe or clack box then being in evidence. No.1621 had one of these boilers from August 1937 to April 1940. Alnmouth, 11th August 1939.

CLASS D 17/1

1620

Gateshead 39.92.

To traffic 12/1892.

REPAIRS:
???. ?/?—?/12/03.**G.**
New cylinders and piston valves.
???. ?/?—?/10/17.**G.**
Superheated boiler fitted.
Dar. 12/1—19/4/23.**G.**
Dar. 6/3—29/5/25.**G.**
Dar. 4/8—28/10/27.**G.**
Dar. 18/2—12/4/30.**G.**
Dar. 29/3—11/5/32.**G.**
Dar. 30/1/34. *Not repaired.*

BOILERS:
G477.
G276 *(new)* ?/12/03.
G963 *(ex spare)* ?/10/17.
G948 *(ex1910)* 19/4/23.
D1981 *(new)* 28/10/27.

SHEDS:
Hull Botanic Gardens.
Bridlington 23/10/33.

CONDEMNED: 5/2/34.
*C.M.E. 9018 History Sheet is
marked 'To be sent to York
Museum LR/1/1/1 30/12/33',
but engine was actually cut up
10/3/34, the tender on 2/11/35.*

1621

Gateshead 1.93.

To traffic 3/1893.

REPAIRS:
???. ?/?—?/8/05. **?.**
Piston valves fitted.
???. ?/?—?/2/09.**G.**
???. ?/?—?/4/14.**G.**
Superheated boiler fitted.
???. ?/?—?/7/21.**G.**
Ghd. 16/5—23/7/23.**G.**
Ghd. 26/2—13/5/24.**G.**
Ghd. 10/7—15/8/24.**H.**
Ghd. 27/2—12/3/25.**L.**
Ghd. 27/7—7/10/27.**G.**
Ghd. 26/11—7/12/28.**L.**
Ghd. 27/3—19/5/30.**G.**

Ghd. 29/7—12/9/32.**G.**
Dar. 2/1—18/2/35.**G.**
Dar. 25/6—20/8/37.**G.**
Dar. 18/4—17/5/40.**G.**
Dar. 18/2—5/3/41.
Change tender.
Dar. 28/12/42—13/2/43.**G.**
Dar. 7—28/7/45.
Restored for Museum.

BOILERS:
G478.
G645 *(new)* ?/2/09.
G404 *(ex1926)* ?/4/14.
G783 *(exD18 1869)* ?/7/21.
D1980 *(new)* 7/10/27.
D814 *(ex1929)* 18/2/35.
D1657 *(ex1624)* 20/8/37.
D1848 *(ex1636)* 17/5/40.
2321 *(from spare)* 13/2/43.

SHEDS:
Gateshead.
Tweedmouth ?/12/24.
Selby 18/5/25.
Tweedmouth 19/1/26.
Alnmouth ?/1/27.

RENUMBERED:
2108 allocatted.

WITHDRAWN: 28/7/45.

1622

Gateshead 2.93.

To traffic 4/1893.

REPAIRS:
???. ?/?—?/6/06.**G.**
???. ?/?—?/6/08.**G.**
Piston valves fitted.
???. ?/?—?/11/13.**G.**
???. ?/?—?/8/15.**G.**
Superheated boiler fitted.
???. ?/?—?/4/20.**G.**
Dar. 4/9—19/11/23.**G.**
Dar. 9/1—27/3/25.**G.**
Dar. 24/9—16/12/27.**G.**
Dar. 20/11—5/2/30.**G.**
Dar. 10/5—21/6/32.**G.**
Dar. 12/2/35. *Not repaired.*

BOILERS:
G479.

G494 *(ex1635)* ?/6/06.
G571 *(new)* ?/6/08.
G569 *(ex1629)* ?/11/13.
G277 *(ex1626)* ?/8/15.
D795 *(new)* ?/4/20.

SHEDS:
Hull Botanic Gardens.
Bridlington ?/?/25.

CONDEMNED: 4/3/35.

1623

Gateshead 3.93.

To traffic 5/1893.

REPAIRS:
???. ?/?—?/3/06.**G.**
???. ?/?—?/6/08. **?.**
Piston valves fitted.
???. ?/?—?/6/15.**G.**
Superheated boiler fitted.
Dar. 25/5—10/8/23.**G.**
Dar. 18/9—24/12/25.**G.**
Dar. 28/7—13/8/26.**L.**
Dar. 20/1—18/4/28.**G.**
Dar. 12—25/5/28.**N/C.**
Dar. 30/6—23/9/30.**G.**

BOILERS:
G480.
G280 *(new)* ?/3/06.
D296 *(new)* ?/6/15.

SHED:
Hull Botanic Gardens.

CONDEMNED: 21/5/32.

1624

Gateshead 5.93.

To traffic 6/1893.

REPAIRS:
???. ?/?—?/2/06. **?.**
Piston valves fitted.
???. ?/?—?/7/08.**G.**
???. ?/?—?/8/21.**G.**
Ghd. 7—14/11/23.**L.**
Ghd. 15/3—19/6/24.**G.**
Ghd. 19/4—27/8/26.**G.**

Ghd. 23/7—14/11/29.**G.**
Superheated boiler fitted.
Ghd. 16/3—22/4/32.**G.**
Dar. 20/11/34—14/1/35.**G.**
Dar. 24/1—14/2/35.**N/C.**
Dar. 27/5—10/7/37.**G.**
Dar. 9/11/38. *Not repaired..*

BOILERS:
G482.
G572 *(new)* ?/7/08.
D50 *(ex1908)* ?/8/21.
D774 *(ex1901)* 14/11/29.
D1657 *(ex1879)* 14/1/35.
2169 *(ex1876)* 10/7/37.

SHEDS:
Tweedmouth.
Alnmouth 8/3/28.

CONDEMNED: 9/11/38.

1625

Gateshead 6.93.

To traffic 6/1893.

REPAIRS:
???. ?/?—?/8/06.**G.**
Piston valves fitted.
???. ?/?—?/1/16.**G.**
Superheated boiler fitted.
Ghd. 26/2—26/5/24.**G.**
Ghd. 2/3—10/6/26.**G.**
Ghd. 23/3—15/6/28.**G.**
Ghd. 27/2—27/3/29.**L.**
Ghd. 25/1—14/3/30.**G.**

BOILERS:
G483.
G282 *(new)* ?/8/06.
G396 *(new)* ?/1/16.

SHEDS:
Gateshead.
Alnmouth ?/12/24.

CONDEMNED: 3/10/32.

WORKS CODES:- Cw - Cowlairs. Dar- Darlington. Don - Doncaster. Ghd - Gateshead. Gor - Gorton. Inv - Inverurie. Nor - Norwich. Str - Stratford.
REPAIR CODES:- **C/H** - Casual Heavy. **C/L** - Casual Light. **G**- General. **H**- Heavy. **H/I** - Heavy Intermediate. **L** - Light. **L/I** - Light Intermediate. **N/C** - Non-Classified.

11

It was customary for the chimney to carry a capuchon or 'windjabber' in North Eastern parlance, all except No.1631 being so fitted at Grouping.

By 1937/1938 No.1624's windjabber had diminished due to corrosion as to be almost non-existent.

On the majority, the safety valves were Ramsbottom type enclosed in a brass trumpet shaped casing.

Only on replacement boilers built between 1927 and 1929 were the Ross 'pop' type fitted. No.1624 had one of these boilers from July 1937 to its withdrawal on 9th November 1938. None ever carried Gresley anti-vacuum valves even with these 1927-1929 boilers.

Normal whistles were two bell-shaped type over the cab roof. A smaller one on the left-hand side gave a shrill note for the guard to apply his brake. A larger one on the driver's side was used for normal warnings. Scarborough, 6th May 1931.

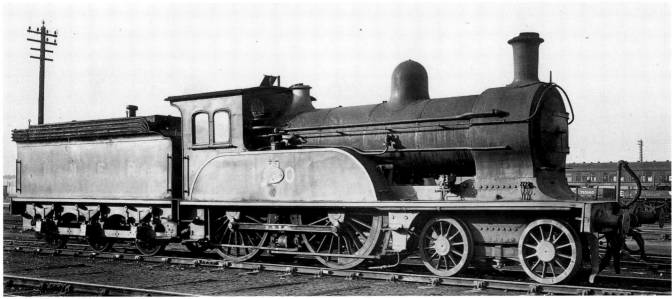

There were some odd variations of whistles. No.1620 changed its left-hand whistle to an organ pipe. No.1623 (*see* photo 31 page XX) changed its right hand one to an organ pipe, whereas No.1627 (*see* page 14) had its whistle sizes reversed. Darlington.

When No.1623 changed whistles the organ pipe was put on the right hand side (as on 1620 - *see* opposite, middle) but not as 1620 in the previous view on page 13.

On No.1627 in 1927 the two whistles had been transposed, the larger one having been put on the fireman's side. Note that the original style chimney without a windjabber is still fitted. Carlisle.

The front end of the engine had a sandwich type buffer beam and taper shank buffers with circular flange. Gateshead, August 1938.

About 1930 Nos.1621, 1624 and 1632 were changed to the Group Standard type buffers which had a square flange and a larger diameter head. York, 1936.

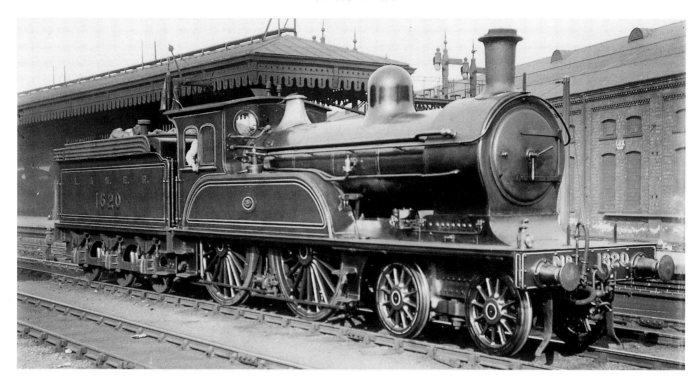

(above) **There was no consistency in the method of fastening the smokebox door. At 1923 there were about half the class with twin handles. York.**

(right) **By April 1930 No.1620 had changed to the other type with wheel and handle.**

Until October 1933, Raven fog signalling apparatus was fitted. The striker for it can be seen just ahead of the front-coupled wheel. King's Cross, 9th August 1924.

1626

Gateshead 7.93.

To traffic 6/1893.

REPAIRS:
???. ?/?—?/4/04.**G.**
Piston valves fitted.
???. ?/?—?/2/15.**G.**
Superheated boiler fitted.
Dar. 7/3—31/5/23.**G.**
Dar. 22/12/25—9/6/26.**G.**
Dar. 26/1—30/3/28.**G.**
Dar. 30/7—27/9/29.**G.**
Dar. 19/10—30/11/31.**G.**

BOILERS:
 G484.
 G277 *(new)* ?/4/04.
 G645 *(ex1621)* ?/2/15.
 G963 *(ex1620)* 31/5/23.
 D1841 *(new)* 9/6/26.

SHEDS:
Hull Botanic Gardens.
Bridlington 1/3/32.

CONDEMNED: 17/5/34.

1627

Gateshead 8.93.

To traffic 6/1893.

REPAIRS:
???. ?/?—?/4/06.**G.**
???. ?/?—?/12/07. **?.**
Piston valves fitted.
???. ?/?—?/2/10.**G.**
???. ?/?—?/6/20.**G.**
Superheated boiler fitted.
???. ?/?—28/8/22.**?.**
Ghd. 10/4—21/6/23.**G.**
Ghd. 24/11/26—2/3/27.**G.**
Dar. 13—29/8/29.**N/C.**
Ghd. 29/8—16/10/30.**G.**

BOILERS:
G485.
G498 *(ex1638)* ?/4/06.
G649 *(new)* ?/2/10.
D809 *(new)* ?/6/20.

SHEDS:
Tweedmouth.
Alnmouth 8/3/28.

CONDEMNED: 12/12/33.

1628

Gateshead 9.93.

To traffic 6/1893.

REPAIRS:
???. ?/?—?/3/05.**G.**
???. ?/?—?/11/06. **?.**
Piston valves fitted.
???. ?/?—?/8/11.**G.**
???. ?/?—?/6/15.**G.**
Superheated boiler fitted.
???. ?/?—?/10/22.**G.**
Dar. 19/6—17/7/23.**L.**
Dar. 18/2—20/5/25.**G.**

BOILERS:
 G486.
 G283 *(new)* ?/3/05.
 G971 *(new)* ?/8/11.
 G427 *(ex spare)* ?/6/15.
D1404 *(new)* ?/10/22.

SHEDS:
Hull Botanic Gardens.
Bridlington ?/?/25.

CONDEMNED: 20/4/27.
*Due to head-on collision with
No.96 outside Hull (Paragon)
station, 14/2/27.*

1629

Gateshead 10.93.

To traffic 6/1893.

REPAIRS:
???. ?/?—?/11/07.**G.**
???. ?/?—?/12/08. **?.**
Piston valves fitted.
???. ?/?—?/4/13.**G.**
???. ?/?—?/6/16.**G.**
Superheated boiler fitted.
Dar. 12/1—28/4/23.**G.**
Dar. 10/2—28/7/26.**G.**
Dar. 5/9—13/11/28.**G.**
Dar. 15/4—29/5/31.**G.**
Dar. 6—14/8/31.**N/C.**
Dar. 30/1—28/5/34.**G.**
Dar. 3/5—15/6/37.**G.**
Dar. 22/11/41—6/1/42.**G.**
Dar. 23/8/45. *Not repaired.*

BOILERS:
 G487.
 G569 *(new)* ?/11/07.
 G278 *(ex1639)* ?/4/13.
 D398 *(new)* ?/6/16.
 D1641 *(ex1924)* 28/5/34.
 D1841 *(ex1905)* 15/6/37.

SHEDS:
Hull Botanic Gardens.
Bridlington ?/?/25.
Hull Botanic Gardens 18/9/39.
Neville Hill 1/6/40.
Selby 17/8/40.
Darlington 2/2/42.
West Auckland 14/2/42.
Middlesbrough 18/5/42.
Newport 25/11/43.

RENUMBERED:
2109 allocated.

CONDEMNED: 12/9/45.

1630

Gateshead 11.93.

To traffic 6/1893.

REPAIRS:
???. ?/?—?/7/08.**G.**
Piston valves fitted.
???. ?/?—?/2/12.**G.**
???. ?/?—?/11/16.**G.**
Superheated boiler fitted.
Dar. 3—26/1/23.**L.**
Dar. 9/1—25/3/24.**G.**
Dar. 25/11/25—30/4/26.**G.**
Dar. 16/5—30/6/28.**G.**
Dar. 17/11/30—13/1/31.**G.**

BOILERS:
G488.
G570 *(new)* ?/7/08.
G283 *(ex1628)* ?/2/12.
D399 *(new)* ?/11/16.
D779 *(exD18 1869)* 13/1/31.

SHEDS:
Hull Botanic Gardens.
Bridlington ?/?/25.

CONDEMNED: 9/12/33.

1631

Gateshead 12.93.

To traffic 6/1893.

REPAIRS:
???. ?/?—?/5/03.**G.**
???. ?/?—?/2/04. **?.**
Piston valves fitted.
???. ?/?—?/11/08.**G.**
???. ?/?—?/4/11.**G.**
Ghd. ?/?—15/9/22.**G.**
Ghd. 10—24/12/23.**L.**
Ghd. 8/5—18/9/25.**G.**

Ghd. 3—7/2/28.**L.**
Ghd. 9/11/28—9/1/29.**G.**
Superheated boiler fitted.
Dar. 7/4—26/5/31.**G.**
Dar. 30/12/32—2/3/33.**G.**
Dar. 1—12/9/33.**L.**
Dar. 26/6/34. *Not repaired.*

BOILERS:
G489.
G275 *(new)* ?/5/03.
G489 *(ex1638)* ?/11/08.
G945 *(new)* ?/4/11.
 2162 *(new)* 9/1/29.
D1390 *(ex1908)* 2/3/33.

SHEDS:
Gateshead.
Selby 31/12/29.

CONDEMNED: 5/7/34.

1632

Gateshead 13.93.

To traffic 9/1893.

REPAIRS:
???. ?/?—?/4/04. **?.**
Piston valves fitted.
???. ?/?—?/1/12.**G.**
???. ?/?—?/9/20.**G.**
Superheated boiler fitted.
Ghd. 30/11/22—2/3/23.**G.**
Ghd. 13/11—8/12/24.**L.**
Ghd. 27/1—15/7/27.**G.**
Ghd. 2/8/29—22/1/30.**G.**
Dar. 28/1—4/2/30.**N/C.**
Dar. 28/6—9/8/32.**G.**
Dar. 2/7—17/8/35.**G.**
Dar. 15/2—16/3/37.**L.**
Dar. 3/11/37. *Not repaired.*

BOILERS:
G490.
 D46 *(new)* ?/1/12.
G941 *(ex spare)* ?/9/20.
 2321 *(new)* 22/1/30.
D1980 *(ex1621)* 17/8/35.

SHEDS:
Tweedmouth.
Alnmouth ?/7/24.
Gateshead ?/1/27.
Darlington 20/3/30.
Hull Botanic Gardens 22/10/32.
Bridlington 10/5/34.

CONDEMNED: 13/11/37.

Lubrication of the cylinders and valves was by NER mechanical type, both on superheated and saturated (*see* page 10, top) engines.

By Grouping, the original tenders had all been fitted with a third coal rail and also a fourth around the coal space. There was also a backing plate to the four rail section. The tenders were 5 tons of coal and 3940 gallons water capacity. Until 1941 the only change was removal of the water pickup gear from 1624's tender in July 1937. Darlington.

From building all had dual brakes, Westinghouse for engine and combined with vacuum ejector for train working. By Grouping a small Westinghouse standpipe was fitted, but the front vacuum connection was still below the buffer beam. They also had a carriage heater connection at the front end.

Beginning during 1929 a vacuum standpipe was put on at the front end and the Westinghouse standpipe was moved to the other side of the coupling hook.

Not all had a Westinghouse standpipe in the 1930's. The photograph on page 17, second from top, shows No.1638 had carried one but by 1932 it only had a vacuum standpipe, the Westinghouse connection being below the buffer beam. Note that a drainpipe has now been fitted to take condensate from the vacuum ejector exhaust. Bridlington.

Sanding was air operated and only fitted in front of the leading coupled wheels. There was no sanding provided for running in reverse. Scarborough, July 1938.

At Grouping, all had full North Eastern green livery with 24in. brass numberplate, which on the right hand side was mounted on the hinged flap giving access to the brake pump. No.1632, ex Gateshead on 2nd March 1923 after general repair, still had this NER livery style, except for the plain ends to buffer beam. No.1620 ex Darlington 19th April 1923, was the first D17 in LNER livery but still with two NER features. The L.& N.E.R. on the tender used 6in. lettering and the buffer beam carried 6in. high characters in NER style shaded transfers. No.1629, ex Darlington 28th April 1923, had similar tender lettering but Group Standard 4½in. figures on the buffer beam and No.1626, out 31st May 1923, was the same as 1629. Darlington continued to put lining on the buffer beam end whilst Gateshead works left them plain. No.1636, ex Gateshead 24th May 1923 had 6in. L.& N.E.R. and the smaller buffer beam figures, as had No.1627, ex Gateshead 21st June 1923. Doncaster.

1633

Gateshead 14.93.

To traffic 9/1893.

REPAIRS:
???. ?/?—?/4/03.**G.**
???. ?/?—?/9/08. **?.**
Piston valves fitted.
???. ?/?—?/1/10.**G.**
???. ?/?—?/3/14.**G.**
Superheated boiler fitted.
Dar. 30/9/22—30/1/23.**G.**
Dar. 29/5—29/10/25.**G.**
Dar. 1/12/27—29/2/28.**G.**
Dar. 26/11/29—24/1/30.**G.**
Dar. 23/2—8/4/32.**G.**
Dar. 8—12/7/32.**N/C.**
Dar. 8/11/34. *Not repaired.*

BOILERS:
G491.
G274 *(new)* ?/4/03.
G646 *(new)* ?/1/10.
G571 *(ex1622)* ?/3/14.
D58 *(ex1924)* 29/10/25.
2320 *(new)* 24/1/30.

SHEDS:
Hull Botanic Gardens.
Bridlington 10/5/34.

CONDEMNED: 19/11/34.

1634

Gateshead 15.93.

To traffic 10/1893.

REPAIRS:
???. ?/?—?/7/04. **?.**
Piston valves fitted.
???. ?/?—?/8/07.**G.**
???. ?/?—?/5/11.**G.**
Ghd. 7/12/23—23/2/24.**G.**
Dar. 6/4—24/8/26.**G.**
Dar. 17/6—23/8/29.**G.**
Superheated boiler fitted.
Dar. 9—26/6/32.**G.**
Dar. 14/12/34. *Not repaired.*

BOILERS:
G492.
G485 *(ex1627)* ?/8/07.
G950 *(new)* ?/5/11.
2169 *(new)* 23/8/29.
D1632 *(ex1638)* 26/6/32.

SHEDS:
Tweedmouth.
Gateshead 1/4/23.
Hull Botanic Gardens 13/2/25.

CONDEMNED: 23/1/35.

1635

Gateshead 16.93.

To traffic 10/1893.

REPAIRS:
???. ?/?—?/2/06.**G.**
???. ?/?—?/3/08. **?.**
Piston valves fitted.
???. ?/?—?/8/19.**G.**
Superheated boiler fitted.
Dar. 29/6—27/9/23.**G.**
Dar. 28/4—26/10/26.**G.**
Dar. 23/11/28—24/1/29.**G.**

BOILERS:
G494.
G281 *(new)* ?/2/06.
D775 *(new)* ?/8/19.

SHEDS:
Hull Botanic Gardens.
Bridlington ?/?/25.

CONDEMNED: 19/10/31.

1636

Gateshead 17.93.

To traffic 11/1893.

REPAIRS:
???. ?/?—?/5/07. **?.**
Piston valves fitted.
???. ?/?—?/4/10.**G.**
???. ?/?—?/8/20.**G.**
Superheated boiler fitted.
Ghd. 2/3—24/5/23.**G.**
Ghd. 8—18/12/23.**L.**
Ghd. 28/2—18/3/24.**L.**
Ghd. 18/4—24/7/25.**G.**
Ghd. 7—22/1/26.**L.**
Ghd. 9/7—30/9/27.**G.**
Ghd. 21/2—8/4/30.**G.**
Dar. 29/9—3/10/30.**N/C.**
Dar. 7/7—12/8/31.**L.**
Dar. 3/10—16/11/33.**G.**
Dar. 2/1—22/2/36.**G.**
Dar. 6/10/38. *Not repaired.*

BOILERS:
G495.
G647 *(new)* ?/4/10.
D45 *(ex1879)* ?/8/20.
D1979 *(new)* 30/9/27.
D1848 *(ex1637)* 16/11/33.

SHEDS:
Gateshead.
Darlington 20/3/30.
Northallerton 1/5/30.
Alnmouth 8/10/32.

CONDEMNED: 7/10/38.

1637

Gateshead 18.93.

To traffic 11/1893.

REPAIRS:
???. ?/?—?/9/04. **?.**
Piston valves fitted.
???. ?/?—?/5/07.**G.**
???. ?/?—?/3/21.**G.**
Superheated boiler fitted.
Ghd. 15/3—23/6/24.**G.**
Dar. 16/2—10/5/27.**G.**
Dar. 2—17/8/28.**N/C.**
Dar. 4/3—29/4/29.**G.**
Dar. 23/12/29—14/1/30.**L.**
Dar. 24/4—18/6/31.**G.**
Dar. 24/7—30/8/33.**H.**
Dar. 10—24/8/34.
Tender only.
Dar. 14/1/35. *Not repaired.*

BOILERS:
G497.
G567 *(new)* ?/5/07.
G951 *(ex1871)* ?/3/21.
D1848 *(new)* 10/5/27.
2092 *(ex1906)* 30/8/33.

SHEDS:
Alnmouth.
Tweedmouth ?/9/24.
Selby 16/5/25.

CONDEMNED: 24/1/35.

1638

Gateshead 19.93.

To traffic 12/1893.

REPAIRS:
???. ?/?—?/12/05.**G.**
Piston valves fitted.
???. ?/?—?/12/07.**G.**
???. ?/?—?/4/10.**G.**
???. ?/?—17/10/22.**?.**
Ghd. 1/11/23—5/5/24.**G.***
Superheated boiler fitted.
Dar. 3/5—12/8/27.**G.**
Dar. 4/2—26/3/30.**G.**
Dar. 8/2—14/3/32.**G.**
Dar. 4/12/34—5/2/35.**G.**
Dar. 3/11/37. *Not repaired.*
* *Sent from Gateshead works to Darlington works 9th January 1924 (possibly for weighing) but was returned to Gateshead the very next day.*

BOILERS:
G498.
G489 *(ex1631)* ?/12/05.
G492 *(ex1634)* ?/12/07.
G650 *(new)* ?/4/10.
D1632 *(new)* 5/5/24.
D775 *(ex1635)* 14/3/32.
D1832 *(ex1874)* 5/2/35.

SHEDS:
Gateshead.
Tweedmouth ?/1/25.
Hull Botanic Gardens 13/2/25.
Bridlington ?/?/25.

CONDEMNED: 13/11/37.

1639

Gateshead 20.93.

To traffic 3/1894.

REPAIRS:
???. ?/?—?/2/05.**G.**
???. ?/?—?/4/07. **?.**
New cylinders fitted.
???. ?/?—?/6/12.**G.**
???. ?/?—?/6/14.**G.**
Superheated boiler fitted.
???. ?/?—?/9/21.**G.**
Dar. 17/10—20/12/23.**G.**
Dar. 17/4—29/7/25.**G.**
Dar. 20/1—10/4/28.**G.**
Dar. 18/8—24/10/30.**G.**
Dar. 27/2/34. *Not repaired.*

BOILERS:
G499.
G278 *(new)* ?/2/05.
G570 *(ex1630)* ?/6/12.
G646 *(ex1633)* ?/6/14.
D48 *(ex1902 & spare)* ?/9/21.

SHEDS:
Hull Botanic Gardens.
Bridlington ?/?/25.

CONDEMNED: 1/3/34.

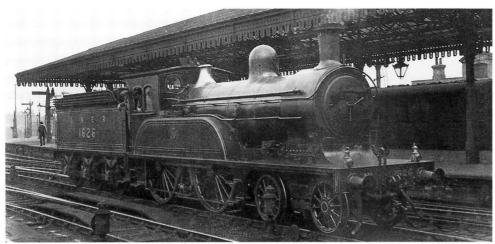

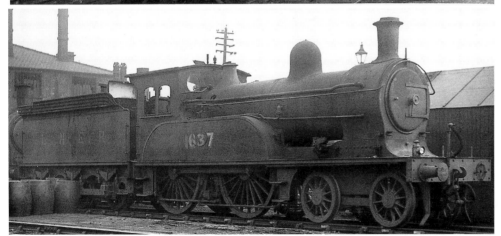

Tender lettering then went to GS 7$\frac{1}{2}$in. size and the full points were discarded. No.1621, ex Gateshead 23rd July 1923, having L&NER. The ampersand was then dropped and No.1623 simply had LNER when ex Darlington on 10th August 1923. During the nearly six months currency of the area Suffix D, Gateshead did not turn out any D17/1's but in 1923 Darlington applied it to Nos.1635 (27th September), 1622 (19th November) and 1639 (20th December). Starting with No.1634 on 23rd February 1924, that engine and the remaining nine, Nos.1624, 1625, 1628, 1630, 1631, 1632, 1633, 1637 and 1638 went straight to this standard style, to which the others adhered at the their next major repair. By the end of 1926 only Nos.1627 and 1632 were not dealt with. No.1627 changed from L.& N.E.R. when out on 2nd March 1927 but No.1632 kept NER livery until it went to Gateshead on 27th January 1927 and was not ex works until 15th July. York, June 1928.

In the June 1928 paint economies the D17/1's were listed to go to black with single red lining, but until March 1929 the number remained on the tender. One from Gateshead works, No.1631 (9th January 1929) and three from Darlington, Nos.1630 (30th June 1928), 1629 (13th November 1928) and 1635 (24th January 1929) got this style. Hull.

From early March 1929 the number was moved on to the engine but Nos.1628 and 1635 never had it there. As the brass beading of the combined splasher was not removed, the number was centred on the splasher, so was ahead of the cab side. Its new position straddled the hinged flap to provide access to the Westinghouse pump but this was just ignored. LNER on tender then came in 12in. tall letters, and eighteen of the class got this style, all then keeping it to withdrawal except Nos.1621 and 1629.

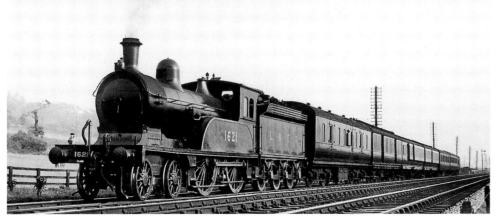

No.1621 seems to have been unusual in the position of its number on the front buffer beam. To clear the two standpipes No. was not used and 1621 was put in its place. It is probable this was done at Gateshead whence 1621 was ex works 12th September 1932. Note that Class D17 is shown which was not used until 1932 the old NE Class M still persisting until into that year.

On 5th March 1941, No.1621 changed its tender to a 3038 gallon type and then ex works on 13th February 1943 it had a boiler with 'pop' valves. The unlined black painting and NE on the tender was kept to withdrawal. Darlington.

When No.1621 was withdrawn on 28th July 1945, Darlington went to considerable trouble and expense to restore the engine to something like its condition at the end of the NER. However, no Raven F.S.A. or tender water pickup apparatus was put back and the front buffers and steel beam were from an earlier period than 1922. Since the 18th July 1947 it has been housed in York, first at Queen Street and now at the NRM. Darlington works, 1947.

At Grouping twenty-two engines had received piston valves and twenty were superheated. No.1927 had been rebuilt and superheated in April 1914. Note the chimney has a capuchon instead of the original brass cap. This engine still had NER livery until it went to works on 5th April 1927. Stratford.

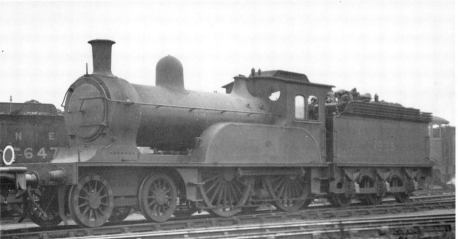

(left) No.1929 got piston valves in August 1924 but did not get a superheater until June 1931. This 13th March 1927 view shows it on loan to the GE Section and with the windjabber taken off by Stratford works, the other two on loan Nos.1880 and 1927 retained their windjabber. Stratford.

(below) No.1929 was the last one to be superheated, ex works on 5th June 1931 and then, apart from the cab roof, Parts 1 and 2 were substantially alike. Note that the windjabber was restored. Scarborough, 11th July 1937.

CLASS D 17/2

1871

Gateshead 7.96.

To traffic 6/1896.

REPAIRS:
???. ?/?—?/9/06.**G.**
???. ?/?—?/5/11.**G.**
???. ?/?—?/9/20.**G.**
Dar. 20/10—30/1/24.**G.**
Ghd. 27/7—12/11/26.**G.**
Ghd. 15/10—2/11/27.**L.**
Ghd. 12/12/29—21/2/30.**G.**
Superheated boiler & piston valves fitted.
Dar. 20/1—8/4/32.**H.**
Dar. 7—14/10/32.**N/C.**
Dar. 12/12/33—25/1/34.**G.**
Dar. 28/4—10/6/36.**G.**
Dar. 10/2—25/3/38.**G.**
Dar. 22/12/41—4/2/42.**G.**
Dar. 3/2/44. *Not repaired.*

BOILERS:
G679.
G692 *(ex1879)* ?/9/06.
G951 *(new)* ?/5/11.
G647 *(ex1636)* ?/9/20.
G975 *(ex spare)* 30/1/24.
2319 *(new)* 21/2/30.
2156 *(ex1901)* 10/6/36.
D1641 *(ex1629)* 25/3/38.
2166 *(ex1879 & spare)* 4/2/42.

SHEDS:
West Hartlepool.
Hull Botanic Gardens 15/4/35.
Bridlington 22/5/35.
Hull Botanic Gardens 16/8/35.
Alnmouth 22/5/41.

RENUMBERED:
2110 allocated.

CONDEMNED: 19/2/44 .

1872

Gateshead 8.96.

To traffic 6/1896.

REPAIRS:
???. ?/?—?/3/04.**G.**
???. ?/?—?/12/10.**G.**

???. ?/?—?/2/14.**G.**
Sup.boiler & p.v. fitted.
Ghd. 13/3—29/5/24.**G.**
Ghd. 17/1—21/4/27.**G.**
Ghd. 31/12/29—5/3/30.**G.**
Dar. 3/11/33. *Not repaired.*

BOILERS:
G680.
G404 *(new)* ?/3/04.
G427 *(ex1876)* ?/12/10.
D292 *(new)* ?/2/14.

SHED:
West Hartlepool.

CONDEMNED: 9/11/33

1873

Gateshead 9.96.

To traffic 6/1896.

REPAIRS:
???. ?/?—?/10/13.**G.**
Sup. boiler & p.v. fitted.
Ghd. 3/6—15/8/24.**G.**
Ghd. 31/8—23/11/26.**G.**
Ghd. 10/5—24/7/29.**G.**
Ghd. 13/4—13/5/32.**G.**
Dar. 22/1—6/3/35.**G.**
Dar. 14/6—6/8/38.**G.**
Dar. 17/4—5/6/42.**G.**
Dar. 16/8—18/9/44.**G.**
Dar. 16/1/48. *Not repaired.*

BOILERS:
G681.
D55 *(new)* ?/10/13.
2166 *(new)* 24/7/29.
2320 *(ex1633)* 6/3/35.
2092 *(ex1908)* 6/8/38.
D1359 *(ex1910 & spare)* 5/6/42.

SHEDS:
West Hartlepool.
Hull Botanic Gardens 15/4/35.
Alnmouth 22/5/41.
York 23/7/45.

RENUMBERED:
2111 17/3/46.

CONDEMNED: 7/2/48

1874

Gateshead 10.96.

To traffic 6/1896.

REPAIRS:
???. ?/?—?/8/10.**G.**
Dar. 20/6—18/9/23.**G.**
Dar. 19/8—16/10/24.**G.**
Piston valves fitted.
Dar. 21/6—12/11/26.**G.**
Dar. 20/8—12/10/28.**G.**
Superheated boiler fitted.
Dar. 4/6—20/8/31.**G.**
Dar. 17/10—1/12/34.**G.**
Dar. 26/10/38. *Not repaired.*

BOILERS:
G683.
G771 *(new)* ?/8/10.
D407 *(ex1907)* 12/10/28.
D1832 *(exD'8 1870)* 20/8/31.
2313 *(ex1⸮ 5)* 1/12/34.

SHEDS:
Scarborougn.
Stockton 18/11/32.
Hull Botanic Gardens 2/10/37.
Bridlington 6/1/38.

CONDEMNED: 29/10/38.

1875

Gateshead 11.96.

To traffic 9/1896.

REPAIRS:
???. ?/?—?/8/07.**G.**
???. ?/?—?/1/10.**G.**
???. ?/?—?/9/15.**G.**
Sup. boiler & p.v. fitted.
Dar. 25/2—28/4/23.**G.**
Dar. 27/11/24—9/4/25.**G.**
Dar. 9/11/26—14/2/27.**G.**
Dar. 30/6—31/8/28.**G.**
Dar. 20/6—9/7/30.**L.**

BOILERS:
G684.
G734 *(ex1904)* ?/8/07.
G732 *(ex spare)* ?/1/10.
D395 *(new)* ?/9/15.

SHED:
Neville Hill.

CONDEMNED: 10/10/31.

1876

Gateshead 12.96.

To traffic 9/1896.

REPAIRS:
???. ?/?—?/11/04.**G.**
???. ?/?—?/11/10.**G.**
???. ?/?—?/5/15.**G.**
Sup. boiler & p.v. fitted.
???. 9/12/22—2/2/23.**L.**
Ghd. 24/7—2/10/23.**G.**
Ghd. 28/9—21/12/25.**G.**
Ghd. 13/1—20/4/28.**G.**
Ghd. 19—26/9/28.**L.**
Ghd. 20/3—5/5/30.**G.**
Ghd. 8—15/5/30.**N/C.**
Ghd. 21—24/12/31.**N/C.**
Ghd. 5/5—20/6/32.**G.**
Dar. 14/11/33—3/1/34.**G.**
Dar. 12/8—16/9/35.**G.**
Dar. 8/4—25/5/37.**G.**
Dar. 27/8—11/10/37.**H.**
Dar. 3/4/43. *Not repaired.*

BOILERS:
G685.
G427 *(new)* ?/11/04.
G693 *(ex spare)* ?/11/10.
D297 *(new)* ?/5/15.
2065 *(new)* 20/4/28.
2169 *(ex1903)* 16/9/35.
2067 *(ex1904 & spare)* 25/5/37.

SHEDS:
Carlisle.
Haymarket 5/9/42.

CONDEMNED: 24/4/43.
(20/4/43 *in Scottish records.*)

1877

Gateshead 13.96.

To traffic 10/1896.

REPAIRS:
???. ?/?—?/12/06.**G.**

WORKS CODES:- Cw - Cowlairs. Dar- Darlington. Don - Doncaster. Ghd - Gateshead. Gor - Gorton. Inv - Inverurie. Nor - Norwich. Str - Stratford.
REPAIR CODES:- **C/H** - Casual Heavy. **C/L** - Casual Light. **G** - General. **H**- Heavy. **H/I** - Heavy Intermediate. **L** - Light. **L/I** - Light Intermediate. **N/C** - Non-Classified.

No.1879, from July 1925 to September 1933, had an exhaust steam injector on the left hand side and so did not have a clack box on the side of the boiler.

(below) Part 2 engines had a cab with a clerestory to the roof, and this had vents on each side, which could be opened for ventilation.

With the vents shut the clerestory had a solid appearance. Darlington, 21st May 1933.

During 1942 four of the five surviving engines had the clerestory removed and a normal roof fitted. These were Nos.1871 and 1905 (February), 1873 and 1902 (June); No.1901 retained the clerestory, even though it was shopped in December 1942.

Note the blackout screen from cab to tender. The absence of vent pipes shows that the water scoop has been removed. Darlington.

The standard whistle arrangement on the Part 2 engines was two-bell shaped whistles on the cab roof with the larger one on the right hand (driver's) side.

1877 cont./
???. ?/?—?/7/11.**G.**
???. ?/?—?/1/16.**G.**
Sup. & p.v. fitted.
Dar. 11/4—28/6/23.**G.**
Dar. 21/10—30/12/24.**G.**
Dar. 28/12/26—25/3/27.**G.**
Dar. 5/12/28—31/1/29.**G.**
Dar. 24/3—12/5/31.**G.**
Dar. 23/10—28/11/33.**G.**
Dar. 18/2—25/3/35.**L.**
Dar. 28/8—4/12/35.**L**
Dar. 24/7—1/9/36.**G.**
Dar. 29/10/38. *Not repaired.*

BOILERS:
G686.
G736 *(ex1906)* ?/12/06.
G963 *(new)* ?/7/11.
G569 *(ex1622)* ?/1/16.
D1640 *(new)* 30/12/24.
D1979 *(ex1636)* 28/11/33.
2088 *(ex1908)* 1/9/36.

SHEDS:
Neville Hill.
Alnmouth 22/2/33.

CONDEMNED: 29/10/38.

1878

Gateshead 14.96.

To traffic 11/1896.

REPAIRS:
???. ?/?—?/5/04.**G.**
???. ?/?—?/4/10.**G.**
???. ?/?—?/4/16. **?.**
Piston valves fitted.
???. ?/?—?/10/20.**G.**
Superheated boiler fitted.
Dar. 31/1—10/4/23.**G.**
Dar. 12/2—8/6/25.**G.**
Dar. 14/4—20/6/28.**G.**
Dar. 25/2—31/3/31.**G.**
Dar. 30/6—8/7/31.**N/C.**
Dar. 31/1/34. *Not repaired.*

BOILERS:
G689.
G680 *(ex1872)* ?/5/04.
G274 *(ex1635)* ?/4/10.
D814 *(new)* ?/10/20.
D399 *(ex1630)* 31/3/31.
SHED:
Scarborough.

CONDEMNED: 2/2/34.

1879

Gateshead 15.96.

To traffic 11/1896.

REPAIRS:
???. ?/?—?/3/06.**G.**
???. ?/?—?/12/11.**G.**
???. ?/?—?/5/20.**G.**
Ghd. 29/3—9/7/23.**G.**
Piston valves fitted.
Ghd. 3/4—28/7/25.**G.**
Superheated boiler fitted.
Dar. 3/8—4/9/25.**N/C.**
Dar. 8—17/9/25.**N/C.**
Ghd. 10/1—14/3/28.**G.**
Ghd. 20/12/28—21/1/29.**L.**
Ghd. 8/8—23/9/30.**G.**
Dar. 30/8—7/9/32.**N/C.**
Dar. 26/9—28/10/33.**G.**
Dar. 21/9—5/11/36.**G.**
Dar. 30/3—7/6/38.**H.**
Dar. 4—12/8/39. *Not repaired.*

BOILERS:
G692.
G766 *(ex1930)* ?/3/06.
D45 *(new)* ?/12/11.
D46 *(ex1632)* ?/5/20.
D1657 *(new)* 28/7/25.
D1358 *(ex1921)* 28/10/33.
D1352 *(ex1910)* 5/11/36.
2166 *(ex1903)* 7/6/38.

SHEDS:
West Hartlepool.
Alnmouth 15/4/35.
Starbeck 31/8/35.

CONDEMNED: 2/8/39 .Stored, then cut up Darlington 2/10/39.

1880

Gateshead 16.96.

To traffic 12/1896.

REPAIRS:
???. ?/?—?/11/04.**G.**
???. ?/?—?/1/11.**G.**
???. ?/?—?/12/18.**G.**
Sup. boiler & p.v. fitted.
Ghd. 2/3—29/5/23.**G.**
Ghd. 22/5—3/6/25.**L.**
Ghd. 27/8—29/9/25.**L.**
Ghd. 22/4—2/8/27.**G.**
Ghd. 23/6—28/8/30.**G.**
Dar. 7—11/1/32.**N/C.**

BOILERS:
G693.
G756 *(ex1926)* ?/11/04.
G275 *(ex spare)* ?/1/11.
D766 *(new)* ?/12/18.

SHEDS:
Gateshead.
Cambridge 24/12/26.
Gateshead 29/3/37.
West Hartlepool 8/2/28.

CONDEMNED: 23/1/33.

1901

Gateshead 8.97.

To traffic 5/1897.

REPAIRS:
???. ?/?—?/2/05.**G.**
???. ?/?—?/3/11.**G.**
???. ?/?—?/8/19.**G.**
Sup. boiler & p.v. fitted.
Ghd. 22/2—20/5/24.**G.**
Ghd. 29/3—22/7/26.**G.**
Ghd. 8/10—29/11/27.**L.**
Ghd. 12/11/28—8/1/29.**G.**
Ghd. 20/1—3/3/31.**G.**
Ghd. 5/9—14/10/32.**G.**
Dar. 24/1—9/3/34.**G.**
Dar. 21/4—5/5/34.**N/C.**
Dar. 4—26/6/34.**L.**
Dar. 11/3—12/4/35.**G.**
Dar. 8/4—26/5/37.**G.**
Dar. 9/1—1/4/41.**L.**
Dar. 24/11—19/12/42.**G.**
Dar. 8/6/45. *Not repaired.*

BOILERS:
G731.
G765 *(ex1925)* ?/2/05.
G941 *(new)* ?/3/11.
D774 *(new)* ?/8/19.
2156 *(new)* 8/1/29.
D1632 *(ex1634)* 12/4/35.
D1981 *(ex1902)* 19/12/42.

SHEDS:
Carlisle.
Hawick 3/9/37.
Carlisle 11/11/37.
Duns 27/4/42.

RENUMBERED:
***2112** allocated.*
CONDEMNED: 21/6/45.

1902

Gateshead 9.97.

To traffic 6/1897.

REPAIRS:
???. ?/?—?/6/05.**G.**
???. ?/?—?/2/10.**G.**
???. ?/?—?/7/12.**G.**
???. ?/?—?/2/20.**G.**
Sup. boiler & p.v. fitted.
Dar. 5/4—29/6/23.**G.**
Dar. 14—17/4/24.**L.**
Dar. 4/1—6/4/27.**G.**
Dar. 17/6—21/8/29.**G.**
Dar. 18/11—31/12/31.**G.**
Dar. 22/5—11/7/33.**H.**
Dar. 1/11—13/12/35.**G.**
Dar. 22/3—20/5/38.**G.**
Dar. 8—22/3/41.
Tender change.
Dar. 28/5—27/6/42.**G.**
Dar. 11/3—1/4/43.**L.**
Dar. 28/4—4/9/44.**L.**
Dar. 8/11—1/12/44.**L.**
Dar. 9/2—9/3/45.**G.**
Dar. 16—21/3/45.**N/C.**
Dar. 18/2—8/3/46.**L.**
Dar. 2/10—2/11/46.**L.**
Dar. 15/1/48. *Not repaired.*

BOILERS:
G732.
G486 *(ex1628)* ?/6/05.
G734 *(ex1875)* ?/2/10.
D48 *(new)* ?/7/12.
D53 *(ex1925)* ?/2/20.
2170 *(new)* 21/8/29.
2065 *(ex1876)* 13/12/35.
D1981 *(ex1924)* 20/5/38.
2319 *(ex1923 & sp.)* 27/6/42.
2063 *(ex1905 & spare)* 9/3/45.

SHEDS:
Scarborough.
Selby 19/11/34.
Scarborough 5/7/37.
Neville Hill 9/1/43.
York 12/3/45.

RENUMBERED:
2112 27/1/46, *originally allocated 2113.*

CONDEMNED: 7/2/48.
Cut up at Darlington.

1903

Gateshead 10.97.

To traffic 6/1897.

REPAIRS:
???. ?/?—?/1/06.**G.**
???. ?/?—?/11/07.**G.**
???. ?/?—?/8/10.**G.**
Dar. 11/3—26/5/24.**G.**

On some, the driver's side bell-shaped whistle was changed to an organ pipe. No.1905 had this style from March 1937 to January 1942.

By April 1928, No.1876 had its smaller whistle on the fireman's side changed to an organ pipe, but a later photograph (*see* page 34, top) shows the bell-shaped device was reinstated.

At some time No.1902 had only a single organ pipe which was on the driver's side.

From May 1938 to May 1942 No.1902 had the standard whistle arrangement. Scarborough, 7th August 1939.

From March 1945 No.1902 had new whistle gear with only a single bell shape. It was renumbered 2112 on 27th January 1946. Note that the Part 2 engines did not get either Gresley anti-vacuum valve, or sight screens on the cab.

A capuchon (windjabber) was a standard fitting on the chimney to withdrawal except on Carlisle based engines from 1935.

In 1935 a move was made to cut down Nos.1876, 1901, 1921, 1924 from 13ft 3in. to 13ft 0in. chimney height by removing their windjabber. These four were at Carlisle shed and could then be permitted to work on the North British section if required.

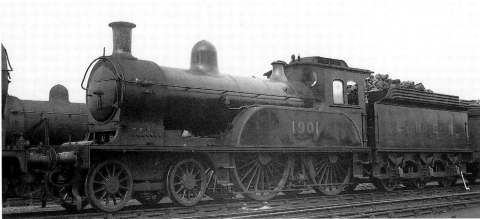

Boilers built until 1927 had Ramsbottom safety valves which were enclosed in a polished brass trumpet shaped cover. They were used on both Parts 1 and 2.

29

The last fourteen boilers, built between January 1928 and December 1929, had Ross 'pop' safety valves, some mounted directly on the firebox.

(above) Some of these boilers seem to have been prepared for a Ramsbottom mounting, as the 'pops' stood higher than normal. Hull Botanic Gardens, September 1938.

In LNER years, most had the smokebox door fastened by two handles. Carlisle London Road, June 1929.

1903 cont./
Dar. 26/8—7/10/25.**L.**
Dar. 6/4—6/7/27.**G.**
Sup. boiler & p.v. fitted.
Dar. 19/11/29—14/1/30.**G.**
Dar. 25/7—6/9/32.**G.**
Dar. 29/3—10/5/35.**G.**
Dar. 2/11/36. *Not repaired.*

BOILERS:
　G733.
　G732 *(ex1902)* ?/1/06.
　G684 *(ex1875)* ?/11/07.
　G772 *(new)* ?/8/10.
　D1404 *(ex1628)* 16/7/27.
　2169 *(ex1634)* 6/9/32.
　2166 *(ex1873)* 10/5/35.

SHEDS:
Scarborough.
Starbeck 22/3/33.
Bradford (Manningham) 14/5/35.
Starbeck 12/8/35.

CONDEMNED: 12/12/36.
5/2/37 York Carr. wks as heating
boiler. To Dar. 5/11/37. Engine c/
u 4/12/37, tender 15/10/38.

_____

1904

Gateshead 11.97.

To traffic 5/1897.

REPAIRS:
???. ?/?—?/1/07.**G.**
???. ?/?—?/6/11.**G.**
???. ?/?—?/9/15.**G.**
Sup. boiler & p.v. fitted.
Ghd. 1/5—1/8/24.**G.**
Ghd. 8/3—1/4/27.**L.**
Dar. 14/10/27—23/2/28.**G.**
Ghd. 21/11—18/12/29.**L.**
Dar. 14/7—14/8/30.**N/C.**
Ghd. 17/9—31/10/30.**G.**
Dar. 6/4—16/5/33.**G.**
Dar. 1/10—19/11/35.**G.**
Dar. 30/9/38. *Not repaired.*

BOILERS:
G734.
G733 *(ex1903)* ?/1/07.
G954 *(new)* ?/6/11.
G971 *(ex1628)* ?/9/15.
2063 *(new)* 23/2/28.
2067 *(ex1907)* 16/5/33.
2321 *(ex1632)* 19/11/35.

SHEDS:
West Hartlepool.
Bridlington 10/12/37.

CONDEMNED: 8/10/38.

1905

Gateshead 12.97.

To traffic 6/1897.

REPAIRS:
???. ?/?—?/2/14.**G.**
Sup. boiler & p.v. fitted.
Dar. 29/10/23—9/1/24.**G.**
Dar. 31/3—10/8/25.**G.**
Dar. 1/7—29/9/27.**G.**
Dar. 29/7—11/12/29.**G.**
Dar. 2/10—5/11/31.**G.**
Dar. 24/2—15/3/33.**L.**
Dar. 4/10—9/11/34.**G.**
Dar. 15/2—20/3/37.**G.**
Dar. 5/1—11/2/42.**G.**
Dar. 2/1—19/2/43.**H.**
Dar. 14—24/9/43.**N/C.**
Dar. 25/11/43. *Not repaired.*

BOILERS:
　G735.
　D60 *(new)* ?/2/14.
　2313 *(new)* 11/12/29.
　D1841 *(ex1626)* 9/11/34.
　2063 *(ex1906)* 20/3/37.
　D1848 *(ex1621)* 19/2/43.

SHEDS:
Neville Hill.
Starbeck 3/10/33.
Hull Botanic Gardens 6/7/35.
Bridlington 6/1/38.
Hull Botanic Gardens 18/9/39.
Neville Hill 1/6/40.
Hull Botanic Gardens 17/8/40.
Selby 9/9/40.
Alnmouth 21/2/42.

RENUMBERED:
2114 allocated.

CONDEMNED: 24/12/43.

_____

1906

Gateshead 13.97.

To traffic 6/1897.

REPAIRS:
???. ?/?—?/5/06.**G.**
???. ?/?—?/10/10.**G.**
Dar. 26/2—26/5/23.**G.**
Dar. 12/3—5/8/25.**G.**
Dar. 7/6—17/8/28.**G.**
Sup. boiler & p.v. fitted.
Dar. 9/3—20/4/31.**G.**
Dar. 14/6—31/7/33.**G.**
Dar. 1/12/36—21/1/37.**G.**
Dar. 9/11/38. *Not repaired.*

BOILERS:
　G736.
　G737 *(ex1907)* ?/5/06.
　G773 *(new)* ?/10/10.
　2092 *(new)* 17/8/28.
　2063 *(ex1904)* 31/7/33.
　2162 *(ex1907)* 21/1/37.

SHEDS:
Scarborough.
West Hartlepool 29/9/34.
Alnmouth 15/4/35.

CONDEMNED: 9/11/38.

_____

1907

Gateshead 14.97.

To traffic 6/1897.

REPAIRS:
???. ?/?—?/6/05.**G.**
???. ?/?—?/3/17.**G.**
Sup. boiler & p.v. fitted.
Dar. 9/1—26/4/24.**G.**
Dar. 21/8—19/11/25.**G.**
Dar. 5/4—8/6/28.**G.**
Dar. 28/1—17/3/31.**G.**
Dar. 6/2—17/3/33.**G.**
Dar. 21/3/35. *Weigh.*
Dar. 26/8—14/10/36.**H.**

BOILERS:
G737.
G279 *(new)* ?/6/05.
D407 *(new)* ?/3/17.
2067 *(new)* 8/6/28.
2162 *(ex1631)* 17/3/33.
2170 *(ex1902)* 14/10/36.

SHEDS:
Scarborough.
West Hartlepool 25/9/34.
Hull Botanic Gardens 6/7/35.

CONDEMNED: 8/10/38.

_____

1908

Gateshead 15.97.

To traffic 6/1897.

REPAIRS:
???. ?/?—?/4/05.**G.**
???. ?/?—?/12/12.**G.**
???. ?/?—?/4/21.**G.**
Dar. 9/1—30/4/23.**G.**
Sup. boiler & p.v. fitted.
Dar. 28/2—31/5/24.**L.**
Dar. 6/4—13/8/25.**G.**

Dar. 17/8—31/10/27.**G.**
Dar. 3/2—21/3/30.**G.**
Dar. 15/11—30/12/32.**G.**
Dar. 13/6—6/8/35.**G.**
Dar. 29/12/36—11/2/37.**L.**
Dar. 12/4—22/7/38.**H.**
Dar. 4/11/38. *Not repaired.*

BOILERS:
　G738.
　G763 *(ex1928)* ?/4/05.
　D50 *(new)* ?/12/12.
　G276 *(ex spare)* ?/4/21.
　D1390 *(new)* 30/4/23.
　2088 *(ex1909)* 30/12/32.
　2092 *(ex1637)* 6/8/35.
　2065 *(ex1902)* 22/7/38.

SHEDS:
West Hartlepool.
Neville Hill ?/6/24.
Bradford (Manningham) 12/8/35.
Starbeck 4/2/38.

CONDEMNED: 4/11/38.

_____

1909

Gateshead 16.97.

To traffic 6/1897.

REPAIRS:
???. ?/?—?/6/11.**G.**
Piston valves fitted.
???. ?/?—?/3/22.**G.**
Ghd. 29/4—28/9/26.**G.**
Dar. 8/8—22/10/28.**G.**
Superheated boiler fitted.
Dar. 9/4—2/7/30.**G.**
Dar. 20/10—22/11/32.**G.**
Dar. 12/12/34—12/2/35.**G.**
Dar. 10/11/37. *Not repaired.*

BOILERS:
　G740.
　G955 *(new)* ?/6/11.
　G774 *(ex1923)* 28/9/26.
　2088 *(new)* 22/10/28.
　D1404 *(ex1903)* 22/11/32.

SHEDS:
Gateshead.
Hull Botanic Gardens 18/2/27.
Starbeck 17/10/32.
Hull Botanic Gardens 6/7/35.
Bridlington 16/8/35.

CONDEMNED: 20/11/37.

_____

1910

Gateshead 17.97.

To traffic 6/1897.

REPAIRS:
???. ?/?—?/12/06.**G.**
???. ?/?—?/4/11.**G.**
???. ?/?—?/8/22.**G.**
Sup. boiler & p.v. fitted.
Ghd. 3—6/7/23.**L.**
Ghd. 11/6—14/8/24.**G.**
Dar. 28/4—7/6/28.**G.**
Dar. 7/7—19/9/30.**G.**
Dar. 9/11—12/12/32.**G.**
Dar. 16/5—25/6/35.**G.**
Dar. 24/11/38. *Not repaired.*

BOILERS:
G742.
G759 *(ex1927)* ?/12/06.
G948 *(new)* ?/4/11.
D1359 *(new)* ?/8/22.
D1352 *(ex1928)* 12/12/32.
D1359 *(ex1921)* 25/6/35.

SHEDS:
Carlisle.
Gateshead ?/7/24.
Hull Botanic Gardens 18/2/27.
Bridlington 6/7/35.

CONDEMNED: 25/11/38.

1921

Gateshead 18.97.

To traffic 6/1897.

REPAIRS:
???. ?/?—?/4/05.**G.**
???. ?/?—?/9/11.**G.**
Ghd. ?/?—30/8/22.**G.**
Sup. boiler & p.v. fitted.
Ghd. 2/9—7/11/24.**G.**
Ghd. 29/1—15/2/26.**L.**
Ghd. 14/3—9/6/27.**G.**
Ghd. 27/8—22/10/29.**G.**
Ghd. 28/10—1/11/29.**N/C.**
Ghd. 5/8—17/9/31.**G.**
Ghd. 14—23/10/31.**N/C.**
Dar. 22/3—4/5/33.**G.**
Dar. 5/2—12/3/35.**G.**
Dar. 11/4—10/5/35.**L.**
Dar. 26/10/36—8/1/37.**G.**
Dar. 18/5—16/7/37.**H.**
Dar. 2/4/43. *Not repaired.*

BOILERS:
G751.
G731 *(ex1901)* ?/4/05.
G975 *(new)* ?/9/11.

D1358 *(new)* 30/8/22.
D1359 *(ex1910)* 4/5/33.
D774 *(ex1624)* 12/3/35.

SHEDS:
Carlisle.
St Margarets 5/9/42.

CONDEMNED: 24/4/43.
(20/4/43 in Scottish records).

1922

Gateshead 19.97.

To traffic 9/1897.

REPAIRS:
???. ?/?—?/10/08.**G.**
???. ?/?—?/1/16.**G.**
Dar. 21/12/23—4/3/24.**G.**
Ghd. 12/4—9/9/26.**G.**
Piston valves fitted.
Ghd. 14/8—19/10/28.**G.**
Superheated boiler fitted.
Dar. 17/9—28/11/30.**G.**

BOILERS:
G752.
G753 *(ex1923 & spare)* ?/10/08.
G954 *(ex1904)* ?/1/16.
D297 *(ex1876)* 19/10/28.

SHEDS:
Starbeck.
West Hartlepool 27/8/27.
Hull Botanic Gardens 11/7/30.

CONDEMNED: 3/10/32.

1923

Gateshead 20.97.

To traffic 9/1897.

REPAIRS:
???. ?/?—?/3/07.**G.**
???. ?/?—?/11/10.**G.**
???. ?/?—?/3/22. **?.**
Piston valves fitted.
Dar. 26/2—21/5/24.**G.**
Superheated boiler fitted.
Dar. 28/12/25—16/4/26.**G.**
Dar. 5/9—28/11/27.**G.**
Dar. 30/7—2/8/29.**N/C.**
Dar. 16—20/9/29.**N/C.**
Dar. 23/4—3/7/30.**G.**
Dar. 16/11/32—12/1/33.**G.**
Dar. 30/8—17/10/34.**G.**
Dar. 4/6—11/7/36.**G.**
Dar. 10/8—11/10/37
Tender only.

BOILERS:
G753.
G686 *(ex1877)* ?/3/07.
G774 *(new)* ?/11/10.
D1639 *(new)* 21/5/24.
D1390 *(ex1631)* 17/10/34.
2319 *(ex1871)* 11/7/36.

SHEDS:
Neville Hill.
Starbeck 3/10/33.
Alnmouth 31/8/35.

CONDEMNED: 8/10/38.

1924

Gateshead 21.97.

To traffic 10/1897.

REPAIRS:
???. ?/?—?/1/06.**G.**
???. ?/?—?/10/13.**G.**
Sup. boiler & p.v. fitted.
Ghd. ?/?—4/10/22.**G.**
Ghd. 6—29/3/23.**L.**
Ghd. 24/7—13/8/23.**L.**
Ghd. 18/12/24—12/3/25.**G.**
Ghd. 18—19/3/25.**N/C.**
Ghd. 20/9—2/12/27.**G.**
Ghd. 19—23/12/27.**L.**
Ghd. 23/4—24/5/28.**L.**
Ghd. 19/3—7/5/30.**G.**
Ghd. 30/3—2/4/31.**N/C.**
Ghd. 18/2—1/4/32.**G.**
Dar. 29/3—15/5/34.**G.**
Dar. 8/2—19/3/36.**G.**
Dar. 8/10/37. *Not repaired.*

BOILERS:
G754.
G751 *(ex1921)* ?/1/06.
D58 *(new)* ?/10/13.
D1641 *(new)* 12/3/25.
D1981 *(ex1620)* 15/5/34.

SHED:
Carlisle.

CONDEMNED: 23/10/37.

1925

Gateshead 22.97.

To traffic 10/1897.

REPAIRS:
???. ?/?—?/11/05.**G.**
???. ?/?—?/2/13.**G.**
???. ?/?—?/10/19.**G.**
Sup. boiler & p.v. fitted.

Ghd. ?/?—29/3/23.**?.**
Dar. 14/9—30/11/23.**G.**
Dar. 29/3—25/6/26.**G.**
Dar. 22/12/27—16/3/28.**G.**
Dar. 22/9—12/11/30.**G.**
Dar. 21/11/33—12/1/34.**G.**
Dar. 14/1—22/2/36.**G.**
Dar. 5/11/38. *Not repaired.*

BOILERS:
G755.
G738 *(ex1908)* ?/11/05.
D53 *(new)* ?/2/13.
D776 *(new)* ?/10/19.
D1640 *(ex1877)* 12/1/34.

SHEDS:
Carlisle.
Bradford (Manningham) 1/7/24.
Neville Hill ?/1/25.
Starbeck 9/10/29.
Bradford (Manningham) 4/2/38.

CONDEMNED: 5/11/38.

1926

Gateshead 23.97.

To traffic 10/1897.

REPAIRS:
???. ?/?—?/7/04.**G.**
???. ?/?—?/1/11.**G.**
???. ?/?—?/1/14.**G.**
Sup.boiler & p.v. fitted.
Ghd. 23/1—25/4/24.**G.**
Ghd. 12/8/26—10/1/27.**G.**
Ghd. 31/7—8/10/28.**G.**
Ghd. 25/11/30—16/1/31.**G.**
Ghd. 18/2—10/3/31.**L.**
Ghd. 6—13/5/31.**L.**

BOILERS:
G756.
G689 *(ex1878)* ?/7/04.
G404 *(ex1872)* ?/1/11.
D54 *(new)* ?/1/14.

SHED:
Carlisle.

CONDEMNED: 24/8/31.

1927

Gateshead 24.97.

To traffic 11/1897.

REPAIRS:
???. ?/?—?/6/06.**G.**
???. ?/?—?/5/10.**G.**

A few did have the wheel and handle fastening for the smokebox door into the 1930's. Note that to at least April 1933 No.1904 still had a brass cap to its chimney, although it also carried a windjabber.

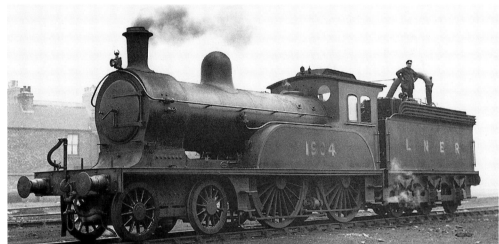

From the middle 1930's the wheel for fastening the smoke box door was discarded and all survivors then had the two handles. No.1872 (*see* page 29, bottom) still had a wheel at its 9th November 1933 withdrawal. Hull Botanic Gardens, September 1938.

The original buffer fitting was the taper shank type with circular flange to the wood sandwich type beam and the majority retained this type. Hull Botanic Gardens, September 1938.

At least ten were changed to Group Standard buffers - 1871, 1872, 1873, 1876, 1879, 1901, 1902, 1904, 1905 and 1930, starting with No.1872 in March 1930. No.1905 was recorded officially as getting them as late as 11th February 1942.

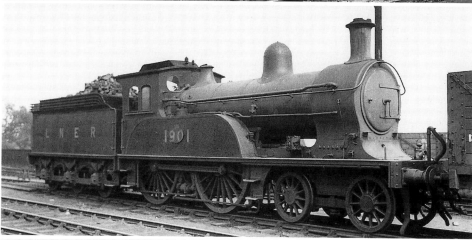

Whether superheated (as here) or saturated (see No.1874 below), a NER designed mechanical lubricator was fitted for the cylinders and valves.

There were also oil boxes on the sides of the smokebox to provide additional lubrication for the front end of the valves.

(below) The normal tender was the 3940 gallons type with three all-round rails and a fourth to the coal space.

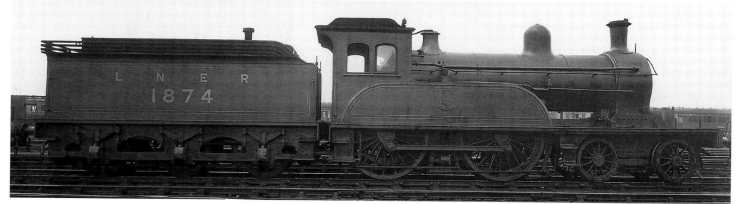

1927 cont./
???. ?/?—?/4/14.**G.**
Sup. boiler & p.v. fitted.
Ghd. 15/11/22—23/2/23.**G.**
Ghd. 2/10—4/11/24.**L.**
Ghd. 5/4—5/8/27.**G.**
Dar. 19/5—19/8/30.**G.**

BOILERS:
G759.
G754 *(ex1924)* ?/6/06.
G742 *(ex spare)* ?/5/10.
D295 *(new)* ?/4/14.

SHEDS:
Gateshead.
Stratford 24/12/26.
Gateshead 11/3/27.
Starbeck 8/2/28.

CONDEMNED: 24/10/32.

___

1928

Gateshead 25.97.

To traffic 11/1897.

REPAIRS:
???. ?/?—?/1/05.**G.**
???. ?/?—?/8/09.**G.**
???. ?/?—?/3/22.**G.**
Sup. boiler & p.v. fitted.
Ghd. 7/5—24/7/24.**G.**
Dar. 16/5—22/8/27.**G.**
Dar. 24/9—8/11/29.**G.**
Dar. 14—30/4/31.**N/C.**

BOILERS:
 G763.
 G685 *(ex1876)* ?/1/05.
 G770 *(new)* ?/8/09.
D1352 *(new)* ?/3/22.

SHEDS:
Carlisle.
Gateshead 24/7/24.
Scarborough 11/7/25.
Gateshead 26/8/25.
Neville Hill 3/3/28.

CONDEMNED: 6/5/32.

___

1929

Gateshead 26.97.

To traffic 11/1897.

REPAIRS:
Ghd. ?/?—12/1/05.**G.**
???. ?/?—?/12/08.**G.**
???. ?/?—?/12/12.**G.**

???. ?/?—17/5/22.**?.**
Ghd. 8/4—13/8/24.**G.**
Piston valves fitted.
Dar. 29/8—30/11/27.**G.**
Dar. 21/4—5/6/31.**G.**
Superheated boiler fitted.
Dar. 26/11/34—15/1/35.**G.**
Dar. 31/7—9/8/35.**L.**
Dar. 22/3—23/5/28.**H.**
Dar. 5/11/38. *Not repaired.*

BOILERS:
 G765.
 G693 *(ex1880)* 12/1/05.
 G679 *(ex spare)* ?/12/08.
 D49 *(new)* ?/12/12.
D814 *(ex1878)* 5/6/31.
D1639 *(ex1923)* 15/1/35.
D814 *(ex1621)* 23/5/38.

SHEDS:
Carlisle.
Gateshead 24/7/24.
Stratford 24/12/26.
Gateshead 29/3/27.
Neville Hill 1/3/28.
Selby 3/10/33.
Scarborough 5/7/37.
Starbeck 20/12/37.

CONDEMNED: 5/11/38.

___

1930

Gateshead 27.97.

To traffic 11/1897.

REPAIRS:
???. ?/?—?/12/05.**G.**

???. ?/?—?/2/14.**G.**
Sup.boiler & p.v. fitted.
Ghd. 9/11/22—22/2/23.**G.**
Ghd. 15/10/25—12/2/26.**G.**
Ghd. 12—31/5/27.**L.**
Ghd. 4/2—9/5/28.**G.**
Ghd. 12/11—29/12/30.**G.**

BOILERS:
G766.
G755 *(ex1925)* ?/12/05.
D287 *(new)* ?/2/14.

SHEDS:
West Hartlepool.
Scarborough 9/7/25.
West Hartlepool 9/10/25.

CONDEMNED: 3/11/33.

___

In 1941 the tenders of Nos.1901 and 1902 were taken to run with new J39 engines and were replaced by 3038 gallons type which had only two coal rails, and no water pick up apparatus.

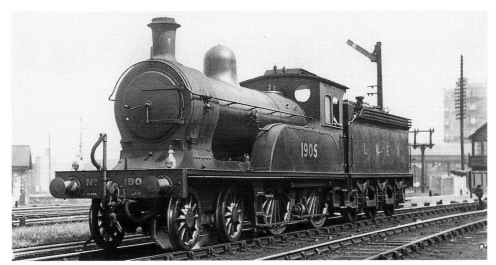

No.1905's original tender was condemned and cut up in October 1931. It was replaced in November 1931 by the tender from scrapped engine No.1619. Although this was also a 3940 gallons type it could be identified because it did not have the fourth rail to the coal space.

Fitted with dual brakes from new, both of the front-end connections were below the buffer beam until well after the Grouping. Scarborough, 6th May 1931.

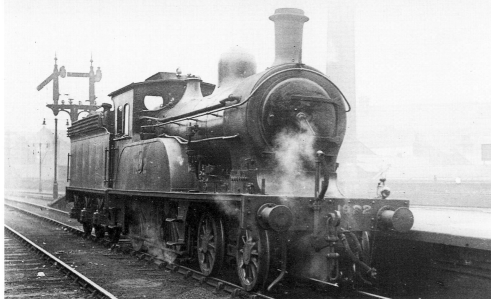

From 1929 a tall vacuum swan-neck standpipe was fitted to the front of the buffer beam. The Westinghouse connection and that for the carriage heating remained below the buffer beam.

Although by 1930 the need for Westinghouse brakes for train working had almost been eliminated, the pump remained for engine brake, power reverse and for air sanding. The front-end brake connection was then removed.

All were fitted with Raven fog signalling apparatus until that system was taken out of use at the end of October 1933. The striker for it was behind the footstep just ahead of the leading coupled wheel on the right hand side (*see* page 34, bottom also).

From about 1930 a small-bore drainpipe was fitted to deal with condensate from the vacuum ejector exhaust pipe. The drain went down from the smokebox through the running plate.

When GS buffers were fitted, a Group Standard coupling hook was put on also - compare with No.1922 opposite, centre, for North Eastern coupling hook.

No.1927 remained in this North Eastern livery until it went to works on 5th April 1927 and only changed to LNER when ex works on 5th August.

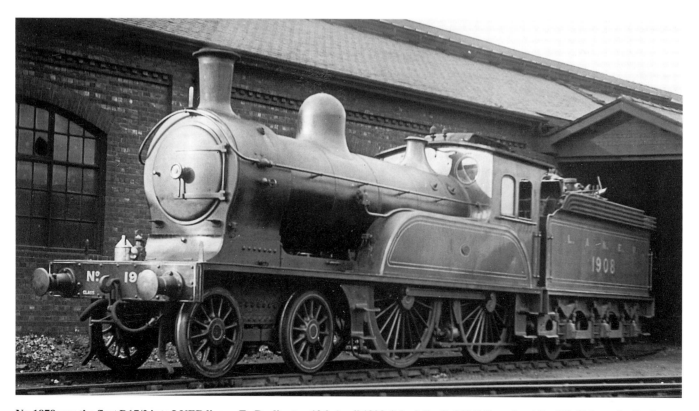

No.1878 was the first D17/2 into LNER livery. Ex Darlington 10th April 1923, it had 6in. L.&N.E.R. and not the GS 4½in. on buffer beam. In 1923, Nos.1875 (28th April) 1908 (30th April) and 1906 (26th May) from Darlington and 1880 (29th May) from Gateshead also got this style, with 4½in. characters on the buffer beam.

Two changes were then made; the full points were discarded and 7½ in. letters were used. Nos. 1877 (28th June) and 1902 (29th June) from Darlington and 1879 (9th July) from Gateshead, all in 1923, had this variation applied. The ampersand was then dropped but from September 1923 to February 1924, area suffix D was added to the number. Five were so treated from Darlington, Nos.1874 (18th September 1923), 1925 (30th November 1923), 1905 (9th January 1924), 1871 (30th January 1924) and from Gateshead 1876 (2nd October 1923). Whitby, June 1925.

From early February 1924 to early June 1928 all were put into this green standard style.

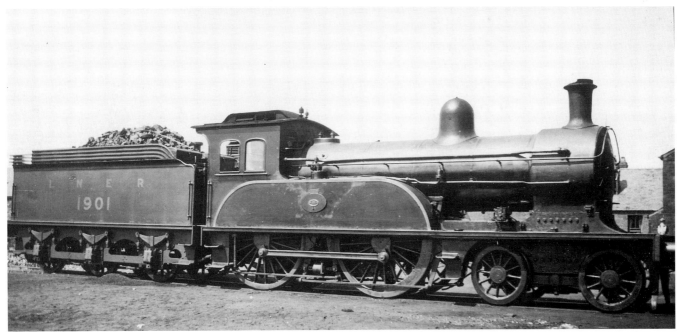

The June 1928 paint economies decreed black with single red lining for D17/2, but until mid-March 1929 the number was still put on the tender, and eight had this style. From Darlington Nos.1906 (17th August 1928), 1875 (31st August 1928), 1874 (12th October 1928), 1909 (22nd October 1928) and 1877 (31st January 1929) and from Gateshead 1926 (8th October 1928), 1922 (19th October 1928) and 1901 (8th January 1929).

The number was then moved to the centre of the combined splasher and the small numberplate was fixed on the frame ahead of the splasher. On the tender side 12in. letters became standard. The single red lining was applied until November 1941 when it became a wartime casualty.

(above) From June 1942 only NE was put on the tender but only four had subsequent heavy repairs at which to get it. These were Nos. 1901 (19th December 1942), 1905 (19th February 1943), 1873 (18th September 1944) and 1902 (9th March 1945). Note the repair date in small figures above the number.

When the 1946 general renumbering was put into effect there were only Nos.1873 and 1902 surviving. No.1873 became 2111 on 17th March 1946 and 1902 changed to 2112 on 27th January 1946 both being Sunday renumberings at York shed and 12in. shaded transfers were used. Both were withdrawn on 7th February 1948 still in unlined black and with only NE on the tender.

40

CLASS D 18

1869

Gateshead 5.96.

To traffic 5/1896.

REPAIRS:
???. ?/?—?/8/10.**G.**
???. ?/?—?/3/20.**G.**
Superheated boiler & piston valves fitted.
Dar. 9/1—29/3/24.**G.**
Dar. 18/5—7/10/26.**G.**
Dar. 27/2—7/5/29.**G.**

BOILERS:
G678.
G783 *(new)* ?/8/10.
D779 *(new)* ?/3/20.

SHED:
Neville Hill.

CONDEMNED: 30/10/30.

1870

Gateshead 6.96.

To traffic 6/1896.

REPAIRS:
???. ?/?—?/9/11.**G.**
Piston valves fitted.
???. ?/?—?/3/15.**G.**
Superheated boiler fitted.
Dar. 20/9—26/11/23.**G.**
Dar. 9/12/25—8/3/26.**G.**
Dar. 14/2—27/4/28.**G.**

BOILERS:
 G682.
 G733 *(exD17/2 1904)* ?/9/11.
 G570 *(exD17/1 1639)* ?/3/15.
D1832 *(new)* 8/3/26.

SHED:
Neville Hill.

CONDEMNED: 30/10/30.

On No.1870 the driver's whistle had been changed to organ pipe. Both had wheel and handle for smokebox door fastening, also buffers with taper shank and circular flange. Their tenders were 3940 gallons type with four coal rails and were fitted with water pick-up apparatus being the first NER tenders to have water scoops.

Schmidt superheaters were fitted, with a steam circulating valve on the left-hand side of the smokebox. Both were always dual braked. No.1870 was the first to get LNER green as 1870D - ex Darlington 26th November 1923 and it remained green to withdrawal on 30th October 1930. Its last repair and painting was five weeks before the June 1928 painting economies came into effect.

At No.1869's last general repair it got a number of changes. The LNER green acquired in March 1924 gave place to black with single red lining and the number was moved on to the combined splasher. LNER in 12in. letters was then put on the tender. At the front a tall vacuum standpipe was put on. No.1869 was also withdrawn on 30th October 1930. Both still had Class Q1 on the front buffer beam.

1619

Gateshead 3.93.

To traffic 5/1893.

REPAIRS:
???. ?/?—?/8/98.**G.**
Rebuilt from a two to three cylinder compound.
???. ?/?—?/9/13.**G.**
Dar. 1/12/22—20/3/23.**G.**
Dar. 3—31/5/24.**L.**
Dar. 14/8—2/9/24.**L.**
Dar. 14/9/26—28/2/27.**G.**

BOILERS:
G481.
G816 *(new)* ?/8/98.
D244 *(new)* ?/9/13.

SHEDS:
Hull Botanic Gardens.
Bridlington ?/1/26.

CONDEMNED: 25/10/30.

(right) **No.1619 was derailed when entering the north end of York station on 31st March 1920. Damage was slight, quickly repaired and it was 1st December 1922 when No.1619 next went into Darlington works. Out on 20th March 1923 it was still in full NER green livery with large brass number plates, polished cap to chimney and Class 3CC on the buffer beam which it kept to withdrawal.**

From 14th September 1926 to 28th February 1927 it was in Darlington works for general repair and painting to LNER green. It lost the large brass number plates and the chimney cap, changing to a chimney with a windjabber. It remained as shown until withdrawal on 25th October 1930. Note the run of the vacuum brake train pipe outside the bogie.

Smith compounds could be worked as a full compound or steam at full pressure could be admitted to the receiver through a small regulator under the driver's control. The change-over valve was on the right hand side of the smokebox. At 1st January 1923 its smokebox door had two handle fastening and the chimney had a polished brass cap.

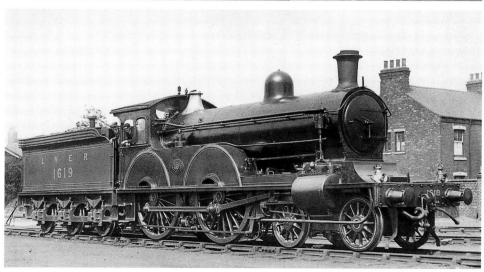

Although the tender was of standard 3940 gallons capacity and had three rails all round, it never had the usual fourth rail added around the coal space.

Dual braked from new, the front-end connections were all below the buffer beam and remained so to withdrawal.

Thirty more engines were built from September 1906 to September 1907 and these were numbered more haphazardly: 476, 592, 707, 708, 711, 712, 713, 723, 724, 725, 1026, 1042, 1051, 1078, 1147, 1184, 1206, 1207, 1209, 1210, 1217, 1223, 1232 to 1236, 1258, 1260, 1665, and 1672. This is No.1206 as at Grouping; superheated in June 1917 and the tender has a fourth coal rail fitted.

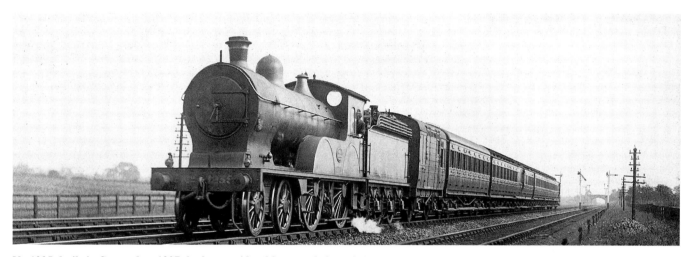

No.1235, built in September 1907, had a considerably extended smokebox to take a Sisterton superheater - the North Eastern's first step in that direction. That particular superheater was taken out in June 1909 and a normal smokebox was put on in November 1911. Into works on 29th September and out on 30th November 1911.

Raven went for superheating with enthusiasm, beginning on No.2013 in October 1912. It was given deeper frames with a convex front end. A smokebox 5ft 1in. long into which a Robinson type superheater was fitted, and a mechanical lubricator was put on to serve the cylinders and piston valves. Note no windjabber yet fitted.

CLASS D 20

2011

Gateshead 12.99.

To traffic 8/1899.

REPAIRS:
???. ?/?—?/3/12.**G.**
???. ?/?—?/10/17.**G.**
Superheated boiler fitted.
???. ?/?—?/10/19.**G.**
Dar. 15/3—13/6/23.**G.**
Dar. 15/12/24—19/3/25.**G.**
Dar. 14/1—26/4/27.**G.**
Dar. 5/9—26/10/28.**G.**
Dar. 12/6—29/8/30.**G.**
Dar. 24/2—20/3/31.**H.**
Dar. 29/3—19/5/32.**G.**
Dar. 12/12/33—8/3/34.**G.**
Dar. 15/9—11/11/36.**G.**
Dar. 5/5—2/8/38.**G.**
Dar. 19/1—11/2/42.**L.**
After collision.
Dar. 17/9—21/11/42.**G.**
Dar. 8/7—15/9/45.**G.**
Dar. 26/5—2/7/48.**G.**

BOILERS:
G911.
D37 *(new)* ?/3/12.
G526 *(ex707)* ?/10/17.
G579 *(ex1042)* ?/10/19.
D1553 *(new)* 19/3/25.
D1541 *(ex2103)* 20/3/31.
2436 *(new)* 19/5/32.
D936 *(ex2018)* 8/3/34.
D1381 *(ex723)* 11/11/36.
2436 *(ex476)* 21/11/42.
2344 *(ex2388)* 2/7/48.

SHEDS:
Neville Hill.
Scarborough 26/11/40.
Selby 12/3/45.

RENUMBERED:
2340 17/11/46.
62340 2/7/48.

CONDEMNED: 27/2/51.

2012

Gateshead 13.99.

To traffic 9/1899.

REPAIRS:
???. ?/?—?/8/05.**G.**
???. ?/?—?/5/14.**G.**
Superheated boiler fitted.
Dar. 1/3—23/5/24.**G.**
Ghd. 28/4—2/9/26.**G.**
Ghd. 14/6—10/8/28.**G.**
Ghd. 24/4—16/6/30.**G.**
Ghd. 12/8—3/10/32.**G.**
Dar. 15/11/34—9/1/35.**G.**
Dar. 31/3—5/5/36.**L.**
Dar. 4/3—6/5/37.**G.**
Dar. 7/2—8/4/41.**G.**
Dar. 26/11—4/12/43.**N/C.**
Dar. 26/10—29/11/44.**G.**
Dar. 30/11—20/12/45.**N/C.**
Dar. 29/4—7/6/47.**G.**
Dar. 20/10—18/11/49.**G.**

BOILERS:
G912.
G919 *(ex2017)* ?/8/05.
D278 *(new)* ?/5/14.
2341 *(new)* 16/6/30.
D1775 *(ex2029)* 8/4/41.
D1547 *(ex1042)* 29/11/44.
2585 *(ex2355)* 7/6/47.
3664 *(ex2345)* 18/11/49 (59A).

SHEDS:
Blaydon
Heaton 6/5/24.
York 16/5/38.
Whitby 1/7/39.
York 11/9/39.
Selby 17/8/40.

RENUMBERED:
2341 27/10/46.
62341 18/11/49.

CONDEMNED: 7/3/51.

2013

Gateshead 14.99.

To traffic 9/1899.

REPAIRS:
???. ?/?—?/6/05.**G.**
???. ?/?—?/10/12.**G.**
Superheated boiler fitted.
???. ?/?—?/7/22.**G.**
Dar. 11/10—21/12/23.**G.**
Dar. 8/12/25—31/3/26.**G.**
Dar. 17/5—6/7/28.**G.**
Dar. 6/10—19/11/30.**G.**
Normal smokebox fitted.
Dar. 23/4—7/6/35.**G.**
Dar. 29/1—10/3/37.**G.**
Dar. 12—25/8/37.**N/C.**
Dar. 20/9—2/11/38.**G.**
Dar. 15/5—27/6/40.**G.**
Dar. 14/1—3/3/41.**H.**
Dar. 5/8—13/9/41.**G.**
Dar. 13/11—18/12/43.**G.**
Dar. 23/10—3/11/44.**L.**
Dar. 11/1—9/2/46.**G.**
Ghd. 17/6—9/7/47.**L.**
Dar. 18/9—22/10/48.**G.**

BOILERS:
G913.
G992 *(ex2026)* ?/6/05.
D39 *(new)* ?/10/12.
G906 *(ex spare)* ?/7/22.
D39 *(ex2102)* 6/7/28.
2339 *(new)* 19/11/30.
2873 *(new)* 10/3/37 (59A).
2869 *(ex1258)* 18/12/43 (59A).
3667 *(new)* 9/2/46 (59A).
3923 *(new)* 22/10/48 (59A).

SHEDS:
Neville Hill.
Scarborough 19/4/24.
Selby 11/2/35.
Hull Botanic Gardens 26/1/46.
Starbeck 29/9/46.
Selby 22/10/50.

RENUMBERED:
2342 8/9/46.
62342 22/10/48.

CONDEMNED: 13/3/51.

2014

Gateshead 15.99.

To traffic 10/1899.

REPAIRS:
???. ?/?—?/7/06.**G.**
???. ?/?—?/1/12.**G.**
???. ?/?—?/10/16.**G.**
Superheated boiler fitted.
Dar. 21/12/22—21/4/23.**G.**
Dar. 14/3—17/7/25.**G.**
Dar. 11/1—29/4/26.**G.**
Dar. 28/2—8/5/28.**G.**
Dar. 2/12/29—21/1/30.**G.**
Dar. 25/1—9/3/32.**G.**
Dar. 30/10—14/12/33.**G.**
Dar. 28/1—12/3/35.**G.**
Dar. 5/10—24/11/36.**G.**
Dar. 13/4—19/5/39.**G.**
Special chimney fitted.
Dar. 2—20/6/39.**N/C.**
Dar. 25/3—16/5/42.**G.**
Dar. 14/3—26/4/44.**L.**
After collision.
Dar. 4/1—3/2/45.**G.**
Dar. 25/4—7/6/47.**G.**
Dar. 14/3—13/4/49.**L.**
Dar. 29/10—30/11/49.**G.**

BOILERS:
G914.
G18 *(ex2108)* ?/7/06.
D36 *(new)* ?/1/12.
G908 *(ex2102)* ?/10/16.
G907 *(ex713)* 21/4/23.
2091 *(new)* 8/5/28.
2323 *(new)* 21/1/30.
2137 *(ex2027)* 14/12/33.
D1439 *(ex712)* 24/11/36.
2344 *(ex1210)* 19/5/39.
2338 *(ex2017)* 16/5/42.
2866 *(ex725)* 3/2/45 (59A).
2443 *(ex2358)* 7/6/47.
2864 *(ex2383)* 30/11/49 (59A).

SHEDS:
Hull Botanic Gardens.
Starbeck 28/8/40.
Selby 1/10/50.
Pickering 29/7/51.
York 1/2/53.
Selby 7/11/54.

RENUMBERED:
2343 5/1/47.
62343 13/4/49.

CONDEMNED: 8/10/56.

2015

Gateshead 16.99.

To traffic 11/1899.

REPAIRS:
???. ?/?—?/1/05.**G.**
???. ?/?—?/1/15.**G.**

WORKS CODES:- Cw - Cowlairs. Dar- Darlington. Don - Doncaster. Ghd - Gateshead. Gor - Gorton. Inv - Inverurie. Nor - Norwich. Str - Stratford.
REPAIR CODES:- **C/H** - Casual Heavy. **C/L** - Casual Light. **G** - General. **H**- Heavy. **H/I** - Heavy Intermediate. **L** - Light. **L/I** - Light Intermediate. **N/C** - Non-Classified.

45

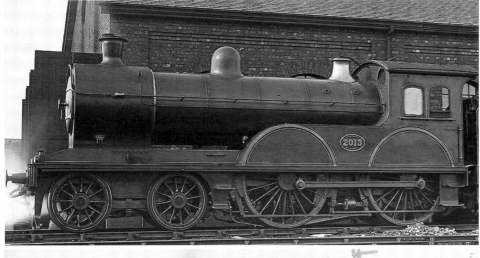

On the left hand side a pyrometer was fitted and for element protection, damper control through the boiler handrail was provided. Note that a windjabber is now fitted.

In July 1922 No.2013 had a boiler change and the boiler put on had a Schmidt type superheater with the usual steam circulating valve on smokebox side for element protection. This enabled the handrail to be made continuous. The extra long smokebox remained and survived general repairs in December 1923, March 1926 and July 1928 and was only changed to normal type at the 6th October to 19th November 1930 repair. Note the steps put on the front of the smokebox. Scarborough, 10th September 1923.

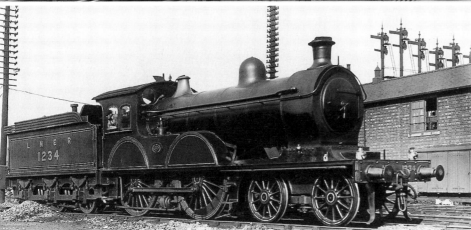

By Grouping, of the sixty engines only Nos.1234 and 2025 were not superheated. No.2025 was fitted when ex works on 6th March 1925 but No.1234 not until 23rd April 1929 and it was the only non-superheated D20 to get LNER livery. Note the short smokebox and no mechanical lubricator fitted.

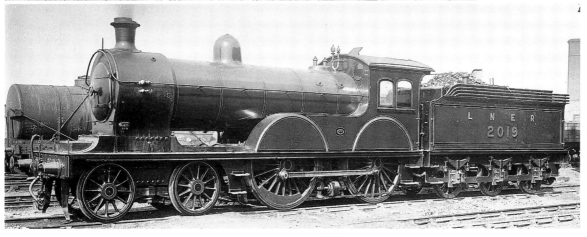

Boilers built up to July 1923 continued to be fitted with a steam circulating valve on the side of the smokebox. No.2019's boiler was one of the final batch of ten and started work on 29th March 1924.

All further new boilers had the Gresley anti-vacuum valve and by June 1924 it was replacing the steam circulating valve on older boilers. Ex works on 20th June 1924, No.1217 had a boiler built in May 1914 which had Ramsbottom safety valves. By the end of 1928 the steam circulating valve had disappeared from D20 class. Darlington, 1925.

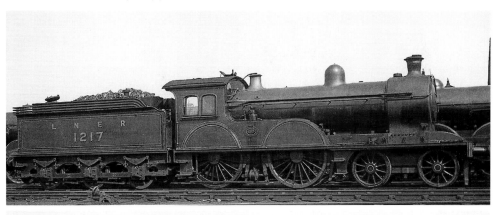

During 1934, the Diagram 59 boiler, used only by D20 class, was redesigned and all boilers built from November 1935 were to Diagram 59A which had a single plate barrel instead of three rings. The only external evidence was slight, the safety valves being $1/4$in. closer together and $7/8$ in. further back with no casing being provided at the base. The whistle was now mounted on an isolating valve and directly on to the firebox. Both Diagram 59 and 59A were fully interchangeable and both types were in use until 1957. Selby, 6th August 1939.

Complaints of indifferent steaming in 1938 led to a change of chimney design. Out on 19th May 1939, No.2014 had a J39 type chimney fitted with a liner and cowl, the windjabber now being discarded. No more D20's were so altered until 1942/1943 when this chimney type was put on Nos.2030 (July 1942), 2105 (August 1942), 476 and 592 (October 1942), 2021 (November 1942), 712 (February 1943) and 723 (March 1943). Others were fitted later but by no means did all of the class receive the J39 type chimney. York, 22nd June 1939, Up *YORKSHIRE PULLMAN*.

By Grouping practically all the class had a chimney with a windjabber except No.2030 which did not get one until ex Gateshead on 2nd December 1926.

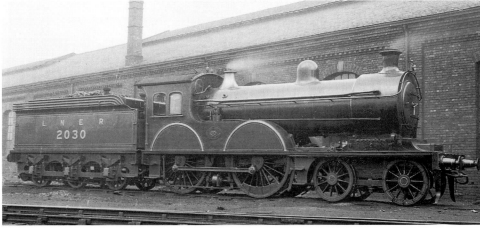

2015 cont./
Superheated boiler fitted.
???. ?/?—7/7/22.**G.**
Ghd. 28/4—7/8/25.**G.**
Ghd. 15/7—8/8/27.**L.**
Ghd. 29/3—5/6/28.**G.**
Ghd. 27/5—22/7/30.**G.**
Ghd. 30/3—8/4/31.**N/C**
Ghd. 12—29/7/32.**L.**
Dar. 23/1—2/3/33.**G.**
Dar. 4/4—27/5/35.**G.**
Dar. 12/7—3/9/37.**G.**
Dar. 20/5—22/6/40.**G.**
Chimney cut to 13'-1".
Dar. 25/11—17/12/41.**L.**
After collision.
Dar. 5/2—1/4/43.**G.**
Dar. 21/5—22/6/46.**G.**
Dar. 3—8/7/46.**N/C.**
Dar. 22/11/48—4/1/49.**G.**

BOILERS:
G917.
G918 *(ex2016)* ?/1/05.
G610 *(ex spare)* ?/1/15.
D1773 *(new)* 7/8/25.
 D986 *(ex1042)* 2/3/33.
 2311 *(ex1672)* 27/5/35.
D2091 *(ex711)* 3/9/37.
 2445 *(ex1217)* 22/6/40.
 3409 *(ex2394)* 22/6/46 (59A).
 2510 *(ex2391)* 4/1/49.

SHEDS:
Tweedmouth.
Alnmouth 4/12/49.
Tweedmouth 23/4/50.
Alnmouth 5/11/50.

RENUMBERED:
 2344 10/11/46.
62344 3/1/49.

CONDEMNED: 28/3/51.

_____

2016

Gateshead 17.99.

To traffic 11/1899.

REPAIRS:
???. ?/?—?/1/05.**G.**
???. ?/?—?/6/10.**G.**
???. ?/?—?/1/16.**G.**
Superheated boiler fitted.
Ghd. 27/7—18/10/23.**G.**
Ghd. 21/1—5/3/25.**G.**
Ghd. 29/10/26—26/1/27.**G.**
Dar. 23/4—25/6/29.**G.**
Dar. 21/9—23/11/31.**G.**
Dar. 30/10—1/12/33.**G.**
Dar. 5/5—25/6/36.**G.**
Dar. 26/4—11/6/38.**G.**

Dar. 13—15/6/38.**N/C.**
Dar. 5/6—4/7/40.**G.**
Dar. 12/11—18/12/43.**G.**
Dar. 19/3—7/4/45.**L.**
Dar. 7/5—12/6/47.**G.**
Dar. 18/8—14/9/49.**G.**
Dar. 21—24/9/49.**N/C.**
Dar. 11—20/10/49.**N/C.**
Dar. 8—14/12/49.**C/L.**
Dar. 9/10—11/11/50.**G.**

BOILERS:
G918.
G920 *(ex2018)* ?/1/05.
G999 *(ex2108)* ?/6/10.
D496 *(new)* ?/1/16.
D573 *(ex2030)* 26/1/27.
D1539 *(ex2019)* 23/11/31.
 2500 *(new)* 1/12/33.
 2512 *(ex2108)* 25/6/36.
D1487 *(ex2108)* 4/7/40.
D1541 *(ex1217)* 18/12/43.
 3664 *(new)* 12/6/47 (59A).
 2725 *(ex2397)* 14/9/49 (59A).
 2866 *(ex2384)* 11/11/50 (59A).
 2866 reno. 24602 11/11/50.

SHEDS:
Gateshead.
Darlington 23/5/27.
York 2/4/28.
Hull Botanic Gardens 3/1/29.
Bridlington 17/7/39.
Northallerton 7/8/49.
Hull Botanic Gardens 8/1/50.
Selby 7/1/51.
York 29/7/51.
Selby 5/2/56.

RENUMBERED:
 2345 1/12/46.
62345 14/9/49.

CONDEMNED: 11/10/56.

_____

2017

Gateshead 18.99.

To traffic 11/1899.

REPAIRS:
???. ?/?—?/5/05.**G.**
???. ?/?—?/12/14.**G.**
Superheated boiler fitted.
Ghd. 15/3—10/7/24.**G.**
Ghd. 17—31/3/26.**L.**
Ghd. 26/1—22/2/27.**L.**
Ghd. 9/1—18/4/28.**G.**
Dar. 9/5—6/8/30.**G.**
Dar. 10/3—27/5/33.**G.**
Dar. 30/11/35—25/1/36.**G.**
Dar. 15/9—31/12/37.**G.**
Dar. 20/12/38—1/2/39.**G.**

Dar. ?/?—?/3/42.**G.**
Dar. 15/11/44. *Not repaired.*

BOILERS:
G919.
G998 *(ex2027)* ?/5/05.
 D344 *(new)* ?/12/14.
D1428 *(ex707)* 6/8/30.
D1553 *(ex1026)* 27/5/33.
 2338 *(ex1026)* 25/1/36.
D2077 *(ex1665)* ?/3/42.

SHEDS:
Tweedmouth.
Hull Botanic Gardens 12/3/28.
York 9/2/34.
Selby 12/7/37.
York 30/1/39.
Scarborough 12/12/42.

RENUMBERED:
2346 *allocated.*

CONDEMNED: 2/12/44.
Cut up at Darlington.

_____

2018

Gateshead 19.99.

To traffic 12/1899.

REPAIRS:
???. ?/?—?/9/04.**G.**
???. ?/?—?/5/08.**G.**
???. ?/?—?/11/11.**G.**
???. ?/?—?/9/13.**G.**
Superheated boiler fitted.
Dar. 3/7—29/9/23.**G.**
Dar. 28/4—14/8/25.**G.**
Dar. 21/4—9/7/26.**L.**
Dar. 10/12/28—14/2/29.**G.**
Dar. 3/6—11/8/31.**G.**
Dar. 22/11—28/12/33.**G.**
Dar. 20/4—30/5/36.**G.**
Dar. 21/3—12/4/38.**N/C.**
Dar. 13/4—7/6/39.**G.**
Dar. 7—18/5/42.**N/C.**
Dar. 30/4—18/6/43.**G.**
Dar. 24—29/7/44.**L.**
Dar. 19/12/46—8/2/47.**G.**
Ghd. 10/1—3/3/48.**L.**
Ghd. 17/6—23/8/48.**L.**
Ghd. 12—28/10/48.**L.**
Dar. 30/1—23/2/50.**C/L.**
Dar. 14/11—15/12/50.**G.**

BOILERS:
G920.
G425 *(new)* ?/9/04.
 G10 *(ex2030)* ?/5/08.
G926 *(ex2027)* ?/11/11.
 D44 *(new)* ?/9/13.
 D43 *(ex725)* 29/9/23.

D337 *(ex2106)* 14/8/25.
D936 *(ex711)* 14/2/29.
D1764 *(ex1235)* 28/12/33.
D1554 *(ex2026)* 30/5/36.
D1439 *(ex2014)* 7/6/39.
 3658 *(new)* 8/2/47 (59A).
 3951 *(new)* 15/12/50 (59A).
 3951 reno.24604 15/12/50.

SHEDS:
York.
Scarborough 29/11/40.
Selby 12/3/45.
Hull Botanic Gardens 26/1/46.
Alnmouth 4/3/46.
Stockton 2/1/49.
Northallerton 20/3/50.

RENUMBERED:
 2347 17/11/46.
62347 23/8/48.

CONDEMNED: 15/11/54.

_____

2019

Gateshead 20.99.

To traffic 12/1899.

REPAIRS:
???. ?/?—?/3/04.**G.**
???. ?/?—?/6/08.**G.**
???. ?/?—?/6/12.**G.**
???. ?/?—?/10/15.**G.**
Superheated boiler fitted.
Dar. 11/1—29/3/24.**G.**
Dar. 6/7—13/8/25.**L.**
Dar. 8/3—30/6/26.**G.**
Ghd. 19—31/8/26.**L.**
Dar. 1/6—7/8/28.**G.**
Dar. 9—17/8/28.**N/C.**
Dar. 21/1—5/2/29.**L.**
Dar. 13/2—6/3/29.**N/C.**
Dar. 21/9—23/11/31.**G.**
Dar. 21/6—4/8/33.**H.**
Dar. 29/10—10/12/34.**G.**
Dar. 30/7—30/9/37.**G.**
Dar. 1/6—2/7/40.**G.**
Dar. 26/5—5/8/43.**G.**
Dar. 20/12/46—1/2/47.**G.**
Dar. 13—21/2/47.**N/C.**
Dar. 23/9—20/10/49.**G.**

BOILERS:
G921.
G341 *(new)* ?/3/04.
 G24 *(ex2109)* ?/6/08.
 G10 *(ex2018)* ?/6/12.
 G544 *(ex713)* ?/10/15.
D1539 *(new)* 29/3/24.
D1515 *(ex708)* 23/11/31.
 D982 *(ex1078)* 10/12/34.
D1783 *(ex1258)* 30/9/37.

The brass cap originally fitted had largely disappeared by 1928 but one survived on No.1258 until May 1934.

From November 1936 No.2024 ran with its windjabber removed and from October 1939 many had them taken off to cut the height to 13ft 0in. and permit wider route availability. So by 1945 a windjabber was a rarity on this class.

As happened so often, there were odd examples; No.62369 (ex 2110) carried a windjabber through to withdrawal on 6th March 1951, as did 62359 (ex 2030) to 26th October 1955, and 62380 (ex 1026) had one to 23rd September 1954. Northallerton.

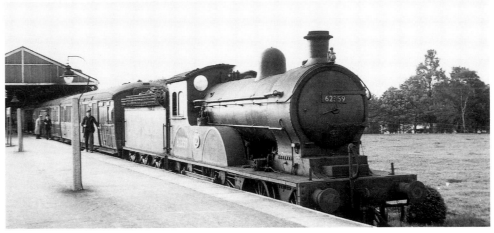

When a superheater was put in the smokebox length became 4ft 1in. instead of 3ft 0³/₄in. and the front portion of the frame had a corresponding extension piece welded in. York.

Beginning with No.2027 in July 1911, twelve of the sixty were fitted with complete new frames which had a level top for the full length and a convex instead of a concave front curve. This had no direct connection with the fitting of a superheater as No.2027 was not superheated until February 1914.

The twelve to get new frames were; Nos.1217, 1665, 2013, 2018, 2020, 2021, 2023, 2024, 2027, 2101, 2104 and 2107, all being done prior to Grouping. No more were modified and the only subsequent change to frames was in connection with rebuilding to Part 2 from 1936.

The cab remained very much in its original form, the wood roof and hinged ventilator being unaltered. A minor addition was the fitting of curved rain strips.

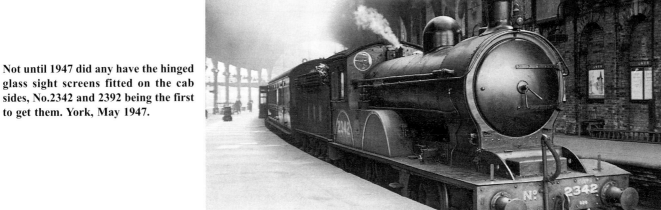

Not until 1947 did any have the hinged glass sight screens fitted on the cab sides, No.2342 and 2392 being the first to get them. York, May 1947.

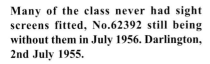

Many of the class never had sight screens fitted, No.62392 still being without them in July 1956. Darlington, 2nd July 1955.

The sixty original boilers and thirty-seven built from 1903 to 1916 for spares and replacements, all had Ramsbottom safety valves in the customary brass trumpet. No.2021 took the last of these boilers to works in December 1936.

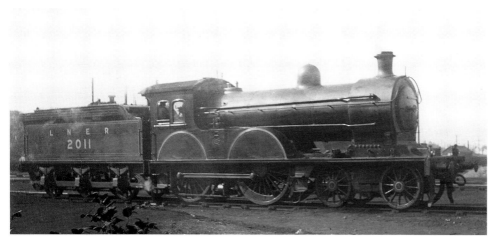

Beginning in May 1919 all subsequent boilers had two Ross 'pop' safety valves and until the Diagram 59 boiler was redesigned in 1934 a shallow circular cover was fitted at their base.

Engines could be seen with either type of safety valves depending on which exchange boiler was available at the time of repair. Gateshead, 3rd August 1924.

Twin bell-shaped whistles were fitted to all when built and these protruded through the cab roof.

2019 cont./
D2091 (ex2015) 2/7/40.
  3650 (ex2027) 1/2/47 (59A).
  3969 (new) 20/10/49 (59A).

SHEDS:
Darlington.
Neville Hill 3/3/34.
Scarborough 26/11/40.
Selby 12/3/45.

RENUMBERED:
2348 24/11/46.
62348 20/10/49.

CONDEMNED: 27/2/51.

2020

Gateshead 21.99.

To traffic 12/1899.

REPAIRS:
???. ?/?—?/11/04.**G.**
???. ?/?—?/5/14.**G.**
Superheated boiler fitted.
Dar. 14/5—31/7/24.**G.**
Dar. 4/4—29/7/27.**G.**
Dar. 14/5—20/7/29.**G.**
Dar. 11/3—25/4/32.**G.**
Dar. 21/2—22/3/34.**G.**
Dar. 3/6—20/10/36.**G.**
Rebuilt to Part 2.
Dar. 18/11/36. Weigh.
Dar. 24/11/36—15/1/37.**N/C.**
Valves adjusted.
Dar. 25/1—16/2/37.**N/C.**
Hot bearings.
Dar. 15/6—6/7/37.**N/C.**
Regulator changed.
Dar. 9/4—7/5/38. *Tender only.*
Dar. 11—30/11/38.**N/C.**
Whistle valve altered.
Dar. 27/12/39—1/5/40.**G.**
Dar. 10/7—14/8/40.**N/C.**
Vacuum brake defective.
Dar. 31/10—16/11/40.**N/C.**
Vacuum brake examination.
Dar. 18/2—9/4/41.**L.**
Frame & buffer beam damaged.
Dar. 18/7—2/9/42.**L/I.**
Dar. 20/3—6/5/44.**G.**
Dar. 23—30/5/45.**N/C.**
Boiler work.
Dar. 22/10—24/12/47.**G.**
Ghd. 23—30/8/49.**C/L.**
Front end collision.
Ghd. 1/2—29/3/50.**G.**

Damage to front buffer beam &
footplate.
Dar. 27/6—20/7/51.**G.**

BOILERS:
G922.
G921 (ex2019) ?/11/04.
D275 (new) ?/5/14.
D985 (ex1260) 29/7/27.
  2314 (ex2022) 25/4/32.
D985 (ex2103) 22/3/34.
  2730 (new) 20/10/36 (59A).
24605 20/7/51 (59A).

SHEDS:
Neville Hill.
Starbeck 18/12/24.
York 6/5/37.
Starbeck 22/9/37.
Gateshead 30/11/40.
Heaton 5/3/45.
Alnmouth 23/7/45.
Blaydon 5/10/47.
Tweedmouth 12/5/48.
Alnmouth 23/10/49.
Gateshead 7/6/53.
Alnmouth 4/10/53.
Blaydon 9/5/54.
Selby 26/6/55.

RENUMBERED:
2349 6/9/46.
62349 30/8/49.

CONDEMNED: 2/2/56.

2021

Gateshead 21.00.

To traffic 8/1900.

REPAIRS:
???. ?/?—?/3/15.**G.**
Superheated boiler fitted.
Dar. 3/4—11/7/23.**G.**
Dar. 17/9—29/11/24.**G.**
Dar. 28/4—30/6/25.**G.**
Dar. 16/8—17/11/27.**G.**
Dar. 6/5—31/7/29.**G.**
Ghd. 30/11/31—20/1/32.**G.**
Dar. 16/12/36—18/2/37.**G.**
Dar. 12—25/8/37.**N/C.**
Dar. 2/2—24/3/39.**G.**
Dar. 18/9—14/11/42.**G.**
Dar. 2/5—30/6/45.**G.**
Dar. 9—18/7/45.**N/C.**
Dar. 25/10/47. *Not repaired.*

BOILERS:
G925.
D341 (new) ?/3/15.
  D37 (ex2028) 29/11/24.
D275 (ex2020) 17/11/27.
  2870 (new) 18/2/37 (59A).
  2140 (ex1210) 30/6/45.

SHEDS:
York.
Scarborough 28/11/40.
Selby 12/3/45.

RENUMBERED:
2350 17/11/46.

CONDEMNED: 20/12/47.
Cut up at Darlington.

2022

Gateshead 22.00.

To traffic 8/1900.

REPAIRS:
???. ?/?—?/1/05.**G.**
???. ?/?—?/2/13.**G.**
Superheated boiler fitted.
???. ?/?—?/3/17.**G.**
Dar. 31/8—28/11/23.**G.**
Dar. 28/4—17/7/25.**G.**
Dar. 7/8—25/8/25.**L.**
Dar. 10/1—30/3/28.**G.**
Dar. 8—19/7/29.**N/C.**
Dar. 25/11/29—14/1/30.**G.**
Dar. 8/3—27/4/32.**G.**
Dar. 14/11—22/12/34.**G.**
Dar. 22/2—13/4/38.**G.**
Dar. 14—26/4/38.**N/C.**
Dar. 29/3—25/5/39.**L.**
After collision.
Dar. 25/10—28/11/40.**G.**
Dar. 22—24/4/41.**N/C.**
Dar. 7/1—4/2/44.**G.**
Dar. 21/11—21/12/46.**G.**
Dar. 13/11—5/12/47.**L.**
Dar. 1—23/12/48.**L.**
Dar. 3/2—21/4/50.**G.**
Ghd. 5—12/7/54.**N/C.**

BOILERS:
G926.
G922 (ex2020) ?/1/05.
  D43 (new) ?/2/13.
D522 (new) ?/3/17.
  D36 (ex1223) 17/7/25.
  2314 (new) 14/1/30.
D987 (ex712) 27/4/32.
  2325 (ex1217) 13/4/38.

  2139 (ex1078) 28/11/40.
D2087 (ex2104) 4/2/44.
D1487 (ex2028) 21/12/46.
  3650 (ex2348) 21/4/50 (59A).

SHEDS:
York.
Middlesbrough 21/1/37.
Alnmouth 18/11/38.
Gateshead 22/5/41.
Alnmouth 11/8/41.
RENUMBERED:
2351 17/11/46.
62351 23/12/48.

CONDEMNED: 22/11/54.

2023

Gateshead 23.00.

To traffic 9/1900.

REPAIRS:
???. ?/?—?/2/05.**G.**
???. ?/?—?/5/12.**G.**
???. ?/?—?/9/21.**G.**
Superheater put in.
Dar. 30/1—29/3/24.**G.**
Dar. 20/2—3/3/25.**L.**
Dar. 8/10—10/11/25.**L.**
Dar. 15/3—29/7/26.**G.**
Dar. 7/12/27—17/1/28.**G.**
Dar. 22/11/28—17/1/29.**G.**
Dar. 18/1—1/2/29.**N/C.**
Dar. 27/3—22/5/31.**G.**
Dar. 27/4—1/6/33.**G.**
Dar. 26/7—2/8/33.**N/C.**
Dar. 17/8/33.**N/C.**
Dar. 29/7—19/9/35.**G.**
Dar. 11/7—29/8/38.**G.**
Dar. 13/8—24/9/41.**G.**
Dar. 14/2—16/3/45.**G.**
Dar. 28/1—8/3/47.**G.**
Dar. 19/9—14/10/49.**G.**

BOILERS:
G928.
G917 (ex2015) ?/2/05.
  D38 (new) ?/5/12.
  2142 (new) 17/1/29.
D1428 (ex2017) 1/6/33.
D987 (ex2022) 29/8/38.
  2137 (ex708) 24/9/41.
D1539 (ex1236) 16/3/45.
  3655 (new) 8/3/47 (59A).
  3659 (ex2358) 14/10/49 (59A).

SHEDS:
Darlington.

WORKS CODES:- Cw - Cowlairs. Dar- Darlington. Don - Doncaster. Ghd - Gateshead. Gor - Gorton. Inv - Inverurie. Nor - Norwich. Str - Stratford.
REPAIR CODES:- **C/H** - Casual Heavy. **C/L** - Casual Light. **G** - General. **H**- Heavy. **H/I** - Heavy Intermediate. **L** - Light. **L/I** - Light Intermediate. **N/C** - Non-Classified.

The boilers built from May 1919 had altered staying to the firebox and the whistles were then placed in front of the cab, but still on the U-shaped mounting. Some earlier boilers retained the cab-roof position (*see also* page 51, bottom) until 1936.

(*above*) A few of these 1919 designed boilers had the larger bell-shape whistle changed to an organ pipe after Grouping.

(*left*) As the U-shape mounting tended to gather water in the bend, from September 1935 a single whistle on a straight pipe over a valve was fitted. At first only a short pipe was used. Selby, October 1948.

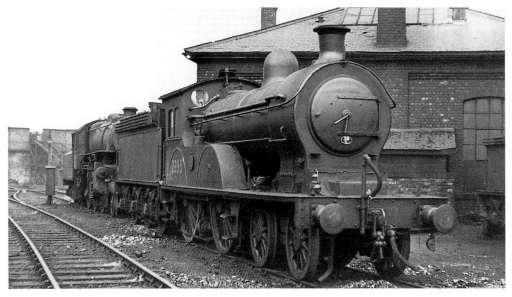

Later the left-hand side whistle was discarded and the smaller bell-shape was moved to the driver's side.

(right) Diagram 59A boilers had a manifold in the cab from which a steam supply was taken and latterly the single whistle was again mounted above the cab roof. Dairycoates, May 1951.

(below) Until 1932 none of the class had lifting holes in the front end of the frames.

2023 cont./
Middlesbrough 16/7/36.
Alnmouth 7/12/38.
Gateshead 22/5/41.
Alnmouth 11/8/41.
Gateshead 7/3/42.
Alnmouth 31/1/44.
Heaton 7/6/53.
Alnmouth 4/10/53.
Gateshead 13/6/54.

RENUMBERED:
2352 24/11/46.
62352 14/10/49.

CONDEMNED: 28/6/54.

_____

2024

Gateshead 24.00.

To traffic 9/1900.

REPAIRS:
???. ?/?—?/10/05.**G.**
???. ?/?—?/3/11.**G.**
???. ?/?—?/1/15.**G.**
Superheated boiler fitted.
Ghd. 20/9—3/10/23.**L.**
Ghd. 29/8—29/12/24.**G.**
Ghd. 16/5—5/8/27.**G.**
Dar. 24/5—31/7/29.**G.**
Dar. 30/9—18/11/30.**H.**
Dar. 12/11—21/12/31.**G.**
Dar. 17/3—14/4/34.**G.**
Dar. 3/9—4/11/36.**G.**
Dar. 21/2—6/4/39.**G.**
Dar. 3/3—29/4/43.**G.**
Dar. 21/3—18/4/46.**G.**
Dar. 30/4—7/5/46.**N/C.**
Dar. 19—27/12/46.**L.**
Dar. 26/3—26/4/47.**L.**
Dar. 26/2—19/3/48.**L.**
Dar. 24/12/48—19/1/49.**G.**

BOILERS:
G930.
G912 *(ex2012)* ?/10/05.
G597 *(ex1260)* ?/3/11.
G613 *(ex1210)* ?/1/15.
D1555 *(new)* 29/12/24.
D573 *(ex2016)* 21/12/31.
2436 *(ex2011)* 14/4/34.
2326 *(ex1236)* 6/4/39.
2869 *(ex2013)* 18/4/46 (59A).
2500 *(ex2390)* 19/1/49.

SHEDS:
Tweedmouth.
Hull Botanic Gardens 4/2/28.
Scarborough 29/11/34.
Hull Botanic Gardens 1/7/35.
Neville Hill 29/5/40.

Hull Botanic Gardens 17/8/40.
Bridlington 18/11/40.
Hull Botanic Gardens 22/5/49.
Bridlington 4/12/49.

RENUMBERED:
2353 1/12/46.
62353 19/1/49.

CONDEMNED: 11/4/51.

_____

2025

Gateshead 25.00.

To traffic 9/1900.

REPAIRS:
???. ?/?—?/12/05.**G.**
???. ?/?—?/9/11.**G.**
Ghd. 19/12/24—6/3/25.**G.**
Superheated boiler fitted.
Ghd. 16/3—22/5/28.**G.**
Ghd. 15/4—22/5/31.**G.**
Ghd. 8—15/6/31.**N/C.**
Ghd. 14/7—12/8/32.**L.**
Dar. 1—8/8/33.**N/C.**
Dar. 9/4—10/5/34.**G.**
Dar. 17/1—27/3/35.**H.**
Dar. 22/5—3/7/36.**G.**
Dar. 24/8—14/9/38.**N/C.**
Dar. 2/8—14/9/39.**G.**
Dar. 14/5—29/6/42.**G.**
Dar. 14/7—1/9/45.**G.**
Dar. 24/12/47—23/1/48.**G.**
Dar. 5—13/2/48.**N/C.**
Ghd. 5—26/10/49.**C/L.**
Ghd. 12—18/10/50.**N/C.**

BOILERS:
G932.
G930 *(ex2024)* ?/12/05.
G614 *(ex1223)* ?/9/11.
D1550 *(new)* 6/3/25.
D529 *(ex1209)* 22/5/31.
2586 *(new)* 10/5/34.
D1554 *(ex2018)* 14/9/39.
2864 *(ex707)* 29/6/42 (59A).
2870 *(ex2021)* 1/9/45 (59A).
2140 *(ex2350)* 23/1/48.

SHEDS:
Tweedmouth.
Alnmouth 14/11/48.

RENUMBERED:
2354 10/11/46.
ᴇ2354 23/1/48.
62354 26/10/49.

CONDEMNED: 2/4/51.

_____

2026

Gateshead 26.00.

To traffic 10/1900.

REPAIRS:
???. ?/?—?/5/05.**G.**
???. ?/?—?/11/12.**G.**
Superheated boiler fitted.
Dar. 4/4—29/6/23.**G.**
Dar. 12/1—13/5/24.**G.**
Dar. 31/7—20/11/25.**G.**
Dar. 17/12/27—28/2/28.**G.**
Dar. 13/1—5/3/30.**G.**
Dar. 16/11/31—7/1/32.**G.**
Dar. 2/1—2/2/34.**G.**
Dar. 24/3—8/5/36.**G.**
Dar. 29/11/38—13/1/39.**G.**
Dar. 19/1—23/3/43.**G.**
Dar. 14/4—4/5/45.**L.**
Dar. 4/12/46—18/1/47.**G.**
Dar. 16/1—3/3/50.**G.**
Dar. 11/11/55.*Not repaired..*

BOILERS:
G992.
G928 *(ex2023)* ?/5/05.
D41 *(new)* ?/11/12.
G908 *(ex2014)* 29/6/23.
D1783 *(new)* 20/11/25.
D944 *(ex724)* 5/3/30.
D1554 *(ex708)* 2/2/34.
2140 *(ex1210)* 8/5/36.
2585 *(ex2028)* 13/1/39.
2726 *(ex2380)* 18/1/47 (59A).
3655 *(ex2352)* 3/3/50 (59A).

SHEDS:
Neville Hill.
Hull Botanic Gardens 30/12/24.
Bridlington 16/5/48.
Alnmouth 3/6/51.

RENUMBERED:
2355 17/11/46.
62355 3/3/50.

CONDEMNED: 14/11/55.
Cut up at Darlington.

_____

2027

Gateshead 27.00.

To traffic 10/1900.

REPAIRS:
???. ?/?—?/3/05.**G.**
???. ?/?—?/7/11.**G.**
???. ?/?—?/2/14.**G.**
Superheated boiler fitted.
Dar. 20/12/23—7/3/24.**G.**

Dar. 26/6—17/7/24.**N/C.**
Dar. 29/9/26—27/1/27.**G.**
Dar. 8/11/28—17/1/29.**G.**
Dar. 5/1—17/2/31.**G.**
Dar. 12/9—16/10/33.**G.**
Dar. 17/8—2/9/34.**L.**
Dar. 10/1—10/3/36.**G.**
Dar. 29/6—31/8/38.**G.**
Dar. 16/9—25/10/41.**G.**
Dar. 5/12/45—24/1/46.**G.**
Dar. 10/10/46. *Not repaired.*

BOILERS:
G998.
G926 *(ex2022)* ?/3/05.
G914 *(ex2109)* ?/7/11.
D271 *(new)* ?/2/14.
D43 *(ex2018)* 27/1/27.
2137 *(new)* 17/1/29.
2344 *(ex1260)* 16/10/33.
D1553 *(ex2017)* 10/3/36.
2324 *(ex1235)* 31/8/38.
D987 *(ex2023)* 25/10/41.
3650 *(new)* 24/1/46 (59A).

SHEDS:
York.
Heaton 16/11/31.
Blaydon 8/3/38.
Tweedmouth 23/1/39.
York 14/10/42.
Starbeck 12/3/45.

RENUMBERED:
2356 *allocated.*

CONDEMNED: 16/11/46.
Cut up at Darlington.

_____

2028

Gateshead 28.00.

To traffic 11/1900.

REPAIRS:
???. ?/?—?/12/05.**G.**
???. ?/?—?/8/12.**G.**
???. ?/?—?/4/18.**G.**
Superheated boiler fitted.
Dar. 21/3—12/6/24.**G.**
Dar. 18/10—24/11/24.**L.**
Ghd. 5/4—28/7/27.**G.**
Ghd. 25/1—3/2/28.**L.**
Ghd. 23/5—31/7/29.**G.**
Ghd. 16/7—7/8/31.**H.**
Ghd. 1—11/9/31.**N/C.**
Dar. 22/9—2/10/31.**N/C.**
Ghd. 24/8—7/10/32.**G.**
Dar. 23/4—23/5/34.**G.**
Dar. 29/1—24/3/36.**G.**
Dar. 7/4—14/5/37.**L.**
Dar. 6/9—20/10/38.**G.**

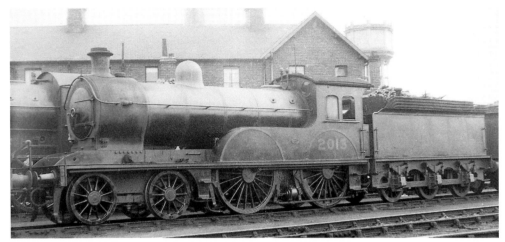

In 1932 a higher capacity overhead crane was installed at Darlington works and from then on, lifting holes were cut into the front end of the frame where suitable.

(above) The original frames with a concave curve at the front, even with the extension part did not permit a strong enough lifting point so no holes were cut into them (*see also* page 58, centre). Botanic Gardens, 24th June 1923.

(right) Many of the class kept the original NER design buffers and coupling hook. Darlington.

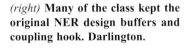

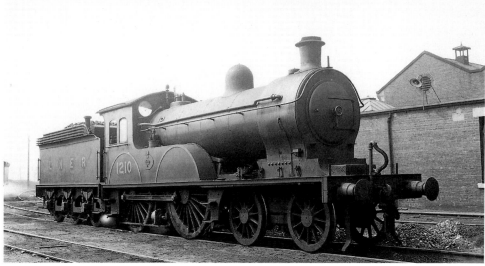

(above) On some, just the hook was changed to the Group Standard design, and this needed wood packing behind the circular flanges of the buffers to compensate for the longer hook. Bridlington, July 1957.

(left) From January 1931, on No.1184, Group Standard buffers and hook were fitted when change was needed, and at least twenty-three D20's were recorded as so fitted.

Apart from nine boilers built in 1932/1933 all had two hand holes on the left hand side for washing out purposes. Darlington, June 1932.

2028 cont./
Dar. 28/11—13/12/38.**N/C.**
Dar. 10/1—3/2/44.**G.**
Dar. 24/2—6/3/44.*Tender only.*
Dar. 31/1—2/2/46.**N/C.**
Dar. 27/9—26/10/46.**G.**
Ghd. 23/9—28/10/49.**C/H.**

BOILERS:
G999.
G30 *(ex2110)* ?/12/05.
G575 *(ex spare)* ?/8/12.
D37 *(ex2011)* ?/4/18.
D47 *(ex1672)* 12/6/24.
D496 *(ex2016)* 28/7/27.
2443 *(new)* 7/10/32.
2585 *(new)* 23/5/34.
2446 *(ex1051)* 20/10/38.
D1487 *(ex2016)* 3/2/44.
2323 *(ex2397)* 26/10/46.

SHEDS:
York.
Gateshead 4/12/24.
Blaydon 2/11/34.
Tweedmouth 24/1/39.
Northallerton 11/3/40.
Gateshead 22/11/40.
Heaton 5/3/45.
Duns 23/7/45.
Tweedmouth 1/2/48.
Alnmouth 5/6/49.

RENUMBERED:
2357 26/10/46.
62357 28/10/49.

CONDEMNED: 8/1/51.

───────────────

2029

Gateshead 29.00.

To traffic 11/1900.

REPAIRS:
???. ?/?—?/5/06.**G.**
???. ?/?—?/3/11.**G.**
???. ?/?—?/5/14.**G.**
Superheated boiler fitted.
Ghd. ?/?—10/8/22.**G.**
Ghd. 8/7—1/10/25.**G.**
Ghd. 15/2—18/4/29.**G.**
Ghd. 5/4—20/5/32.**G.**
Dar. 7/11/34—4/1/35.**G.**
Dar. 3/2—1/4/38.**G.**
Dar. 5/11—26/12/40.**G.**
Chimney cut to 13'-1".
Dar. 11/11—15/12/44.**G.**
Dar. 18/1—22/2/47.**G.**
Dar. 17/8—17/9/49.**G.**
Dar. 24/9—11/10/49.**N/C.**

BOILERS:
G4.
G932 *(ex2025)* ?/5/06.
G585 *(ex1217)* ?/3/11.
G608 *(ex1235)* ?/5/14.
D1763 *(new)* 1/10/25.
D933 *(ex707)* 4/1/35.
D1775 *(ex1672)* 1/4/38.
2325 *(ex2022)* 26/12/40.
2443 *(ex1665)* 15/12/44.
3659 *(new)* 22/2/47 (59A).
2586 *(ex2362)* 17/9/49.

SHEDS:
Tweedmouth.
Alnmouth 21/10/38.
Tweedmouth 7/12/38.
Alnmouth 23/4/50.
Tweedmouth 5/11/50.
Alnmouth 1/4/51.

RENUMBERED:
2358 18/8/46.
62358 17/9/49.

CONDEMNED: 19/10/54.

───────────────

2030

Gateshead 30.00.

To traffic 12/1900.

REPAIRS:
???. ?/?—?/1/07.**G.**
???. ?/?—?/2/18.**G.**
Superheated boiler fitted.
Ghd. 5/9—16/10/23.**L.**
Ghd. 2/6—2/9/24.**G.**
Ghd. 18/8—2/12/26.**G.**
Ghd. 26/2—4/6/29.**G.**
Ghd. 13/8—24/9/31.**G.**
Ghd. 5—9/10/31.**N/C.**
Ghd. 23/3—8/4/32.**L.**
Ghd. 23/12/32.**N/C.**
Dar. 9/11/33—23/2/34.**G.**
Dar. 23/9—5/11/36.**G.**
Dar. 11/7—31/8/38.**G.**
Dar. 6/3—2/5/40.**L.**
After collision.
Dar. 25/10/40.*Weigh.*
Dar. 24—28/6/41.**N/C.**
Dar. 27/5—11/7/42.**G.**
Dar. 26/6—1/9/45.**G.**
Dar. 26/10—8/12/45.**L.**
After collision.
Dar. 21/1—23/2/49.**G.**
Dar. 1—8/3/49.**N/C.**

BOILERS:
G10.
G4 *(ex2029)* ?/1/07.
D573 *(new)* ?/2/18.

D522 *(ex2022)* 2/12/26.
2510 *(new)* 23/2/34.
D1554 *(ex2025)* 11/7/42.
2869 *(ex2353)* 23/2/49 (59A).

SHEDS:
Gateshead.
West Hartlepool 15/4/35.
Middlesbrough 29/3/38.
Stockton 31/5/39.
Northallerton 16/10/39.
Stockton 16/7/42.
Newport 30/5/45.
Northallerton 1/9/45.
West Hartlepool 12/9/45.
Hull Botanic Gardens 20/5/49.
Northallerton 4/12/49.
West Auckland 26/10/52.
West Hartlepool 2/11/52.
Northallerton 16/5/54.
Neville Hill 26/6/55.

RENUMBERED:
2359 24/11/46.
62359 23/2/49.

CONDEMNED: 26/10/55.

───────────────

2101

Gateshead 31.00.

To traffic 12/1900.

REPAIRS:
???. ?/?—?/12/10.**G.**
???. ?/?—?/4/19.**G.**
Superheater put in.
???. ?/?—?/5/22.**G.**
Dar. 12/1—29/5/24.**G.**
Dar. 28/4—26/6/25.**G.**
Dar. 17/5—31/8/26.**G.**
Dar. 12/10—10/11/26.**L.**
Dar. 19/1—10/4/28.**G.**
Dar. 4/12/29—5/2/30.**G.**
Dar. 24/3—7/4/30.**N/C.**
Dar. 15/6—26/7/32.**G.**
Dar. 15/1—23/2/35.**G.**
Dar. 23/2—14/5/37.**G.**
Dar. 16/5—29/6/39.**G.**
Dar. 27/7—11/12/42.**G.**
Rebuilt to Part 2.
Dar. 13/12/44—18/1/45.**G.**
Dar. 26/1—3/2/45.**N/C.**
Dar. 12/8/47—9/1/48.**G.**
Ghd. 11—19/12/50.**L.**
Dar. 10/6—5/7/52.**G.**
Dar. 7—9/7/52.**N/C.**

BOILERS:
G11.
G906 *(new)* ?/12/10.
D1381 *(new)* ?/5/22.

D341 *(ex2021)* 26/6/25.
D2079 *(new)* 10/4/28.
2139 *(ex711)* 26/7/32.
2087 *(ex1184)* 23/2/35.
2322 *(ex2110)* 14/5/37.
2504 *(ex1206)* 29/6/39.
3960 *(new)* 5/7/52 (59A).
3960 reno. 24606.

SHEDS:
York.
Hull Botanic Gardens 9/2/34.
Starbeck 19/2/35.
Hull Botanic Gardens 28/8/40.
Bridlington 18/11/40.
Blaydon 13/12/47.
Alnmouth 2/1/49.
Gateshead 7/6/53.
Alnmouth 4/10/53.
Gateshead 13/6/54.
Alnmouth 10/10/54.

RENUMBERED:
2360 27/4/46.
62360 5/7/52.

CONDEMNED: 23/10/56.
Originally condemned 18/9/47,
but this was later cancelled, and
No.2360 got a general repair.

───────────────

2102

Gateshead 32.00.

To traffic 12/1900.

REPAIRS:
???. ?/?—?/2/11.**G.**
???. ?/?—?/6/16.**G.**
Superheated boiler fitted.
???. ?/?—?/10/22.**G.**
Dar. 23/2—15/5/24.**G.**
Dar. 9/4—27/8/26.**G.**
Dar. 24/3—1/6/28.**G.**
Dar. 25/7—26/9/30.**G.**
Dar. 9/1—8/2/33.**G.**
Dar. 12/5—17/7/34.**H.**
Dar. 12/3—17/5/35.**G.**
Dar. 3/6—17/7/35.**H.**
New coupled wheel tyres.
Dar. 12/7—14/9/37.**G.**
Dar. 1/6—2/8/39.**G.**
Dar. 10/6—17/8/43.**G.**
Ghd. 7/2—3/4/47.**L.**
Dar. 2—27/2/48.**G.**

BOILERS:
G12.
G908 *(new)* ?/2/11.
G909 *(ex2105)* ?/6/16.
D39 *(ex2013)* ?/10/22.
D2087 *(new)* 1/6/28.

2102 cont./
D1547 *(ex1078)* 8/2/33.
D1487 *(ex724)* 17/7/34.
D1515 *(ex1232)* 14/9/37.
  2446 *(ex2382)* 27/2/48.

SHEDS:
Hull Botanic Gardens.
Selby 14/11/48.

RENUMBERED:
  2361 1/12/46.
ᴇ**2361** 27/2/48.

CONDEMNED: 27/2/51.

_____

2103

Gateshead 34.00.

To traffic 12/1900.

REPAIRS:
???. ?/?—?/3/11.**G.**
???. ?/?—?/7/18.**G.**
Superheated boiler fitted.
Dar. 24/3—31/5/24.**G.**
Dar. 28/6—5/8/24.**L.**
Dar. 21/1—8/6/27.**G.**
Dar. 19/12/28—22/2/29.**G.**
Dar. 20/10—4/12/30.**G.**
Dar. 7/4—27/5/32.**G.**
Dar. 31/1—1/3/34.**G.**
Dar. 13/9—12/12/35.**G.**
Dar. 14—20/12/35.**N/C.**
Dar. 28/2—6/5/36.**L.**
Dar. 21/9—24/12/36.**L.**
Dar. 15/2—6/4/37.**N/C.**
Dar. 22/6—15/7/37.**N/C.**
Dar. 11/8/37. *Tender weigh.*
Dar. 30/1—21/3/39.**G.**
Dar. 27/8—9/10/40.**H.**
Dar. 19/3—29/4/41.**L.**
Dar. 19/5—10/7/43.**G.**
Dar. 21/12/44—5/1/45.**N/C.**
Dar. 4/5—1/6/46.**G.**
Dar. 13—20/6/46.**N/C.**
Dar. 19/5—18/6/49.**G.**

BOILERS:
  G13.
  G11 *(ex2101)* ?/3/11.
  G541 *(ex712)* ?/7/18.
  D1541 *(new)* 31/5/24.
  D1487 *(ex1051)* 4/12/30.
  D985 *(ex2020)* 27/5/32.
  2323 *(ex2014)* 1/3/34.
  2725 *(new)* 12/12/35 (59A).
  2586 *(ex723)* 1/6/46.
  3927 *(new)* 18/6/49 (59A).

SHEDS:
Hull Botanic Gardens.

Neville Hill 20/1/26.
Hull Botanic Gardens 4/2/26.
Neville Hill 30/5/40.
Hull Botanic Gardens 17/8/40.
Alnmouth 5/10/47.
Bridlington 7/8/49.
Alnmouth 23/4/50.

RENUMBERED:
  2362 17/11/46.
62362 18/6/49.

CONDEMNED: 11/4/51.

_____

2104

Gateshead 35.00.

To traffic 2/1901.

REPAIRS:
???. ?/?—?/3/09.**G.**
???. ?/?—?/8/14.**G.**
Superheated boiler fitted.
???. ?/?—?/9/20.**G.**
Dar. 9/1—21/4/23.**G.**
Dar. 21/5—15/8/24.**G.**
Ghd. 20/4—4/8/27.**G.**
Dar. 20/6—11/7/28.**L.**
Ghd. 6/6—4/12/29.**G.**
Ghd. 11/4—23/5/32.**G.**
Ghd. 2—9/6/32.**N/C.**
Dar. 6/3—28/5/34.**G.**
Dar. 9/2—26/4/37.**G.**
Dar. 24/4—30/5/40.**G.**
Water scoop taken off.
Dar. 17/2—29/3/41.**L.**
After collision.
Dar. 8/12/43—8/1/44.**G.**
Dar. 14/6—13/7/46.**G.**
Ghd. 23/9—17/10/47.**L.**
Dar. 12/2/48. *Weigh.*
Dar. 22/12/48—26/1/49.**G.**

BOILERS:
  G14.
  G425 *(ex2018)* ?/3/09.
  G585 *(ex2029)* ?/8/14.
  D991 *(new)* ?/9/20.
  D47 *(ex2028)* 4/8/27.
  2308 *(new)* 4/12/29.
  2339 *(ex2013)* 26/4/37.
  2087 *(ex1184)* 30/5/40.
  D1375 *(ex1207)* 8/1/44.
  2326 *(ex2024)* 13/7/46.
  3409 *(ex2344)* 26/1/49 (59A).

SHEDS:
York.
Gateshead 4/12/24.
Starbeck 15/4/35.
Selby 18/12/49.

RENUMBERED:
  2363 17/11/46.
62363 26/1/49.

CONDEMNED: 20/3/51.

_____

2105

Gateshead 36.00.

To traffic 3/1901.

REPAIRS:
???. ?/?—?/3/11.**G.**
???. ?/?—?/7/15.**G.**
Superheated boiler fitted.
???. ?/?—?/7/22.**G.**
Ghd. 8/5—24/7/24.**G.**
Ghd. 27/8—10/9/25.**L.**
Ghd. 7/10/26—3/2/27.**G.**
Ghd. 31/10—19/11/28.**L.**
Ghd. 15/3—27/5/29.**G.**
Ghd. 24/7—31/8/31.**G.**
Ghd. 1—7/4/32.**N/C.**
Dar. 15/9—25/10/33.**G.**
Dar. 12/4—7/6/35.**G.**
Dar. 15/3—6/8/37.**G.**
Dar. 13/9—27/10/39.**G.**
Dar. 27/6—1/8/42.**G.**
Dar. 10/10—11/11/44.**G.**
Dar. 17/1/45. *Weigh.*
Dar. 9/8/47. *Not repaired.*

BOILERS:
  G15.
  G909 *(new)* ?/3/11.
  G522 *(ex1260)* ?/7/15.
  D1409 *(new)* ?/7/22.
  D537 *(ex1258)* 31/8/31.
  2142 *(ex2023)* 25/10/33.
  2079 *(ex707)* 6/8/37.
  2314 *(ex2106)* 27/10/39.
  D1773 *(ex592)* 1/8/42.
  2512 *(ex1051)* 11/11/44.

SHEDS:
Gateshead.
Starbeck 15/4/35.

RENUMBERED:
2364 15/12/46.

CONDEMNED: 7/10/47.
Cut up at Darlington.

_____

2106

Gateshead 1.01.

To traffic 3/1901.

REPAIRS:
???. ?/?—?/2/15.**G.**
Superheated boiler fitted.
Dar. 27/10/22—20/2/23.**G.**
Dar. 5/5—20/6/24.**G.**
Dar. 25/3—11/8/25.**G.**
Dar. 27/10/27—13/1/28.**G.**
Dar. 14—20/3/29.**N/C.**
Dar. 18/9—6/11/29.**G.**
Dar. 4/12/31—22/1/32.**G.**
Dar. 7/7—4/8/33.**H.**
Dar. 30/4—31/5/34.**G.**
Dar. 25/2/36. *Weigh.*
Dar. 2/10—18/12/36.**G.**
Dar. 8/2—2/3/38.**L.**
Dar. 23/6—12/8/39.**G.**
Dar. 7/5—20/6/41.**G.**
Dar. 19/9—20/10/45.**G.**
Dar. 11/11—18/12/48.**G.**

BOILERS:
  G16.
  D337 *(new)* ?/2/15.
  D1381 *(ex2101)* 11/8/25.
  D1555 *(ex2024)* 22/1/32.
  2314 *(ex2020)* 31/5/34.
  D1539 *(ex2110)* 12/8/39.
  2341 *(ex2012)* 20/6/41.
  2324 *(ex1235)* 20/10/45.
  3667 *(ex2342)* 18/12/48 (59A).

SHEDS:
Darlington.
Alnmouth 7/11/38.
Gateshead 11/8/41.
Newport 13/2/43.
Stockton 5/11/45.
West Hartlepool 6/10/46.
Stockton 21/6/47.
Hull Botanic Gardens 22/5/49.
Alnmouth 4/12/49.
Bridlington 23/4/50.
Alnmouth 5/11/50.

RENUMBERED:
  2365 27/10/46.
62365 18/12/48.

CONDEMNED: 4/4/51.

_____

2107

Gateshead 2.01.

To traffic 3/1901.

REPAIRS:
???. ?/?—?/6/09.**G.**
???. ?/?—?/4/15.**G.**
Superheated boiler fitted.
Ghd. 9/10—28/12/23.**G.**
Ghd. 13/4—5/8/26.**G.**
Ghd. 11—13/8/26.**L.**

On the right hand side were two similar hand holes placed nearer the cab front to give the desirable staggered effect.

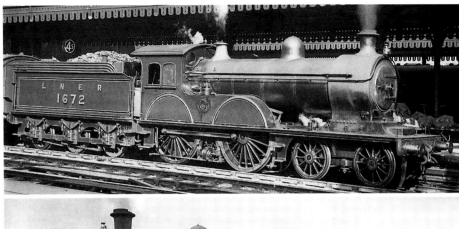

On four boilers built during April and May 1932 (Nos.2436, 2443, 2445, 2446), and five built during April and May 1933 (Nos.2500, 2504, 2507, 2510, 2512), there was a change to four plugs on the left hand side of the firebox. These nine boilers did not have a cover to the base of the safety valves. Leeds.

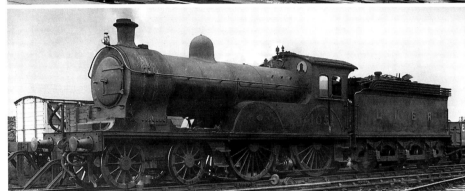

The 1932 and 1933 built boilers were fitted with three plugs on the right hand side of the firebox, pitched between the four on the opposite side.

These nine boilers served until the 1950's and no change was made to the washout plugs. Two of them were re-numbered by British Railways in the series they used from August 1950. Engine No.62388 had boiler 24600 when both were condemned on 26th April 1954 but the last of the batch, renumbered 24611 went out of stock with Part 2 engine No.62375 on 7th May 1957. Darlington.

When the revised boiler to Diagram 59A was introduced in November 1935 there was reversion to two hand holes on the left hand side of the firebox. Diagram 59A boilers also had two hand holes on the right hand side. Leeds (City), July 1956.

Although not fitted when built, most had steps welded to each side of the smokebox front plate before Grouping. No.713 was most unusual in getting its LNER livery on 16h February 1925 - before getting the steps.

The front plate of the smokebox of all the class when new was secured to the wrapper by an internal angle iron, which gave a sharp right-angled corner on the outside; No.1184 still had one as late as 1931.

From about 1915 the smokebox front plates had the edge flanged to fit inside the wrapper and all were duly changed to this type when replacement was needed.

For smokebox door fastening the original provision was a pair of handles and these were still carried by the majority of the class at the end of the North Eastern.

In early LNER years quite a number had a wheel instead of one handle, but there was a steady reversion to two handles although No.2101 carried a wheel until February 1937.

2107 cont./
Ghd. 7/2—24/4/29.**G.**
Ghd. 29/9—5/11/31.**G.**
Ghd. 20—25/11/31.**N/C.**
Dar. 27/11/33—2/1/34.**G.**
Dar. 6—30/11/34.**L.**
Dar. 24/8—30/10/36.**G.**
Dar. 7/10—17/11/37.**L.**
Dar. 27/9—3/11/38.**H.**
Dar. 15/5—18/6/40.**G.**
Dar. 24/6—4/7/40.**N/C.**
Dar. 15/12/42—22/6/43.**G.**
Dar. 13—26/7/43.**N/C.**
Dar. 26/1—2/3/46.**G.**
Ghd. 12—29/5/47.**L.**
Dar. 25/8—24/9/48.**G.**

BOILERS:
G17.
G341 *(ex2019)* ?/6/09.
G597 *(ex2024)* ?/4/15.
D1501 *(new)* 28/12/23.
D1409 *(ex2105)* 5/11/31.
D1501 *(ex1210)* 2/1/34.
D1764 *(ex1672)* 18/6/40.
D1783 *(ex1234)* 22/6/43.
3652 *(new)* 2/3/46 (59A).
2436 *(ex2340)* 24/9/48.

SHEDS:
Gateshead.
Starbeck 21/5/37.
Selby 15/8/48.

RENUMBERED:
2366 22/12/46.
62366 24/9/48.

CONDEMNED: 13/3/51.

2108

Gateshead 3.01.

To traffic 4/1901.

REPAIRS:
???. ?/?—?/2/06.**G.**
???. ?/?—?/3/10.**G.**
???. ?/?—?/11/15.**G.**
Superheated boiler fitted.
Dar. 13/9/22—9/1/23.**G.**
Dar. ?/6—29/6/32.**L.**
Dar. 19/12/24—18/3/25.**G.**
Dar. 25/2—11/6/26.**G.**
Dar. 9/8—31/10/27.**G.**
Dar. 14/2—7/3/28.**N/C.**
Dar. 6/6—23/8/29.**G.**
Dar. 3/5—12/6/31.**G.**
Dar. 2/5—24/6/32.**G.**
Dar. 15/2—16/3/34.**G.**
Dar. 27/4—17/6/36.**G.**
Dar. 22/10—15/12/37.**G.**

Dar. 30/5—29/6/40.**G.**
Dar. 21/5—1/7/41.**L.**
After falling into a bomb crater 16/4/41.
Dar. 24/12/43—28/1/44.**G.**
Dar. 3/10—8/11/44.**L.**
Dar. 11/12/47. *Not repaired.*

BOILERS:
G18.
G999 *(ex2028)* ?/2/06.
G14 *(ex2104)* ?/3/10.
D491 *(new)* ?/11/15.
2512 *(new)* 16/3/34.
D1764 *(ex2018)* 17/6/36.
D1487 *(ex2102)* 15/12/37.
D1501 *(ex2107)* 29/6/40.
3412 *(new)* 28/1/44 (59A).

SHEDS:
Neville Hill.
Scarborough 30/11/40.
Hull Botanic Gardens 15/10/42.

RENUMBERED:
2367 15/12/46.

CONDEMNED: 17/1/48.
Cut up at Darlington.

2109

Gateshead 4.01.

To traffic 4/1901.

REPAIRS:
???. ?/?—?/8/07.**G.**
???. ?/?—?/3/11.**G.**
???. ?/?—?/11/12.**G.**
Superheated boiler fitted.
Dar. 6/12/22—20/3/23.**G.**
Dar. 24/9—18/12/24.**G.**
Dar. 15/1—28/4/26.**G.**
Dar. 24/8—27/10/26.**L.**
Dar. 18/2—5/5/28.**G.**
Dar. 26/8—16/10/30.**G.**
Dar. 8/2—22/3/33.**G.**
Dar. 19/3—2/5/35.**G.**
Dar. 11/12/36—19/2/37.**G.**
Dar. 22/2—4/3/37.**N/C.**
Dar. 22/5—4/8/39.**G.**
Dar. 6—29/5/43.**L.**
Dar. 1/5/44. *Not repaired.*

BOILERS:
G24.
G914 *(ex spare)* ?/8/07.
G13 *(ex2103)* ?/3/11.
D40 *(new)* ?/11/12.
D341 *(ex2101)* 5/5/28.
2338 *(new)* 16/10/30.
D1775 *(ex1232)* 22/3/33.

D1541 *(ex1665)* 2/5/35.
2507 *(ex725)* 19/2/37.
2322 *(ex2101)* 4/8/39.

SHEDS:
Neville Hill.
Hull Botanic Gardens 22/4/31.
Neville Hill 30/5/40.
Hull Botanic Gardens 17/8/40.
Selby 9/9/40.
Scarborough 5/3/42.
Hull Botanic Gardens 15/10/42.

RENUMBERED:
2348 *allocated.*

CONDEMNED: 10/6/44.
Cut up at Darlington.

2110

Gateshead 5.01.

To traffic 5/1901.

REPAIRS:
???. ?/?—?/9/05.**G.**
???. ?/?—?/3/11.**G.**
???. ?/?—?/9/17.**G.**
Superheated boiler fitted.
Dar. 13/6—10/9/24.**G.**
Dar. 17—24/10/24.**L.**
Dar. 17/3—29/6/27.**G.**
Ghd. 15/5—21/8/29.**G.**
Ghd. 11/2—23/3/32.**G.**
Dar. 21/4—27/5/33.**H.**
Dar. 13/4—10/5/34.**G.**
Dar. 11—17/5/34.**N/C.**
Dar. 3/2—10/3/37.**G.**
Dar. 22/6—12/8/39.**G.**
Dar. 19/6—11/9/43.**G.**
Dar. 8/1—13/2/48.**G.**
Dar. 24/2—1/3/48.**N/C.**
Ghd. 6/10—4/11/49.**C/H.**

BOILERS:
G30.
G913 *(ex2013)* ?/9/05.
G907 *(new)* ?/3/11.
D499 *(new)* ?/9/17.
D1439 *(ex1210)* 23/3/32.
2322 *(ex1223)* 10/5/34.
D1539 *(ex708)* 10/3/37.
2507 *(ex2109)* 12/8/39.
2135 *(ex2374)* 13/2/48.

SHEDS:
Darlington.
York 2/4/28.
Hull Botanic Gardens 3/1/29.
Gateshead 11/1/29.
Selby 2/10/36.
Hull Botanic Gardens 26/11/40.

Selby 14/11/48.
Starbeck 17/9/50.

RENUMBERED:
2369 22/12/46.
E2369 13/2/48
62369 4/11/49.

CONDEMNED: 6/3/51.

476

Gateshead 53.

To traffic 9/1906.

REPAIRS:
???. ?/?—?/3/13.**G.**
???. ?/?—?/6/15.**G.**
Superheated boiler fitted.
???. ?/?—?/4/22.**G.**
Dar. 15/9—27/11/24.**G.**
Dar. 8/12/25—24/2/26.**G.**
Dar. 25/3—9/4/26.**L.**
Dar. 21/11/28—24/1/29.**G.**
Dar. 29/1—11/2/29.**N/C.**
Dar. 10/3—29/4/31.**N/C.**
Audible signalling app. fitted.
Dar. 22/6—9/7/31.**N/C.**
Ghd. 9/12/31—27/1/32.**G.**
Ghd. 20—22/4/32.**N/C.**
Dar. 16/5—5/7/35.**G.**
Dar. 24/2—7/4/37.**G.**
Dar. 28/12/38—6/1/39.**N/C.**
Dar. 22/4—19/5/39.**G.**
Dar. 24/3—15/4/42.*Tender only.*
Dar. 10—18/7/42.**N/C.**
Dar. 27/8—5/10/42.**G.**
Dar. 26/10—29/11/45.**G.**
Dar. 11/11—5/12/47.**G.**
Dar. 25/8/49.*Weigh.*

BOILERS:
G516.
G548 *(ex725)* ?/3/13.
G341 *(ex2107)* ?/6/15.
D1375 *(new)* ?/4/22.
D1550 *(ex1207)* 5/7/35.
2436 *(ex2024)* 19/5/39.
2510 *(ex2030)* 5/10/42.
2341 *(ex2106)* 29/11/45.
2339 *(ex2381)* 5/12/47.

SHEDS:
Darlington.
Heaton 27/11/33.
Haverton Hill 11/6/36.
Middlesbrough 6/10/36.
Stockton 31/5/39.
Northallerton 16/10/39.
Stockton 28/2/42.
Northallerton 25/1/43.
Newport 27/5/44.

(above) **Until March 1945 the smokebox door had a flat flange which made the seal by pressure against the ring riveted to the smokebox front plate. Darlington works.**

(right) **Starting in March 1945, with No.2023, a larger diameter door was introduced with the edge flanged at a right angle. The channel shaped front ring was then welded on and it housed packing into which the rim of the door was pressed. No.2027 got this type of door when ex works 24th January 1946 when a Diagram 59A boiler was put on. With this type of door it was usual to fit a new type chimney with liner and cowl (*see also* page 47, 2nd from bottom). Arthington, with 511.**

The larger door, with pressed joint ring was also used for Diagram 59 boilers when replacement was needed. No.2363 (when still No.2104) got the larger door on 13th July 1946. Starbeck, June 1947.

As a consequence of damage from a collision in March 1944, No.2014 (62343 later) had its brass splasher beading taken off, the only Part 1 engine to lose it. However, the number was still displayed in the same position as it was with beading and was never centred on the cab which it could have been.

During the war, and after, many had the beading covered by black paint, but there was no deliberate attempt to have it removed. Darlington.

Where shed staff had enough interest, it was an easy job to remove the paint from the beading and many D20's still had it polished in their final years despite much less attention to general cleaning. Dairycoates, 17th May 1951.

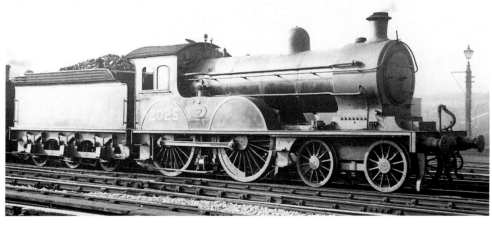

Until after the 1939-1945 war there was no provision for sanding when running in reverse, only air-operated sanding in front of the leading coupled wheels.

Changed duties after the war led to No.2011 being the first to have rear sanding fitted when ex works on 15th September 1945. Nos.2363, 2366 and 2373 were also soon fitted likewise.

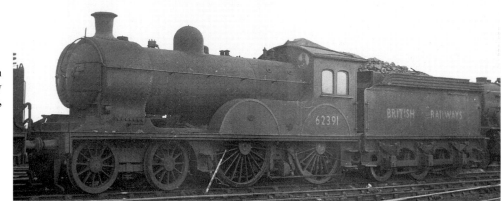

Addition of sanding for running in reverse then became generally fitted on the survivors. Newport, September 1949.

The Diagram 59 boilers had a tall dome cover slightly tapered towards the top.

At least the first eight Diagram 59A boilers - those built in December 1935 (3) and in January 1937 (5) had the same type of dome cover.

From September 1943 the dome cover on all further Diagram 59A boiler was made larger in diameter but not so tall, although there was no change in the height of the dome itself. Leeds.

Until the end of October 1933 all the D20's were fitted with Raven's fog signalling apparatus. The striking toggle could be seen just ahead of the leading coupled wheel on the right hand side. Darlington.

From March 1931 to April 1932 No.476 was equipped for trials of Gresham & Craven's system of automatic train control, for which the striker was under the cab. After the Raven system was discarded in October 1933, the apparatus was taken off and D20 class took no further part in attempts made to solve this problem. Darlington.

476 cont./
Starbeck 5/3/45.

RENUMBERED:
2370 17/11/46.

CONDEMNED: 19/4/51.

_____

592

Gateshead 54.

To traffic 9/1906.

REPAIRS:
???. ?/?—?/9/10.**G.**
???. ?/?—?/2/15.**G.**
Superheated boiler fitted.
Ghd. ?/?—29/11/22.**G.**
Ghd. 29/4—5/8/25.**G.**
Ghd. 20/1—13/4/28.**G.**
Ghd. 29/3—21/5/30.**G.**
Ghd. 27/10—22/12/32.**G.**
Dar. 14/8—15/11/35.**G.**
Dar. 19/8—12/10/37.**H.**
Dar. 20/12/38—28/1/39.**G.**
Dar. 3/3—9/10/42.**G.**
Rebuilt to Part 2.
Dar. 10—29/1/44.**L.**
Dar. 15/5—15/6/46.**G.**
Dar. 28/6—6/7/46.**N/C.**
Dar. 27/9—22/10/48.**G.**
Dar. 16—27/11/48.**N/C.**

BOILERS:
G522.
 G17 *(ex spare)* ?/9/10.
 G516 *(ex spare)* ?/2/15.
D1439 *(new)* 29/11/22.
 D502 *(ex1147)* 21/5/30.
 2323 *(ex2103)* 15/11/35.
D1773 *(ex1209)* 12/10/37.
 2308 *(ex711)* 9/10/42.
 3654 *(new)* 15/6/46 (59A).
 3653 *(ex2373)* 22/10/48 (59A).

SHEDS:
Tweedmouth.
Alnmouth 17/6/39.
Heaton 24/7/39.
Alnmouth 23/7/45.
Blaydon 5/10/47.
Alnmouth 5/6/49.
Tweedmouth 15/3/53.
Gateshead 7/6/53.
Alnmouth 4/10/53.

RENUMBERED:
 2371 12/5/46.
 62371 22/10/48.

CONDEMNED: 19/10/54.

_____

707

Gateshead 55.

To traffic 10/1906.

REPAIRS:
???. ?/?—?/10/17.**G.**
Superheated boiler fitted.
???. ?/?—?/9/22.**G.**
Dar. 23/2—16/5/24.**G.**
Dar. 8/2—10/6/26.**G.**
Dar. 2—15/7/26.**L.**
Dar. 15/7—24/8/27.**L.**
Ghd. 3/7—18/9/28.**G.**
Dar. 7/4—4/7/30.**G.**
Dar. 22/3—2/5/32.**G.**
Dar. 11/10—19/11/34.**G.**
Dar. 2/12/36—4/2/37.**G.**
Dar. 24/5—10/6/37.**N/C.**
Dar. 21/1—16/3/39.**G.**
Dar. 2/5—12/6/40.*Tender only.*
Dar. 29/4—1/6/42.**G.**
Dar. 14/2—4/4/45.**G.**
Dar. 26/1—27/2/48.**G.**
Dar. 12—19/3/48.**N/C.**
Dar. 29/9—25/10/52.**G.**
Dar. 27—30/10/52.**N/C.**

BOILERS:
 G526.
 G535 *(ex725)* ?/10/17.
D1428 *(new)* ?/9/22.
 D933 *(ex1042)* 4/7/30.
D2079 *(ex1042)* 19/11/34.
 2864 *(new)* 4/2/37 (59A).
 2344 *(ex2014)* 1/6/42.
 2137 *(ex2023)* 4/4/45.
 2870 *(ex2354)* 27/2/48 (59A).
 3967 *(new)* 25/10/52 (59A).
 3967 reno.24607.

SHEDS:
York.
Selby 3/10/33.
Hull Botanic Gardens 14/11/48.
West Hartlepool 22/5/49.
Northallerton 27/5/51.
West Hartlepool 20/12/53.
Neville Hill 26/6/55.
Bridlington 10/6/56.

RENUMBERED:
 2372 17/11/46.
 ᴇ2372 27/2/48.
 62372 25/10/52.

CONDEMNED: 5/11/56.

_____

708

Gateshead 56.

To traffic 10/1906.

REPAIRS:
???. ?/?—?/4/12.**G.**
???. ?/?—?/1/21.**G.**
Superheated boiler fitted.
Dar. 1/2—16/4/24.**G.**
Dar. 31/3—24/8/26.**G.**
Dar. 17/5—18/7/28.**G.**
Dar. 11/3—7/5/31.**G.**
Dar. 27/11/33—3/1/34.**G.**
Dar. 26/11/36—19/1/37.**G.**
Dar. 31/7—10/9/41.**G.**
Dar. 14—29/8/42.**L.**
Dar. 8/3—6/4/46.**G.**
Dar. 2/9—1/10/48.**G.**
Dar. 4—31/10/52.**C/L.**
Dar. 3—6/11/52.**N/C.**
Dar. 4—11/12/52.**N/C.**
Dar. 17/2/53. *Not repaired.*

BOILERS:
 G533.
 G581 *(ex1147)* ?/4/12.
 G593 *(ex spare)* ?/1/21.
D1515 *(new)* 16/4/24.
D1554 *(ex1026)* 7/5/31.
D1539 *(ex2016)* 3/1/34.
 2137 *(ex2014)* 19/1/37.
 2500 *(ex1236)* 10/9/41.
 3653 *(new)* 6/4/46 (59A).
 3652 *(ex2366)* 1/10/48 (59A).
 3652 reno.24608 31/10/52.

SHEDS:
York.
Scarborough 19/4/24.
York 20/5/40.
Starbeck 12/3/45.
Northallerton 3/6/51.

RENUMBERED:
 2373 17/11/46.
 62373 1/10/48.

CONDEMNED: 23/2/53.
Cut up at Darlington.

_____

711

Gateshead 57.

To traffic 10/1906.

REPAIRS:
???. ?/?—?/11/12.**G.**
???. ?/?—?/5/15.**G.**
Superheated boiler fitted.
???. ?/?—?/6/19.**G.**
Dar. 6/10—14/12/23.**G.**
Dar. 12/8—9/9/24.**L.**
Dar. 7/2—9/7/25.**H.**
Dar. 27/10/26—28/2/27.**G.**
Dar. 1/11—27/12/28.**G.**
Dar. 11/6—15/8/30.**G.**
Dar. 1/6—11/7/32.**G.**

Dar. 12/9—5/10/34.**L.**
Dar. 8/3—12/6/37.**G.**
Dar. 26/6—12/8/39.**G.**
Dar. 7/7—13/8/42.**G.**
Dar. 6—26/10/43.**L.**
Dar. 3/4—10/5/44.**G.**
Dar. 28/5—25/6/45.**L.**
Dar. 18/11—24/12/47.**G.**
Dar. 18/4—20/5/50.**G.**

BOILERS:
 G535.
 G30 *(ex2028)* ?/11/12.
 G547 *(ex724)* ?/5/15.
 D936 *(new)* ?/6/19.
 2139 *(new)* 27/12/28.
 2091 *(ex724)* 11/7/32.
 2308 *(ex2104)* 12/6/37.
 2314 *(ex2105)* 13/8/42.
 2135 *(ex1184)* 10/5/44.
 2512 *(ex2364)* 24/12/47.
 2726 *(ex2355)* 20/5/50 (59A).

SHEDS:
York.
Scarborough 5/7/37.
Selby 28/3/38.

RENUMBERED:
 2374 14/4/46.
 62374 20/5/50.

CONDEMNED: 14/10/54.

_____

712

Gateshead 58.

To traffic 11/1906.

REPAIRS:
???. ?/?—?/7/18.**G.**
Superheated boiler fitted.
???. ?/?—?/7/20.**G.**
Dar. 22/2—9/5/23.**G.**
Dar. 6/2—11/5/25.**G.**
Dar. 30/4—12/8/27.**G.**
Dar. 13/2—9/3/28.**L.**
Dar. 13/3—10/5/29.**G.**
Dar. 8/12/31—15/2/32.**G.**
Dar. 24/5—30/6/34.**G.**
Dar. 6/7—24/9/36.**G.**
Dar. 15/3—12/4/38.**N/C.**
Dar. 14/6—31/7/39.**G.**
Dar. 5/1—27/2/43.**G.**
Dar. 24/12/45—9/2/46.**G.**
Dar. 16—23/2/46.**N/C.**
Dar. 27/2—8/3/46.**N/C.**
Dar. 16/6—9/10/48.**G.**
Rebuilt to Part 2.
Dar. 17/8—11/9/53.**G.**

BOILERS:
 G541.

712 cont./

G548 *(ex713)* ?/7/18.
D987 *(new)* ?/7/20.
D1381 *(ex2106)* 15/2/32.
D1439 *(ex2110)* 30/6/34.
D1409 *(ex1223)* 24/9/36.
  3405 *(ex1217)* 9/2/46 (59A).
  24611 *(ex spare)* 11/9/53.

SHEDS:
Hull Botanic Gardens.
York 15/6/25.
Scarborough 7/2/30.
Starbeck 14/9/34.
Bridlington 17/4/50.
Alnmouth 3/6/51.
Gateshead 7/6/53.
Alnmouth 4/10/53.
Gateshead 13/6/54.
Alnmouth 10/10/54.

RENUMBERED:
2375 12/5/46.
62375 8/10/48.

CONDEMNED: 7/5/57.

713

Gateshead 59.

To traffic 11/1906.

REPAIRS:
???. ?/?—?/8/15.**G.**
Superheated boiler fitted.
???. ?/?—?/1/18.**G.**
???. ?/?—?/12/22.**G.**
Dar. 11/11/24—16/2/25.**G.**
Dar. 5/10/26—10/2/27.**G.**
Dar. 20/11/28—24/1/29.**G.**
Dar. 3/12/30—29/1/31.**G.**
Dar. 25/3—10/4/31.**N/C.**
Dar. 20/5—20/6/32.**H.**
Dar. 28/4—20/6/33.**G.**
Dar. 26/6—2/9/36.**G.**
Dar. 16/8—30/9/37.**H.**
Dar. 8/6—3/8/38.**G.**
Dar. 14/6—18/8/39.**N/C.**
Dar. 4/6—15/7/40.**H.**
Dar. 24/9—12/10/40.**L.**
Dar. 19/11—26/12/41.**G.**
Dar. 25/1—19/2/44.**G.**
Dar. 28/5—6/6/45.**N/C.**
Dar. 13/9—31/10/47.**G.**
Dar. 18—28/11/47.**N/C.**
Dar. 3—24/12/47.**N/C.**

BOILERS:
  G544.

G548 *(ex476)* ?/8/15.
G907 *(ex2110)* ?/1/18.
G909 *(ex2102)* ?/12/22.
  2140 *(new)* 24/1/29.
  2326 *(ex1207)* 20/6/33.
D985 *(ex2020)* 2/9/36.
  2142 *(ex2105)* 30/9/37.
  3414 *(new)* 19/2/44 (59A).

SHEDS:
York.
Selby 5/7/37.
York 12/7/37.
Selby 8/3/38.

RENUMBERED:
2376 12/5/46.

CONDEMNED: 27/2/51.

723

Gateshead 60.

To traffic 11/1906.

REPAIRS:
???. ?/?—?/2/20.**G.**
Superheated boiler fitted.
Ghd. 23/2—18/5/23.**G.**
Ghd. 18/10—12/11/24.**H.**
Ghd. 25/4—16/8/29.**G.**
Ghd. 4/7—1/8/30.**H.**
Ghd. 23—31/3/31.**N/C.**
Ghd. 20/4—27/5/32.**G.**
Dar. 2/8—15/9/34.**G.**
Dar. 11/9—3/11/36.**G.**
Dar. 6/9—13/10/39.**G.**
Chimney cut to 13'-1".
Dar. 21/1—8/3/43.**G.**
Dar. 16/2—16/3/46.**G.**
Dar. 4/5/49. *Not repaired.*

BOILERS:
  G545.
D982 *(new)* ?/2/20.
D499 *(ex2110)* 27/5/32.
D1381 *(ex712)* 15/9/34.
  2135 *(ex1236)* 3/11/36.
  2586 *(ex2025)* 13/10/39.
  2079 *(ex1232)* 16/3/46.

SHEDS:
Tweedmouth.
Scarborough 9/7/25.
Tweedmouth 1/10/25.
Alnmouth 26/2/44.

RENUMBERED:
2377 22/12/46.

CONDEMNED: 23/5/49.
Cut up at Darlington.

724

Gateshead 61.

To traffic 12/1906.

REPAIRS:
???. ?/?—?/2/15.**G.**
Superheated boiler fitted.
???. ?/?—?/12/19.**G.**
Dar. 4/7—26/9/23.**G.**
Dar. 18/4—21/8/25.**G.**
Dar. 16/1—24/3/28.**G.**
Dar. 10/12/29—30/1/30.**G.**
Dar. 26/5—1/7/32.**G.**
Dar. 1/5—9/6/34.**G.**
Dar. 11/6—21/9/37.**G.**
Dar. 7/10—28/11/41.**G.**
Dar. 28/3—4/6/45.**G.**
Dar. 10/12/48—26/2/49.**G.**
Ghd. 1/12/50—5/1/51.**C/H.**
Dar. 7/7—19/8/53.**G.**

BOILERS:
  G547.
G425 *(ex2104)* ?/2/15.
D944 *(new)* ?/12/19.
  2091 *(ex2014)* 30/1/30.
D1487 *(ex2103)* 1/7/32.
  2443 *(ex2028)* 9/6/34.
D1555 *(ex1235)* 28/11/41.
  2338 *(ex2014)* 4/6/45.
  3935 *(new)* 26/2/49 (59A).
  3959 *(new)* 5/1/51 (59A).
  3959 reno.24603.
  3952 *(new)* 19/8/53 (59A).
  3952 reno.24610.

SHEDS:
York.
Scarborough 19/4/24.
Selby 17/8/40.

RENUMBERED:
2378 15/12/46.
62378 26/2/49.

CONDEMNED: 6/11/56.

725

  Gateshead 62.

To traffic 12/1906.

REPAIRS:
???. ?/?—?/12/12.**G.**
???. ?/?—?/8/17.**G.**
Superheated boiler fitted.
Dar. 26/5—14/8/23.**G.**
Dar. 12/2—5/8/25.**G.**
Dar. 20/12/27—28/3/28.**G.**
Dar. 24/2—16/4/31.**G.**
Dar. 24/4—14/6/33.**G.**
Dar. 9/12/36—10/2/37.**G.**
Dar. 2—18/6/37.**N/C.**
Dar. 18/11—6/12/38.**N/C.**
Dar. 7/2—2/4/40.**H.**
Dar. 27/11/40—10/1/41.**G.**
Dar. 4/12/44—10/1/45.**G.**
Dar. 6/9—17/10/47.**G.**
Dar. 9—10/2/48.**N/C.**
Dar. 24/6—18/8/48.**L.**
After collision.

BOILERS:
  G548.
G535 *(ex711)* ?/12/12.
D43 *(ex2022)* ?/8/17.
D41 *(ex2026)* 14/8/23.
  2077 *(new)* 28/3/28.
  2507 *(new)* 14/6/33.
  2866 *(new)* 10/2/37 (59A).
D1775 *(ex2012)* 10/1/45.
  2314 *(ex2383)* 17/10/47.

SHEDS:
Neville Hill.
Scarborough 21/1/26.
Selby 13/8/34.
Scarborough 11/2/35.
York 20/5/40.
Starbeck 12/3/45.
York 5/10/47.
Hull Botanic Gardens 14/11/48.
Stockton 22/5/49.
West Hartlepool 20/3/50.

RENUMBERED:
2379 5/1/47.
ᴇ**2379** 10/2/48.
62379 18/8/48.

CONDEMNED: 10/4/51.

1026

Gateshead 63.

To traffic 2/1907.

REPAIRS:
???. ?/?—?/5/11.**G.**
???. ?/?—?/3/14.**G.**
Superheated boiler fitted.

WORKS CODES:- Cw - Cowlairs. Dar- Darlington. Don - Doncaster. Ghd - Gateshead. Gor - Gorton. Inv - Inverurie. Nor - Norwich. Str - Stratford.
REPAIR CODES:- **C/H** - Casual Heavy. **C/L** - Casual Light. **G** - General. **H**- Heavy. **H/I** - Heavy Intermediate. **L** - Light. **L/I** - Light Intermediate. **N/C** - Non-Classified.

70

All were dual brake fitted from new, and except for seven, the vacuum, Westinghouse and carriage heating connections at the front end were all below the buffer beam at Grouping.

The seven which differed, Nos.476, 1026, 1042, 1258, 2019, 2021 and 2106 had a short standpipe for the Westinghouse brake connection. This was removed in 1929 when a vacuum standpipe was put on, except on No.1258 (*see* page 49, top) which carried both standpipes until November 1934. York.

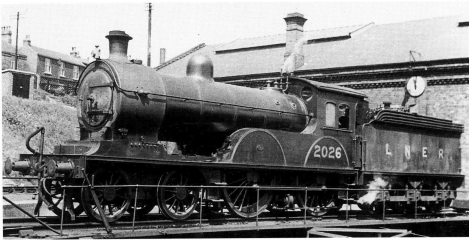

From December 1928, a standpipe was fixed to the front of the buffer beam for the vacuum brake and all soon acquired it. Scarborough.

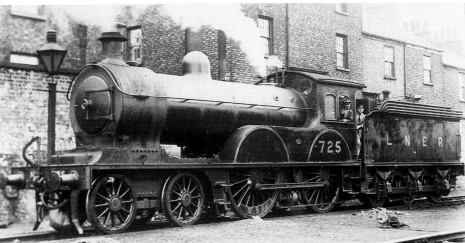

By 1930, Westinghouse brake for train working had largely gone out of use, and the front end connection for it was removed. Sheffield Neepsend.

Until into the 1930's no drain pipe was provided for the vacuum ejector exhaust pipe but by 1933 a drain pipe was being fitted. It emerged from the right hand side of smokebox and dropped down through the running plate to discharge on to the track.

(centre) The installation of a superheater was accompanied by the fitting of an NER design mechanical lubricator to serve the pistons and valves. Carlisle London Road, April 1928.

(below) Seventeen engines, Nos.711, 1042, 1217, 2013, 2016, 2018, 2020, 2021, 2022, 2023, 2024, 2026, 2029, 2101, 2104, 2107, 2109 were fitted on the front of the leading splasher with an oil box having two feeds to lubricate the horn cheeks. In addition, No.2027 had been provided with them in July 1911 but lost them about 1920-1923 and No.1665 *(see* page 50, centre) carried them on the inside face of the splasher.

1026 cont./
Dar. 9/1—30/4/23.**G**.
Dar. 20/5—8/6/23.**L**.
Dar. 13/7—9/8/23.**L**.
Dar. 20/2—20/5/25.**G**.
Dar. 11/8—18/9/25.**L**.
Dar. 21/1—12/5/27.**G**.
Dar. 20/10—14/12/28.**G**.
Dar. 9/3—24/4/31.**G**.
Dar. 23/2—5/4/33.**G**.
Dar. 21/10—19/12/35.**G**.
Dar. 7—24/12/36.**N/C**.
Push-Pull regulator fitted.
Dar. 13/4—3/5/37.**N/C**.
Push-Pull regulator taken off.
Dar. 20/1—8/3/38.**G**.
Dar. 6—18/10/38.**N/C**.
Dar. 10/12/40—6/2/41.**L**.
Dar. 8/6—8/8/42.**G**.
Dar. 18/4—10/5/45.**N/C**.
Dar. 4/11—14/12/46.**G**.
Dar. 4—14/11/47.**L**.
Dar. 15/9—14/10/49.**G**.

BOILERS:
  G575.
  G913 *(ex2110)* ?/5/11.
  G625 *(ex1672)* ?/3/14.
  D1554 *(new)* 20/5/25.
  D1553 *(ex2011)* 24/4/31.
    2338 *(ex2109)* 5/4/33.
    2726 *(new)* 19/12/35 (59A).
    2445 *(ex2015)* 14/12/46.
    3964 *(new)* 14/10/49 (59A).

SHEDS:
York.
Neville Hill 19/4/24.
Hull Botanic Gardens 30/12/24.
Neville Hill 4/2/26.
Hull Botanic Gardens 22/4/31.
Starbeck 16/7/36.
York 6/7/39.
West Hartlepool 8/7/39.
Darlington 27/5/40.
Gateshead 22/11/40.
Newport 13/2/43.
Starbeck 5/3/45.
Alnmouth 5/10/47.
Gateshead 13/6/54.

RENUMBERED:
  2380 24/2/46.
  62380 14/10/49.

CONDEMNED: 23/9/54.

These oil boxes for the horn cheeks were fitted to all twelve engines which got the Raven type frames. The boxes were fitted before Grouping and the only LNER change seems to be that No.2027 lost them and that No.592 had them fitted after May 1928 but still whilst a Part 1 engine.

In August 1936 No.1223 was fitted with bronze axleboxes for its coupled wheels and these were fed from a fountain type lubricator in the cab. Note the loop in the feed pipe to avoid an air-lock. Similarly fitted were Part 1 engines Nos.2107 (October 1936), 2011,2024 (November 1936), 1051,2106 (December 1936), 2013 (March 1937) and 2015 (September 1937).

Both sides were of course equipped but except for Part 2 engines, this change did not extend beyond the eight Part 1 engines listed.

1042

Gateshead 64.

To traffic 3/1907.

REPAIRS:
???. ?/?—?/6/19.**G.**
Superheated boiler fitted.
Dar. 23/6—14/10/24.**G.**
Dar. 18—24/11/24.**N/C.**
Dar. 8/12/25—8/3/26.**G.**
Dar. 13/10—3/12/26.**H.**
Dar. 5/9—25/10/28.**G.**
Dar. 25/3—29/5/30.**G.**
Dar. 3/11—6/12/32.**G.**
Dar. 24/9—25/10/34.**G.**
Dar. 5/8/36. *Weigh.*
Dar. 6/5—25/6/37.**G.**
Dar. 4/1—22/2/38.**L.**
Dar. 17/6/38. *Weigh.*
Dar. 18/6—26/7/40.**G.**
Dar. 26/2—16/3/44.**L.**
After collision.
Dar. 26/7—26/8/44.**G.**
Dar. 27/4—12/5/45.**L.**
Dar. 7/10—14/11/47.**G.**
Dar. 3—29/4/50.**G.**
Dar. 22/2—27/3/54.**G.**

BOILERS:
G579.
D933 *(new)* ?/6/19.
D986 *(ex1665)* 29/5/30.
2079 *(ex2101)* 6/12/32.
D1547 *(ex2102)* 25/10/34.
2339 *(ex1672)* 26/8/44.
D1775 *(ex2379)* 14/11/47.
2585 *(ex2341)* 29/4/50.
24614 *(ex spare)* 27/3/54 (59A).

SHEDS:
Darlington.
Starbeck 24/11/38.
Neville Hill 31/7/43.
Selby 12/3/45.
Starbeck 12/5/46.
Selby 29/11/47.
Hull Botanic Gardens 10/6/56.
Alnmouth 22/9/57.

RENUMBERED:
2381 24/2/46.
62381 29/4/50.

CONDEMNED: 19/11/57.

1051

Gateshead 73.

To traffic 6/1907.

REPAIRS:
???. ?/?—?/7/11.**G.**
???. ?/?—?/2/14.**G.**
Superheated boiler fitted.
Ghd. 25/4—27/7/23.**G.**
Dar. 9/1—14/2/25.**L.**
Ghd. 2/12/25—19/2/26.**G.**
Dar. 4/9—26/10/28.**G.**
Dar. 7/8—16/9/29.**G.**
Dar. 29/9—6/11/30.**G.**
Dar. 16/1—28/2/33.**G.**
Dar. 26/11/34—21/1/35.**G.**
Dar. 15/10—24/12/36.**G.**
Fountain lubricator &
bronze axleboxes fitted.
Dar. 27/7—6/9/38.**G.**
Dar. 20/5—2/7/41.**G.**
Dar. 26/1—25/2/44.**G.**
Dar. 29/12/47—30/1/48.**G.**

BOILERS:
G608.
G932 *(ex2029)* ?/7/11.
D270 *(new)* ?/2/14.
D1487 *(new)* 27/7/23.
D344 *(ex2017)* 6/11/30.
2446 *(new)* 28/2/33.
D1553 *(ex2027)* 6/9/38.
2512 *(ex2016)* 2/7/41.
2446 *(ex2028)* 25/2/44.
3412 *(ex2367)* 30/1/48 (59A).

SHEDS:
Gateshead.
Hull Botanic Gardens 22/3/27.
Selby 14/11/48.

RENUMBERED:
2382 3/3/46.
ᴇ2382 30/1/48.

CONDEMNED: 21/2/51.

1078

Gateshead 74.

To traffic 6/1907.

REPAIRS:
???. ?/?—?/4/11.**G.**
???. ?/?—?/6/14.**G.**
Superheated boiler fitted.
Ghd. 13/3—6/6/24.**G.**
Ghd. 17/10—4/11/24.**L.**
Ghd. 15/9/26—13/1/27.**G.**
Ghd. 1/3—13/5/29.**G.**
Ghd. 27/9—4/10/29.**L.**
Ghd. 20/3—11/4/30.*Tender.*
Ghd. 27/10—7/11/30.**L.**
Ghd. 16/6—22/7/32.**G.**
Dar. 5/10—3/11/34.**G.**
Dar. 30/1—9/3/35.**N/C.**
Dar. 17/7—21/8/35.**H.**
Dar. 11/10/35.*Weigh..*
Dar. 14/6—1/7/37.*Tender*
change.
Dar. 10/1—19/2/38.**G.**
Dar. 18/9—21/10/40.**G.**
Dar. 6—23/11/40.**N/C.**
Dar. 30/6—5/8/44.**G.**
Dar. 19/12/45—25/1/46.**L.**
Dar. 22/2—6/4/46.**L.**
Dar. 12/8—27/9/47.**G.**
Dar. 1/9—1/10/49.**G.**
Dar. 3—6/10/49.**N/C.**
Dar. 28/2—16/4/55.**H/I.**

BOILERS:
G610.
G912 *(ex2024)* ?/4/11.
G589 *(ex1236)* ?/6/14.
D1547 *(new)* 6/6/24.
D982 *(ex723)* 22/7/32.
D1555 *(2106)* 3/11/34.
2139 *(ex1147)* 19/2/38.
2311 *(ex1209)* 21/10/40.
2314 *(ex711)* 5/8/44.
2864 *(ex2392)* 27/9/47 (59A).
3980 *(new)* 1/10/49 (59A).
3980 reno.24617 16/4/55.

SHEDS:
Heaton.
Darlington 27/11/33.
Alnmouth 7/11/38.
Gateshead 11/8/41.
Bridlington 1/1/44.
Hull Botanic Gardens 4/12/49.
Alnmouth 3/6/51.

RENUMBERED:
2383 10/2/46.
62383 1/10/49.

CONDEMNED: 2/5/57.

1147

Gateshead 65.

To traffic 3/1907.

REPAIRS:
???. ?/?—?/12/11.**G.**
???. ?/?—?/1/17.**G.**
Superheated boiler fitted.
Ghd. ?/?—9/11/22.**G.**
Ghd. 23/8—24/9/23.**L.**
Ghd. 2/4—6/8/25.**G.**
Dar. 14/9—22/10/26.**L.**
Ghd. 18/1—2/5/28.**G.**
Ghd. 19/2—27/3/30.**G.**
Dar. 24/1—4/3/35.**G.**
Dar. 12/10—24/12/37.**G.**
Dar. 20/2—30/3/40.**L.**

Dar. 15/12/41—6/1/42.**L.**
Dar. 26/10/42. *Not repaired.*

BOILERS:
G581.
G593 *(ex1236)* ?/12/11.
D502 *(new)* ?/1/17.
2324 *(new)* 27/3/30.
2139 *(ex2101)* 4/3/35.
D1763 *(ex1184)* 24/12/37.

SHEDS:
Gateshead.
Scarborough 9/7/30.
Selby 13/8/34.
Scarborough 19/11/34.
West Hartlepool 19/6/39.

CONDEMNED: 9/1/43.
Cut up at Darlington.

1184

Gateshead 75.

To traffic 6/1907.

REPAIRS:
???. ?/?—?/11/11.**G.**
???. ?/?—?/6/14.**G.**
Superheated boiler fitted.
Ghd. 20/3—20/6/23.**G.**
Ghd. 2/4—13/7/25.**G.**
Ghd. 20/7—24/8/26.**L.**
Ghd. 15/11/28—11/1/29.**G.**
Ghd. 1/12/30—21/1/31.**G.**
Ghd. 16—25/2/31.**N/C.**
Ghd. 26/8—24/9/31.**H.**
Dar. 4—14/7/32.**N/C.**
Dar. 23/1—14/3/33.**G.**
Dar. 10/12/34—1/2/35.**G.**
Dar. 21/11—9/12/35.*Tender.*
Dar. 29/5—24/6/36.**L.**
Dar. 31/10—17/12/36.**L.**
After collision.
Dar. 19/10—3/12/37.**G.**
Dar. 21/11/38—6/1/39.**N/C.**
Dar. 4/3—9/4/40.**G.**
Dar. 4—9/7/42.**N/C.**
Dar. 18/1—15/2/44.**G.**
Dar. 23/5—21/6/47.**G.**
Dar. 14/8—16/9/50.**G.**
Dar. 18—21/9/50.**N/C.**
Dar. 25/3—9/4/54.**N/C.**
Dar. 12/8/55. *Not repaired.*

BOILERS:
G611.
G930 *(ex2025)* ?/11/11.
D329 *(new)* ?/6/14.
2135 *(new)* 11/1/29.
2087 *(ex2102)* 14/3/33.
D1763 *(ex2029)* 1/2/35.

The horn cheek lubrication from oil boxes was retained to withdrawal, No.62381 (ex 1042) still having them in August 1952 as shown here. Selby.

The tender normally used was the NER standard 3940 gallons type with three rails all round and an extra one around the coal space.

In 1937 an instruction was issued that water pick-up gear was no longer required and was to be removed. No.2105, in July 1937, was the first to lose it and No.1234 did so in February 1938 but it was 1945 before the job was completed. Absence of vent pipes at the front of the tender was an indication that the gear had gone. York.

At the tender end a short Westinghouse standpipe was usual and this was retained long after the Westinghouse train braking had ceased although the connecting hose had gone. York, April 1949.

In May 1949 No.62397's tender had a new body put on to the existing frame and wheels. The style was the same as the LNER standard 3500 gallon type but these rebuilt tenders carried 3900 gallons of water and 6¼ tons of coal. This one alone got BRITISH RAILWAYS put on it. The tender remained with No.62397 until withdrawal in February 1957.

Between September 1949 and June 1950 nine more tenders were rebuilt in the same way, and these got the large BR emblem. Even with this substantial alteration, the redundant short standpipe which had been used for Westinghouse braking was not disturbed, and NE buffers remained. The engines to which these other nine rebuilt tenders were attached were: Nos.62341 (November 1949), 62348 (October 1949), 62351 (April 1950), 62353 (January 1950), 62355 (March 1950), 62358 (September 1949), 62380 (October 1949), 62381 (April 1950), 62386 (June 1950). Except for the tender on No.62381, which was transferred to no.62392 in November 1952, all remained paired with their engines to withdrawal, in two cases for as little as sixteen months. Four saw further use behind other D20 class engines, Nos.62343 (March 1956 - ex 62355), 62374 (April 1952 - ex 62353), 62383 (April 1955 - ex 62380), 62387 (April 1954 - ex 62386), all to withdrawal.

Until after Grouping all were in fully lined NER green livery but only a few still had the brass cap on the chimney. The last to get this style of painting was No.2109, ex Darlington 20th March 1923. Prudhoe, June 1920.

Whilst standards for Group livery were still under discussion, No.2106 was ex Darlington on 20th February 1923 without any change to the engine livery but a very noticeable change on the tender. North Eastern and the armorial gave place to N.E.R. above 12in. figures showing the engine number, although the engine kept its large brass number plates. York.

(above) The first post-Grouping style of 6in. L.& N.E.R. was applied to eleven engines from Darlington in 1923: Nos.2104 and 2014 (21st April), 1260 (25th April), 1026 (30th April) and 712 (9th May). From Gateshead, also in 1923; Nos.1665 (11th April), 1206 (24th April), 723 (18th May), 1236 (6th June), 1209 (16th June) and 1184 (20th June).

(right) This is one of the very rare examples of a North Eastern engine and tender number being at variance. The engine is No.2024 but the tender is No.723. Both were shedded at Tweedmouth but the switch probably occurred when both were in Gateshead works. Engine No.723 was in for a heavy repair on 18th October to 12th November 1924 whilst engine No.2024 was in for a general from 29th August to 29th December 1924. The pairing shown here was still to be seen in Edinburgh on 21st February 1926! Haymarket.

Full points were then discarded on the tender lettering but the next five engines painted in 1923 kept the ampersand. Darlington did Nos.2011 (13th June), 2026 (29th June) and 2021 (11th July); Gateshead did 1051 (27th July) and 1235 (17th August). Before the suffix was used, the ampersand was dropped but in this short period only LNER 725, ex Darlington on 14th August 1923, was so painted.

During the period from September 1923 to February 1924, when the area suffix was being applied, Darlington put it on five, all during 1923; Nos.724 (26th September), 2018 (29th September), 2022 (28th November), 711 (14th December), 2013 (21st December) whilst Gateshead only used it on two, both in 1923: Nos.2016 (18th October) and 2107 (28th December).

(left) In addition to the exceptional case of No.725 on 14th August 1923, there were thirty-six which went straight to LNER green livery between 7th March 1924 (No.2027) and 1st October 1925 (No.2029).

(bottom) The June 1928 economies decreed black for D20 class but until March 1929 the number remained on tender, and no less than twenty were so treated, fifteen at Darlington: [1928] Nos. 2013 (6th July), 708 (18th July), 2019 (7th August), 1042 (25th October), 2011 (26th October), 1051 (26th October), 1026 (14th December), 711 (27th December), 1232 (29th December), [1929] Nos.2023 (17th January), 2027 (17th January), 476 (24th January), 713 (24th January), 2018 (14th February), 2103 (22nd February). The five done by Gateshead were; Nos.2012 (10th August 1928), 1209 (28th August 1928), 707 (18th September 1928), 1235 (8th November 1928) and 1184 (11th January 1929).

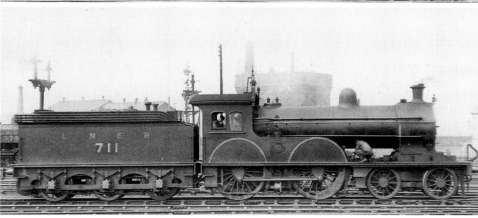

1184 cont./
2087 *(ex2101)* 3/12/37.
2135 *(ex723)* 9/4/40.
2873 *(ex2013)* 15/2/44 (59A).
2866 *(ex2343)* 21/6/47 (59A).
3929 *(new)* 16/9/50 (59A).
3929 reno.24601.

SHEDS:
Gateshead.
Stockton 15/4/35.
Newport 17/2/43.
Stockton 23/2/44.
Newport 5/11/45.
Northallerton 15/12/45.
Newport 18/2/46.
Stockton 4/3/46.
West Hartlepool 6/10/46.
Selby 4/1/48.
Starbeck 9/1/49.
Selby 22/5/49.
Starbeck 17/7/49.
Selby 1/10/50.

RENUMBERED:
2384 3/2/46.
62384 16/9/50.

CONDEMNED: 15/8/55.
Cut up at Darlington.

1206

Gateshead 66.

To traffic 4/1907.

REPAIRS:
???. ?/?—?/5/11.**G.**
???. ?/?—?/5/13.**G.**
???. ?/?—?/6/17.**G.**
Superheated boiler fitted.
Ghd. 7/2—24/4/23.**G.**
Ghd. 24/11/24—5/1/25.**L.**
Ghd. 17/4—22/7/25.**G.**
Ghd. 11/1—5/4/28.**H.**
Ghd. 28/1—11/3/30.**G.**
Dar. 22/5—9/6/33.**N/C.**
Dar. 5/1—7/2/34.**G.**
Dar. 6/5—28/6/37.**G.**
Dar. 27/4—9/6/39.**G.**
Dar. 16/1/41. *Weigh.*
Dar. 12/2—27/3/42.**G.**
Dar. 12/2—3/3/44.**L.**
Dar. 12/1/45. *Not repaired.*

BOILERS:
G582.
G610 *(ex1078)* ?/5/11.
G622 *(ex1665)* ?/5/13.
D507 *(new)* ?/6/17.
2504 *(new)* 7/2/34.
D1550 *(ex476)* 9/6/39.

SHEDS:
Gateshead.
Scarborough 11/7/30.
Starbeck 30/9/35.

RENUMBERED:
2385 *Allocated.*

CONDEMNED: 31/1/45.
Cut up at Darlington.

1207

Gateshead 76.

To traffic 8/1907.

REPAIRS:
???. ?/?—?/4/13.**G.**
Superheated boiler fitted.
???. ?/?—28/12/22.**G.**
Ghd. 1/2—1/4/24.**G.**
Ghd. 29/12/24—14/1/25.**L.**
Ghd. 8/10/27—10/1/28.**G.**
Ghd. 18—26/5/28.**L.**
Ghd. 31/1—13/3/30.**G.**
Ghd. 26/11—14/12/31.**L.**
Dar. 24/4—7/6/33.**G.**
Dar. 26/3—30/7/35.**G.**
Dar. 26/6—26/10/36.**H.**
Dar. 17/2—29/6/38.**G.**
Dar. 29/6—8/7/38.**N/C.**
Dar. 2/5—1/6/39.**N/C.**
Dar. 27/8/42—9/10/43.**G.**
Dar. 8/3—21/4/45.**G.**
Dar. 28/4—5/5/45.**N/C.**
Dar. 22—26/5/45.**N/C.**
Dar. 7/1—6/2/48.**G.**
Dar. 17/5—17/6/50.**G.**
Dar. 22/9—17/10/53.**G.**
Dar. 27—28/10/53.**N/C.**
Ghd. 2—16/3/54.**N/C.**

BOILERS:
G612.
D42 *(new)* ?/4/13.
D270 *(ex1051)* 1/4/24.
2326 *(new)* 13/3/30.
D1550 *(ex1258)* 7/6/33.
D1375 *(ex476)* 30/7/35.
3408 *(new)* 9/10/43 (59A).
2325 *(ex2395)* 6/2/48.
2873 *(ex62392)* 17/6/50 (59A).
24612 *(ex spare)* 17/10/53 (59A).

SHEDS:
Heaton.
York 16/11/31.
Selby 10/6/39.

RENUMBERED:
2386 7/4/46.
ᴇ2386 6/2/48.
62386 17/6/50.

CONDEMNED: 19/10/56.

1209

Gateshead 67.

To traffic 4/1907.

REPAIRS:
???. ?/?—?/2/13.**G.**
???. ?/?—?/10/17.**G.**
Superheated boiler fitted.
Ghd. 26/3—16/6/23.**G.**
Ghd. 28/4—6/8/25.**G.**
Ghd. 17/11—7/12/27.**L.**
Ghd. 8/6—28/8/28.**G.**
Ghd. 1/7—20/8/30.**G.**
Ghd. 10/9—28/10/31.**L.**
Dar. 1/3—20/4/33.**G.**
Dar. 4/3—20/4/35.**G.**
Dar. 8—19/7/35.**N/C.**
Dar. 5/8/36. *Weigh.*
Dar. 1/10/36. *Weigh.*
Dar. 30/7—24/9/37.**G.**
Dar. 3/3/39. *Weigh.*
Dar. 18/6—20/7/40.**G.**
Dar. 3—31/3/44.**G.**
Dar. 12/4—14/5/48.**G.**
Dar. 25/5—29/6/48.**N/C.**
Dar. 22/3—17/4/54.**G.**
Dar. 20—27/4/54.**N/C.**

BOILERS:
G583.
G533 *(ex708)* ?/2/13.
D529 *(new)* ?/10/17.
D560 *(ex1236)* 20/8/30.
D1773 *(ex2015)* 20/4/33.
2311 *(ex2015)* 24/9/37.
2323 *(ex1234)* 20/7/40.
2139 *(ex2022)* 31/3/44.
3408 *(ex2386)* 14/5/48 (59A).
24615 *(ex spare)* 17/4/54 (59A).

SHEDS:
Gateshead.
West Hartlepool 15/4/35.
Newport 17/2/43.
West Hartlepool 25/11/43.
Selby 26/9/48.
Hull Botanic Gardens 14/11/48.
Bridlington 22/5/49.
Alnmouth 7/8/49.
Heaton 7/6/53.
Selby 26/6/55.
Alnmouth 23/6/57.

RENUMBERED:
2387 5/5/46.
62387 14/5/48.

CONDEMNED: 2/9/57.

1210

Gateshead 77.

To traffic 8/1907.

REPAIRS:
???. ?/?—?/3/14.**G.**
Superheated boiler fitted.
???. ?/?—7/11/22.**G.**
Ghd. 6/12/24—5/2/25.**G.**
Ghd. 13/10/27—30/1/28.**G.**
Ghd. 15/5—3/7/30.**G.**
Ghd. 25/11/31—3/2/32.**H.**
Dar. 26/9—28/10/33.**G.**
Dar. 15/1—21/3/36.**G.**
Dar. 16—24/6/38.**N/C.**
Dar. 28/2—14/4/39.**G.**
Dar. 27/7—7/9/42.**L/I.**
Dar. 16/3—20/4/45.**G.**
Dar. 11—18/5/45.**N/C.**
Dar. 7—21/6/45.**L.**
Dar. 30/10—30/11/46.**L.**
Dar. 30/3—30/4/48.**G.**
Dar. 12—19/5/48.**N/C.**
Dar. 25/5—2/6/48.**N/C.**
Dar. 10/8—6/9/50.**G.**
Dar. 21—29/9/50.**N/C.**
Dar. 11/8—13/9/52.**N/C.**
Dar. 13/4/54. *Not repaired.*

BOILERS:
G613.
D273 *(new)* ?/3/14.
D42 *(ex1207)* 5/2/25.
D991 *(ex2104)* 30/1/28.
D1439 *(ex592)* 3/7/30.
D1501 *(ex2107)* 3/2/32.
2140 *(ex713)* 28/10/33.
2344 *(ex2027)* 21/3/36.
2140 *(ex2026)* 14/4/39.
2344 *(ex707)* 20/4/45.
2507 *(ex2369)* 30/4/48.
2512 *(ex2374)* 6/9/50.
2512 reno.24600.

SHEDS:
Tweedmouth.
Blaydon 18/1/40.
Gateshead 1/3/41.
Stockton 12/2/44.
Newport 23/2/44.
Stockton 30/5/45.
Northallerton 6/10/46.
West Hartlepool 27/5/51.
Northallerton 26/10/52.
Tyne Dock 18/1/53.
Northallerton 15/3/53.

RENUMBERED:
2388 23/6/46.
62388 30/4/48.

CONDEMNED: 26/4/54.
Cut up at Darlington.

From mid-March 1929, the number was moved to the engine. As the splasher beading was retained the number was placed inside it, and the small number plate was moved forward. Some then had it centred on the combined splasher. Scarborough.

On others the small number plate was centred on the leading splasher.

(below) One small consequence of the change from green to black was that Darlington no longer put a lined panel on the ends of the buffer beam.

The single red lining was not applied after November 1941 and from July 1942 to January 1946 only NE was put on the tender.

Starting with No.1232 on 7th February 1946, LNER was restored and during that year the class was renumbered 2340 to 2397. No.708 became 2373 on Sunday 17th November 1946 at Starbeck shed. York.

When No.1042 was renumbered to 2381 on Sunday 24th February 1946 at Selby shed, 8inch stencils were used but it seems to have been the only one done in this manner. Starbeck, June 1947.

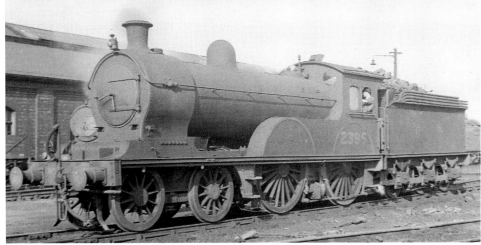

The renumbering of 1260 to 2395 at Starbeck shed on Sunday 31st March 1946 was more representative of how the job was done. The new number was painted in the same size and style as the transfer figures but without any shading. The buffer beam numbers were however shaded type.

1217

Gateshead 68.

To traffic 5/1907.

REPAIRS:
???. ?/?—?/2/11.**G.**
???. ?/?—?/12/14.**G.**
Superheated boiler fitted.
Dar. 29/3—20/6/24.**G.**
Dar. 15/12/27—28/2/28.**G.**
Dar. 13/3—26/4/29.**G.**
Dar. 20/5—29/8/30.**G.**
Dar. 12/1—17/2/33.**G.**
Dar. 14—17/11/33.**N/C.**
Dar. 18/10—17/12/35.**G.**
Dar. 11/1—26/2/38.**G.**
Dar. 19/4—17/5/40.**G.**
Dar. 19/8—28/9/43.**G.**
Ghd. 22/6—7/7/44.**S/L.**
Dar. 30/11/45—12/1/46.**G.**
Dar. 30/5—2/7/48.**G.**
Dar. 3/9/54. *Not repaired.*

BOILERS:
G585.
G920 *(ex2016)* ?/2/11.
D333 *(new)* ?/12/14.
2325 *(new)* 29/8/30.
2445 *(ex1234)* 26/2/38.
D1541 *(ex1232)* 17/5/40.
3405 *(new)* 28/9/43 (59A).
3647 *(new)* 12/1/46 (59A).

SHEDS:
Darlington.
Starbeck 9/10/34.
Selby 10/6/51.
Neville Hill 6/7/52.

RENUMBERED:
2389 31/3/46.
62389 2/7/48.

CONDEMNED: 6/9/54.
Cut up at Darlington

1223

Gateshead 78.

To traffic 9/1907.

REPAIRS:
???. ?/?—?/8/11.**G.**
???. ?/?—?/12/16.**G.**
Superheated boiler fitted.
???. ?/?—27/9/22.**G.**
Ghd. 22/3—4/5/23.**H.**
Ghd. 16—26/7/23.**L.**
Ghd. 6/1—17/4/25.**G.**
Ghd. 25/5—12/9/27.**G.**
Ghd. 24/11/27.**N/C.**

Ghd. 23/2—8/3/28.**L.**
Ghd. 15/10/29—22/1/30.**G.**
Ghd. 26/1—4/3/32.**G.**
Dar. 22/6—13/7/33.**L.**
Dar. 8/1—14/2/34.**G.**
Dar. 15/6—8/8/36.**G.**
Dar. 17/10—26/11/38.**G.**
Dar. 29/12/42—15/2/43.**G.**
Dar. 14/8/44. *Weigh.*
Dar. 26/2/45. *Weigh.*
Dar. 11/1—9/2/46.**L.**
Dar. 11/10—9/11/46.**G.**
Dar. 15/11/48. *Not repaired.*

BOILERS:
G614.
G588 *(ex1232)* ?/8/11.
D36 *(ex2014)* ?/12/16.
D273 *(ex1210)* 17/4/25.
2322 *(new)* 22/1/30.
D1409 *(ex2107)* 14/2/34.
2500 *(ex2016)* 8/8/36.
D1428 *(ex2023)* 26/11/38.
2500 *(ex708)* 9/11/46.

SHEDS:
Gateshead.
West Hartlepool 15/4/35.
Stockton 21/6/47.

RENUMBERED:
2390 31/3/46.

CONDEMNED: 29/11/48.
Cut up at Darlington.

1232

Gateshead 69.

To traffic 5/1907.

REPAIRS:
???. ?/?—?/6/11.**G.**
???. ?/?—?/3/18.**G.**
Superheated boiler fitted.
Ghd. 28/7—24/8/23.**L.**
Ghd. 10/1—25/3/24.**G.**
Dar. 21/12/26—19/5/27.**G.**
Dar. 7/11—29/12/28.**G.**
Dar. 8/8—30/9/30.**G.**
Dar. 3/11—11/12/32.**G.**
Dar. 1/11—20/12/34.**G.**
Dar. 14/5—2/7/37.**G.**
Dar. 14/3—17/4/40.**G.**
Dar. 14—28/7/41.**N/C.**
Dar. 2/1—7/2/46.**G.**
Dar. 6—20/12/46.**L.**
Dar. 20/4/48. *Weigh.*
Dar. 26/4/48. *Weigh.*
Dar. 13/10—5/11/48.**G.**
Dar. 18—27/11/48.**N/C.**
Dar. 24/3—9/4/49.**N/C.**

BOILERS:
G588.
G582 *(ex1206)* ?/6/11.
G588 *(ex spare)* ?/3/18.
D1775 *(new)* 19/5/27.
D1783 *(ex1665)* 11/12/32.
D1515 *(ex2019)* 20/12/34.
D1541 *(ex2109)* 2/7/37.
2079 *(ex2105)* 17/4/40.
2510 *(ex476)* 7/2/46.
3925 *(new)* 5/11/48 (59A).

SHEDS:
Heaton.
York 6/5/24.
Starbeck 21/6/37.
York 24/9/37.
Pickering 16/11/40.
Darlington 2/2/42.
Middlesborough 14/2/42.
Newport 17/2/43.
Northallerton 18/2/46.

RENUMBERED:
2391 28/4/46.
62391 5/11/48.

CONDEMNED: 7/6/51.

1234

Gateshead 70.

To traffic 5/1907.

REPAIRS:
???. ?/?—?/7/11.**G.**
Dar. 12/3—29/5/24.**G.**
Dar. 28/12/26—30/4/27.**G.**
Dar. 5/10—28/11/27.**L.**
Dar. 5/3—23/4/29.**G.**
Superheated boiler fitted.
Dar. 16/6—24/8/31.**G.**
Dar. 13/4—30/5/33.**G.**
Dar. 1/9—3/11/33.**H.**
Dar. 2/5—12/7/35.**G.**
Dar. 18/11/37—4/2/38.**G.**
Dar. 7—9/2/38.**N/C.**
Dar. 12/6—11/7/40.**G.**
Dar. 15—19/7/40.**N/C.**
Dar. 6/5/43. *Not repaired.*

BOILERS:
G589.
G911 *(new)* ?/7/11.
D337 *(ex2018)* 23/4/29.
2445 *(new)* 30/5/33.
2323 *(ex592)* 4/2/38.
D1783 *(ex2019)* 11/7/40.

SHEDS:
Hull Botanic Gardens.
Bridlington 11/9/39.

CONDEMNED: 22/5/43.
Cut up at Darlington.

1235

Gateshead 79.

To traffic 9/1907.

REPAIRS:
Ghd. ?/?—?/6/09.**?.**
Sisterson superheater removed.
Ghd. 29/9—30/11/11.**G.**
Long smokebox shortened.
???. ?/?—?/11/13.**G.**
Superheated boiler fitted.
???. ?/?—24/2/22.**G.**
Ghd. 11/5—17/8/23.**G.**
Ghd. 21/10—20/11/24.**L.**
Ghd. 16/4—19/8/26.**G.**
Ghd. 20/9—8/11/28.**G.**
Ghd. 20/8—9/10/30.**G.**
Ghd. 12—20/5/32.**N/C.**
Dar. 20/9—24/10/33.**G.**
Dar. 21/2—29/3/35.**G.**
Dar. 27/2—31/3/36.**L.**
After collision.
Dar. 7/2—29/3/38.**G.**
Dar. 22/9—7/11/41.**G.**
Dar. 8—30/10/43.**L.**
Dar. 27/9—25/10/44.**L.**
After collision.
Dar. 23/8—22/9/45.**G.**
Dar. 22/5—5/7/47.**G.**
Dar. 21/7—19/8/47.**N/C.**
Ghd. 19/10—5/11/48.**L.**
Dar. 13/4—18/5/50.**G.**
Dar. 30/5—8/6/50.**N/C.**

BOILERS:
G616 *(superheated).*
G608 *(ex1051; sat.)* 30/11/11.
G612 *(ex1207)* ?/11/13.
D1764 *(new)* 19/8/26.
2077 *(ex725)* 24/10/33.
2324 *(ex1147)* 29/3/35.
D1555 *(ex1078)* 29/3/38.
2324 *(ex2027)* 7/11/41.
2864 *(ex2025)* 22/9/45 (59A).
2873 *(ex2384)* 5/7/47 (59A).
2443 *(ex62343)* 18/5/50.

SHEDS:
Gateshead.
West Hartlepool 15/4/35.
Darlington 21/5/40.
Gateshead 22/11/40.
Starbeck 9/12/40.
Selby 10/6/51.

RENUMBERED:
2392 28/4/46.
62392 5/11/48.

When Darlington's stock of shaded transfers was exhausted in 1947 they changed to yellow painted and unshaded Gill sans but with modified 6 and 9. No.2395, ex works 9th January 1948, was one of the last to get LNER. Reston, July 1949.

From 19th to 26th January 1948, No.2395 was in works again for a non-classified repair during which its tender was changed. That put on was without either LNER or BRITISH RAILWAYS and had been spare from September 1947.

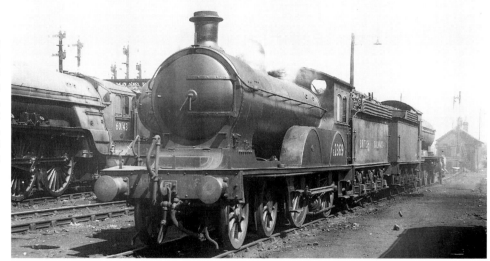

On 23rd January 1948 No.ᴇ2354 was ex works still in unlined black but with BRITISH RAILWAYS on the tender. Six others also got this style in 1948: Nos.2382 (30th January), 2386 (6th February), 2379 (10th February), 2369 (13th February), 2361 and 2372 (27th February). Note the 6 and 9 were the modified style of Gill sans. York.

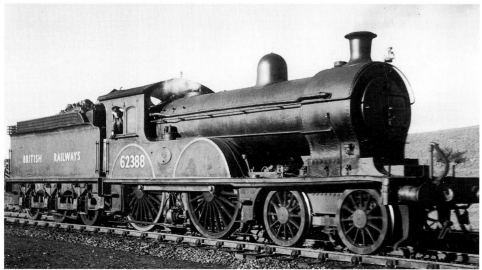

On 30th April 1948 No. 62388 was the first D20 ex works with a full BR number. That one and 62387, ex works 14th May 1948, were the only two to have a full BR number painted on the buffer beam by Darlington. From a light repair at Gateshead, on 5th November 1948, No.62392 had this style for the engine but retained LNER on the tender. Northallerton, 10th April 1950.

From a light repair on 13th April 1949 by Darlington, No.62343 came out with its BR number, including 6in. correct Gill sans on the cab, but still with LNER on the tender.

Cast iron smokebox number plates were used on D20 class from 2nd July 1948 and at first with a modified 6 and 9 on them. No.62340, ex works 2nd July 1948, was the only one to have the smokebox plate fixed above the hinge strap.

Ex Darlington also on 2nd July 1948, No.62389 had the plate below the top hinge strap in what became the standard position for subsequent fittings. Bradford (Forster Square), April 1950.

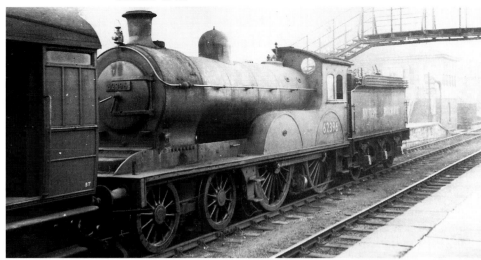

Beginning with No.62396, ex works 9th October 1948, the correct Gill sans 6 and 9 were used both on the splasher and on the smokebox plate.

From 17th September 1949 the BR emblem superseded BRITISH RAILWAYS on the tender, No.62358 being the first D20 to be so done. That one got the 28in. high emblem. The next one 62352, out 14th October 1949, had the 15½in. high emblems. Alnmouth, 16th April 1952.

The last two to have heavy repairs, Nos.62383 ex works 16th April 1955 and 62396, ex works 18th June 1955, both got the 28in. emblems, but there was not any recognisable pattern as to which size was used. Ten are known to have carried the larger size, and six the smaller version.

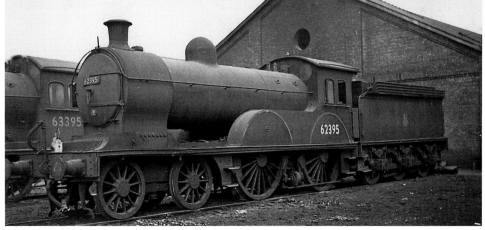

Ex works in January 1948, No.2395 remained as shown on page 83, and did not get its BR number 62395 until 20th June 1953 when out from general repair, as shown here. It had no further major repairs before withdrawal on 20th November 1957 as the last of the class. Selby, March 1955.

In July 1957 Nos.62381 and 62396 were taken out of store at Dairycoates to help with the summer traffic. Their appearance was so bad that a Darlington painter was sent to apply a coat of unlined black. He also put on the BR crest introduced in April that year.

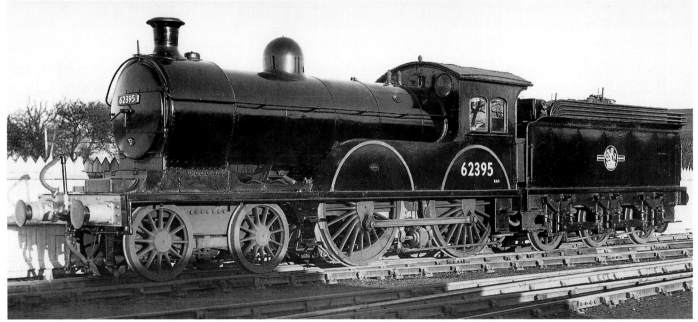

(above) Withdrawn on 20th November 1957, No.62395 reached Darlington early in December and, as the last North Eastern passenger engine in service, it was repainted, on one side only for this official photograph to be taken. Note the 1957 crest was applied. Darlington.

(left) This was the engine, already thirty-seven years old, which was chosen in 1936 for modernisation, but apart from the front bogie, the coupled wheels plus the frame and wheels of the tender, everything else was new.

1235 cont./
CONDEMNED: 31/5/54.

1236

Gateshead 71.

To traffic 6/1907.

REPAIRS:
???. ?/?—?/10/11.**G.**
???. ?/?—?/6/13.**G.**
???. ?/?—?/12/17.**G.**
Superheated boiler fitted.
Ghd. 22/3—6/6/23.**G.**
Ghd. 16—25/1/24.**L.**
Ghd. 28/4—7/9/25.**G.**
Ghd. 17/3—8/6/28.**G.**
Ghd. 21/5—16/7/30.**G.**
Dar. 2/3—21/4/33.**G.**
Dar. 4/7—2/9/34.**G.**
Dar. 7/7—2/9/36.**G.**
Dar. 6/1—14/2/39.**G.**
Dar. 30/6—20/8/41.**G.**
Dar. 7—24/4/42.**L.**
Dar. 16—27/3/43.**L.**
Dar. 6/1—9/2/45.**G.**
Dar. 30/10/47. *Not repaired.*

BOILERS:
G593.
G589 *(ex1234)* ?/10/11
G583 *(ex1209)* ?/6/13.
D560 *(new)* ?/12/17.
D991 *(ex1210)* 16/7/30.
2135 *(ex1184)* 21/4/33.
2326 *(ex713)* 2/9/36.
2500 *(ex1223)* 14/2/39.
D1539 *(ex2106)* 20/8/41.
2077 *(ex2017)* 9/2/45.

SHEDS:
Gateshead.
Starbeck 15/4/35.

RENUMBERED:
2393 31/3/46.

CONDEMNED: 20/12/47.
Cut up at Darlington.

1258

Gateshead 80.

To traffic 9/1907.

REPAIRS:
???. ?/?—?/6/12.**G.**
???. ?/?—?/11/17.**G.**
Superheated boiler fitted.
???. ?/?—21/12/22.**G.**
Ghd. 24/7—14/8/23.**L.**

Ghd. 10/1—28/3/25.**G.**
Ghd. 24/1—11/5/28.**G.**
Ghd. 29/11/29—17/1/30.**G.**
Ghd. 8/5—19/6/31.**G.**
Ghd. 6—17/7/31.**L.**
Dar. 17/3—4/5/33.**G.**
Dar. 19/11/34—26/1/35.**G.**
Dar. 14/12/36—17/2/37.**G.**
Dar. 29/6—16/7/37.**N/C.**
Dar. 7/1—15/2/39.**G.**
Dar. 16—22/2/39.**N/C.**
Dar. 25/2—4/4/41.**G.**
Dar. 28/10—27/11/43.**G.**
Dar. 5/4/46. *Not repaired.*

BOILERS:
G618.
G616 *(ex1235)* ?/6/12.
D537 *(new)* ?/11/17.
D1550 *(ex2025)* 19/6/31.
D560 *(ex1209)* 4/5/33.
D1783 *(ex1232)* 26/1/35.
2869 *(new)* 17/2/37 (59A).
3409 *(new)* 27/11/43 (59A).

SHEDS:
Gateshead.
Starbeck 23/5/36.

RENUMBERED:
2394 31/3/46.

CONDEMNED: 4/5/46.
Cut up at Darlington.

1260

Gateshead 72.

To traffic 6/1907.

REPAIRS:
???. ?/?—?/12/10.**G.**
???. ?/?—?/11/14.**G.**
Superheated boiler fitted.
???. ?/?—?/6/20.**G.**
Dar. 18/1—25/4/23.**G.**
Dar. 12/1—29/4/25.**G.**
Dar. 12/3—19/5/26.**L.**
Dar. 28/2—15/7/27.**G.**
Dar. 6/3—17/5/29.**G.**
Dar. 19/11/30—20/1/31.**G.**
Dar. 11/5—28/7/33.**G.**
Dar. 30/7—13/9/35.**G.**
Dar. 25/1—18/3/38.**G.**
Dar. 22/7—3/9/41.**G.**
Dar. 5—12/9/41.**N/C.**
Dar. 19/12/44—25/1/45.**G.**
Dar. 8—15/2/45.**N/C.**
Dar. 6/12/47—9/1/48.**G.**
Dar. 19—26/1/48.**N/C.**
Dar. 20/5—20/6/53.**G.**
Dar. 22—25/6/53.**N/C.**

BOILERS:
G597.
G522 *(ex592)* ?/12/10.
G618 *(ex spare)* ?/11/14.
D985 *(new)* ?/6/20.
D271 *(ex2027)* 15/7/27.
2344 *(new)* 20/1/31.
D991 *(ex1236)* 28/7/33.
D1553 *(ex1051)* 3/9/41.
2325 *(ex2029)* 25/1/45.
2341 *(ex2370)* 9/1/48.
3954 *(new)* 20/6/53 (59A).
3954 reno.24609.

SHEDS:
York.
Starbeck 12/3/45.
Selby 23/4/50.
York 2/12/56.
Alnmouth 16/6/57.

RENUMBERED:
2395 31/3/46.
62395 20/6/53.

CONDEMNED: 20/11/57.

1665

Gateshead 81.

To traffic 9/1907.

REPAIRS:
???. ?/?—?/6/12.**G.**
???. ?/?—?/8/20.**G.**
Superheated boiler fitted.
Ghd. 22/11/22—11/4/23.**G.**
Dar. 28/8—29/11/25.**G.**
Dar. 28/5—16/7/26.**G.**
Dar. 10/1—21/4/28.**G.**
Dar. 11/6—20/7/28.**L.**
Dar. 17/2—7/4/30.**G.**
Dar. 5/4—4/7/32.**G.**
Dar. 28/2—20/4/35.**G.**
Dar. 2/3—7/7/38.**G.**
Dar. 8—22/7/38.**N/C.**
Dar. 15/11—22/12/41.**G.**
Dar. 23/10—23/11/44.**G.**
Dar. 29/11—5/12/44.**N/C.**
Dar. 3/8—9/10/48.**G.**
Ghd. 23/6—2/7/54.**N/C.**
Dar. 14/5—18/6/55.**G.**
Dar. 2—12/7/55.**N/C.**

BOILERS:
G622.
G611 *(ex1184)* ?/6/12.
D986 *(new)* ?/8/20.
D1783 *(ex2026)* 7/4/30.
D1541 *(ex2011)* 4/7/32.
2077 *(ex1235)* 20/4/35.
2443 *(ex724)* 22/12/41.

2322 *(ex2109)* 23/11/44.
24616 *(ex spare)* 18/6/55 (59A).

SHEDS:
Gateshead.
York 6/5/24.
Selby 30/1/39.
Hull Botanic Gardens 26/1/46.
Alnmouth 4/3/46.
Tweedmouth 5/6/49.
Alnmouth 23/10/49.
Hull Botanic Gardens 4/12/49.
Alnmouth 3/6/51.
Tweedmouth 13/7/52.
Alnmouth 15/3/53.
Gateshead 13/6/54.
Alnmouth 10/10/54.
Selby 26/6/55.
Hull Botanic Gardens 10/6/56.
Alnmouth 22/9/57.

RENUMBERED:
2396 17/8/46.
62396 8/10/48.

CONDEMNED: 19/11/57.

1672

Gateshead 82.

To traffic 9/1907.

REPAIRS:
???. ?/?—?/8/13.**G.**
Superheated boiler fitted.
Dar. 19/2—30/4/24.**G.**
Dar. 24/4—11/6/25.**G.**
Dar. 8/11/27—10/2/28.**G.**
Dar. 8/11—27/12/29.**G.**
Dar. 26/2—15/4/32.**G.**
Dar. 2/4—18/5/35.**G.**
Dar. 8—25/6/37. *Tender only.*
Dar. 29/11/37—8/2/38.**G.**
Dar. 1/5—2/6/40.**G.**
Dar. 22/4—18/5/44.**G.**
Dar. 14/8—14/9/46.**G.**
Dar. 17—18/7/47.**N/C.**
Ghd. 3—25/11/47.**L.**
Ghd. 22/4—27/5/49.**G.**
Dar. 15—24/8/51.**C/L.**
Dar. 31/8—21/9/53.**C/L.**
After collision.
Dar. 29/1/57. *Not repaired.*

BOILERS:
G625.
D47 *(new)* ?/8/13.
D44 *(ex2018)* 30/4/24.
2311 *(new)* 27/12/29.
D1775 *(ex2109)* 18/5/35.
D1764 *(ex2108)* 8/2/38.
2339 *(ex2104)* 2/6/40.

1672 cont./
  2323 *(ex1209)* 18/5/44.
  2725 *(ex2103)* 14/9/46 (59A).
  3949 *(new)* 27/5/49 (59A).
  3949 reno.24613 21/9/53.

SHEDS:
York.
Darlington 1/5/30.
Starbeck 25/11/38.
Newport 17/2/43.
Northallerton 27/5/44.
Newport 1/9/45.
West Hartlepool 12/10/45.
Northallerton 18/2/46.
Bridlington 7/8/49.
Starbeck 17/4/50.
York 17/9/50.
Selby 1/10/50.
Neville Hill 6/7/52.
Bridlington 10/6/56.

RENUMBERED:
  2397 20/1/46.
  62397 27/5/49.

CONDEMNED: 4/2/57.
Cut up at Darlington.

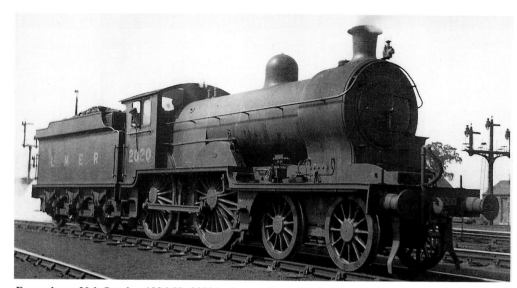

Ex works on 20th October 1936, No.2020 had a new Diag. 59A boiler, new frames, new cylinders of the same size but now with 10in. instead of 8¾in. piston valves and the maximum travel increased to 6in. A new cab had a different window arrangement at the front and sides, and the new tender body was and remained unique in having a solid coping stepped out on both sides and at the rear. Coal capacity was unaltered but water capacity dropped to 3600 gallons with pick-up gear being retained.

The driving position was changed from right to left hand side and cab side sight screens were fitted. The Westinghouse brake was changed to all vacuum and sanding became steam instead of air-operated. The buffers and hook became the Group Standard type. For the coupled wheels, bronze axle boxes were fitted with lubrication from a fountain type in the cab. Note the inverted U-shaped loops on the feed pipes to avoid air locks. Cylinder lubrication was altered from NER to a Wakefield mechanism, now driven from the right hand leading coupling rod pin.

On the 2nd September 1942 No.2020 was ex works in unlined black and with only NE on the tender. Its chimney had been changed to one with a liner. Note that at the 1936 rebuilding, a steel buffer beam had replaced the previous sandwich type.

88

Renumbered 2349 on 6th September 1946, it had LNER restored in Gill sans lettering at a general repair from 22nd October 1947 to 24th December 1947. Following a front end collision, it was out of Gateshead works on 30th August 1949 from a casual/light repair with its BR number but still with LNER on the tender. No smokebox number plate was put on at that repair. Heaton, 25th June 1950.

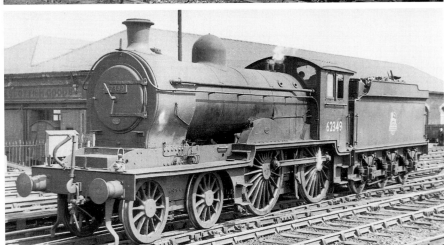

At its last general repair from 27th June to 20th July 1951, the Diagram 59A boiler carried from 1936 was changed to one built in November 1945 which had the shorter, wider dome cover and a whistle above the cab roof instead of on the firebox. LNER on the tender then gave way to the BR large emblem and a smokebox plate was fitted. Note that it kept the original design small smokebox door to its withdrawal on 2nd February 1956.

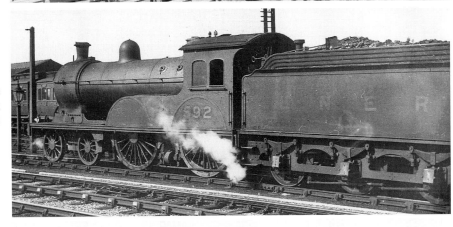

Before Gresley died in April 1941, no more rebuilding of D20 class took place, but a move was begun on 20th June 1941 and No.592 of Part 1 was the next alteration.

Ex works on 9th October 1942, No.592 had the new cylinder and piston valve arrangement but it did not differ very much in appearance from its later Part 1 guise. Note it had lost the beading from the rear splasher and had already acquired GS buffers.

At rebuilding, No.592 retained the Diagram 59A boiler, original splashers and cab with no changes to the tender. It was altered to left hand drive and had deeper frames behind the smokebox, also lubrication was changed to the fountain type. Darlington.

No.592 was renumbered 2371 on 12th May 1946 and was then in works from 15th May to 15th June 1946 for a general repair during which it changed to a Diagram 59A boiler with a shorter, wider dome cover. Its twin whistles were superseded by a single one mounted above the cab roof; LNER was restored on the tender. Unlike No.2020, the other three rebuilds to Part 2 retained their Westinghouse brake equipment.

(below) Ex works 22nd October 1948, No.62371 included correct Gill sans 6 in its BR number and on its smokebox number plate, and it remained as shown until withdrawal on 19th October 1954. Whittingham, February 1953.

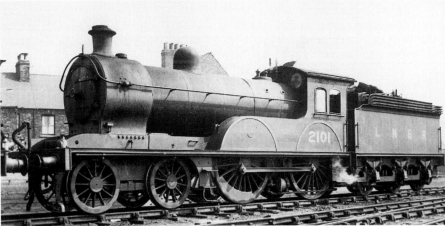

This Part 1 engine was the next to be rebuilt and as it already had the deeper type of frame, these needed no alteration.

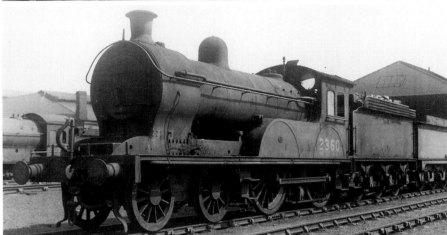

No.2101 was rebuilt to Part 2 on 11th December 1942 and became No.2360 at Bridlington shed on 27th April 1946. On rebuilding it kept its Diagram 59 boiler but the twin whistles were changed to a single one still mounted on the firebox, but on a pipe which put it above cab roof level. Note it had one of the boilers with washout plugs.

At its last repair from 10th June to 5th July 1952, it changed to its BR number with the correct 6 included and from LNER to the smaller size BR emblem. A new 59A boiler, built in March 1949, was put on and it also got the larger diameter smokebox door with pressed joint ring. Note that no sight screens were fitted and it remained like this until withdrawn on 23rd October 1956. Botanic Gardens, August 1952.

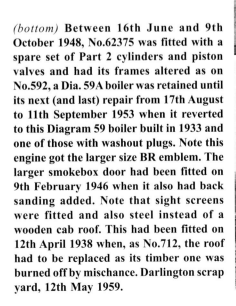

(bottom) Between 16th June and 9th October 1948, No.62375 was fitted with a spare set of Part 2 cylinders and piston valves and had its frames altered as on No.592, a Dia. 59A boiler was retained until its next (and last) repair from 17th August to 11th September 1953 when it reverted to this Diagram 59 boiler built in 1933 and one of those with washout plugs. Note this engine got the larger size BR emblem. The larger smokebox door had been fitted on 9th February 1946 when it also had back sanding added. Note that sight screens were fitted and also steel instead of a wooden cab roof. This had been fitted on 12th April 1938 when, as No.712, the roof had to be replaced as its timber one was burned off by mischance. Darlington scrap yard, 12th May 1959.

Between August 1912 and July 1915 all ten D21's were superheated, the smokebox being lengthened to 4ft 3½in. By Grouping, the whole class had been fitted with steps on the front plate to give easier access to the top lamp iron. The boilers used on this class had three hand holes on the right hand side of the firebox for washout purposes. York.

On the left hand side of the boiler there were two hand holes, pitched opposite the spaces on the right hand side. In total twenty-four boilers were built for this class, twenty-two with Schmidt superheaters and two with the Robinson type header but there was no external difference.

The ten original boilers and the two spares built in 1912 had Ramsbottom safety valves and as superheaters were put into them, the two 1912 spares remained in use until 1929 and 1931. Engines 1239, 1243, 1245 and 1246 could be seen in LNER livery still with Ramsbottom valves.

CLASS D 21

1237

Darlington.

To traffic 11/1908.

REPAIRS:
Dar.?/? —?/4/13.**G**.
Dar.?/? —?/7/15.**G**.
Superheated boiler fitted.
Dar.?/? —?/1/20.**G**.
Dar.?/? —?/8/21.**G**.
Dar. 5/3—27/6/24.**G**.
Dar. 30/11/26—22/3/27.**G**.
Dar. 4/3—25/4/29.**G**.
Dar. 17/2—12/3/30.**L**.
Dar. 13/1—25/2/31.**G**.
Dar. 14/11/32—10/1/33.**G**.
Dar. 3/10—17/11/34.**G**.
Dar. 13/7—28/8/36.**G**.
Dar. 28/4—1/7/37.**N/C**.
Dar. 21/9—9/12/39.**G**.
Dar. 27/5—12/7/41.**L**.
Tender changed to G.N. type.
Dar. 29/12/42—18/2/43.**G**.
Dar. 23/2/45. *Not repaired.*

BOILERS:
D1975.
D1978 *(ex1240)* ?/4/13.
D1981 *(ex1240)* ?/7/15.
D1978 *(ex1245)* ?/1/20.
D1264 *(new)* ?/8/21.
D1240 *(ex1246)* 25/4/29.
D1269 *(ex1243)* 25/2/31.
D1264 *(ex1238)* 10/1/33.
D1240 *(ex1238)* 17/11/34.
2329 *(ex1246)* 28/8/36.

SHEDS:
York.
Neville Hill 29/12/24.

RENUMBERED:
2217 *allocated.*

CONDEMNED: 19/3/45.
Cut up at Darlington.

1238

Darlington.

To traffic 12/1908.

REPAIRS:
Dar.?/? —?/12/12.**G**.
Superheated boiler fitted.
Dar.?/? —?/2/20.**G**.
Dar.?/? —?/6/22.**G**.
Dar. 27/3—31/5/23.**G**.
Dar. 15/1—7/3/24.**G**.
Dar. 16/4—19/8/25.**G**.
Dar. 28/8—30/9/25.**L**.
Dar. 16/4—24/6/29.**G**.
Dar. 19/2—12/5/32.**G**.
Dar. 1/2—8/3/34.**G**.
Dar. 30/8—8/11/35.**G**.
Dar. 8/7—19/10/36.**L**.
Dar. 7/3—27/5/38.**G**.
Dar. 23/4—21/5/41.**N/C**.
Tender changed to G.N. type.
Dar. 16/6—17/8/42.**G**.
Dar. 25/1—4/2/44.**L**.
After collision.
Dar. 17/2/45. *Not repaired.*

BOILERS:
D1976.
D1977 *(ex1239)* ?/12/12.
 D126 *(ex1242)* ?/2/20.
D1980 *(ex1244)* ?/6/22.
D1294 *(new)* 31/5/23.
D1264 *(ex1237)* 24/6/29.
D1240 *(ex1237)* 12/5/32.
D1210 *(ex1243)* 8/3/34.
D1294 *(ex1243)* 8/11/35.

SHEDS:
York.
Neville Hill 14/1/25.
Starbeck ?/2/25.
Neville Hill 5/11/28.

RENUMBERED:
2218 *Allocated.*

CONDEMNED: 3/3/45.
Cut up at Darlington.

1239

Darlington.

To traffic 12/1908.

REPAIRS:
Dar.?/? —?/9/12.**G**.
Dar.?/? —?/6/14.**G**.
Superheated boiler fitted.
Dar.?/? —?/8/21.**G**.
Dar. 9/3—28/6/24.**G**.
Dar. 12/10/26—17/2/27.**G**.
Dar. 13/11/28—16/1/29.**G**.
Dar. 7—21/1/30.**L**.
Dar. 19/2—21/3/32.*Tender only.*
Dar. 16/1—16/2/33.**G**.
Dar. 25/10—24/12/35.**G**.
Dar. 27/2—15/4/36.**L**.
Dar. 25/4—6/7/38.**G**.

Dar. 14/3—28/4/41.**N/C**.
Tender changed to G.N. type.
Dar. 19/11/42. *Not repaired.*

BOILERS:
D1977.
D1982 *(ex1244)* ?/9/12.
D1983 *(ex spare)* ?/6/14.
D1258 *(new)* ?/8/21.
 D121 *(ex1243)* 17/2/27.
D1160 *(ex1241)* 16/1/29.
D1269 *(ex1237)* 16/2/33.
D1311 *(ex1240)* 24/12/35.

SHEDS:
York.
Hull Botanic Gardens ?/2/25.
Neville Hill 22/4/31.

CONDEMNED: 24/12/42.
Cut up at Darlington.

1240

Darlington.

To traffic 3/1909.

REPAIRS:
Dar.?/? —?/2/13.**G**.
Dar.?/? —?/4/15.**G**.
Superheated boiler fitted.
Dar.?/? —?/1/22.**G**.
Dar. 13/3—22/5/24.**G**.
Dar. 29/12/26—30/4/27.**G**.
Dar. 29/4—28/6/29.**G**.
Dar. 21/4—29/5/31.**G**.
Dar. 7/9—16/10/33.**G**.
Dar. 17/9—1/11/35.**G**.
Dar. 24/7—8/10/36.**L**.
Dar. 21/5—1/7/37.**H**.
Dar. 13/7—11/8/37.**L**.
Dar. 16/11/38—28/2/39.**G**.
Dar. 21/3—15/4/40.**L**.
Dar. 18/12/40—30/1/41.**L**.
Dar. 7/3—2/5/41.**L**.
Tender changed to G.N. type.
Dar. 31/8—24/10/42.**G**.
Dar. 27/4/44. *Not repaired.*

BOILERS:
D1978.
D1981 *(ex1243)* ?/2/13.
D1975 *(ex spare)* ?/4/15.
D1292 *(new)* ?/1/22.
D1294 *(ex1238)* 28/6/29.
D1311 *(ex1241)* 16/10/33.
D1210 *(ex1238)* 1/11/35.
D1269 *(ex1246)* 28/2/39.

SHEDS:
Hull Botanic Gardens.
Neville Hill 1/4/25.
Hull Botanic Gardens 20/1/26.
Neville Hill 22/4/31.

RENUMBERED:
2219 *allocated.*

CONDEMNED: 20/5/44.
Cut up at Darlington.

1241

Darlington.

To traffic 6/1909.

REPAIRS:
Dar.?/? —?/10/12.**G**.
Dar.?/? —?/5/15.**G**.
Superheated boiler fitted.
Dar.?/? —?/1/21.**G**.
Dar. 15/1—30/4/23.**G**.
Dar. 5—16/5/23.**N/C**.
Dar. 10/2—11/5/25.**G**.
Dar. 6/7—22/10/26.**G**.
Dar. 23/3—24/5/28.**G**.
Dar. 5/1—16/2/31.**G**.
Dar. 9—21/3/32.**N/C**.
Dar. 4/4—1/5/33.**H**.
Dar. 24/8—25/9/33.**G**.
Dar. 30/10—19/12/35.**G**.
Dar. 9/4—5/5/37.**L**.
Dar. 13/9—23/12/38.**G**.
Dar. 21/5—9/7/41.**L**
Tender changed to G.N. type.
Dar. 2—17/10/41.**N/C**.
Dar. 12—24/3/43. *Not repaired.*

BOILERS:
D1979.
D1980 *(ex1242)* ?/10/42.
D1976 *(ex1243)* ?/5/15.
D1160 *(new)* ?/1/21.
D1311 *(new)* 24/5/28.
D1258 *(ex1245)* 25/9/33.

SHEDS:
York.
Starbeck 19/9/25.

CONDEMNED: 19/3/43. *In
transfers. Deleted from stock.
24/3/43 Engine & a spare NE type
tender sent to Fishguard via
Banbury for air target practice.
Returned to Darlington July 1943
and cut up there in January 1944.*

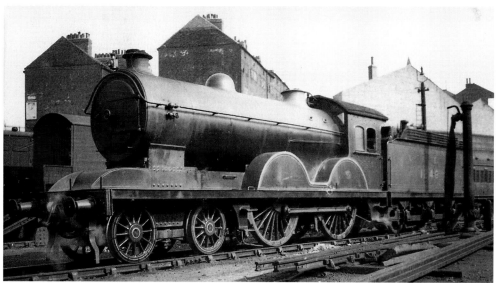

Until January 1929 all the D21's had a steam circulating valve on the left hand side of the smokebox for protection of the elements. The blower control rod was through the left hand boiler handrail. Nottingham (Victoria).

An instruction of July 15th 1927 decreed that Gresley anti-vacuum valves were to be fitted but the first was not to get one until No.1239 was ex works on 16th January 1929 (*see* page 100, bottom). All then duly got that type.

Until October 1933 all were fitted with Raven fog signalling apparatus for which the striker was under the cab, just behind the rear coupled wheels.

The normal whistle fitting was one large and one small bell shape type on a U-mounting in front of the cab. Smokebox door fastening was originally two handles but in LNER days all except 1244 carried a wheel and handle. Until 1932 the front end of the frames did not have lifting holes. Scarborough.

(right) By the mid-1930's there were some changes. Nos.1237, 1240, 1244 and 1246 had the larger whistle changed to an organ pipe. The wheel on the smokebox door was replaced by another handle and lifting holes were put on from 1932.

(below) All were dual brake fitted and until 1929 the front end connections were below the buffer beam.

1242

Darlington.

To traffic 6/1909.

REPAIRS:
Dar.?/? —?/9/12.**G.**
Superheated boiler fitted.
Dar.?/? —?/12/17.**G.**
Dar. 4/4—30/6/23.**G.**
Dar. 26/5—30/9/26.**G.**
Dar. 16/2—7/3/28.**L.**
Dar. 20/1—4/3/30.**G.**
Dar. 9—15/5/30.**N/C.**
Dar. 21/8—9/9/30.**N/C.**
Dar. 1/11—13/12/32.**G.**
Dar. 2/7—29/8/35.**G.**
Dar. 8/6—20/8/37.**H.**
Dar. 2/5—11/6/38.**G.**
Dar. 7/6—6/7/40.**N/C.**
Dar. 9/6—26/7/41.**L.**
Tender changed to G.N. type.
Dar. 27/11/41—6/1/42. *Tender only.Tender top & back holed by an unexploded bomb.*
Dar. 29/9—3/12/42.**G.**
Dar. 6/12/45. *Not repaired.*

BOILERS:
D1980.
 D126 *(new)* ?/9/12.
D1979 *(ex1246)* ?/12/17.
D1303 *(new)* 30/6/23.
 2334 *(new)* 4/3/30.
D1160 *(ex1245)* 29/8/35.
 2334 *(ex1243)* 11/6/38.

SHEDS:
Starbeck.
Neville Hill 12/3/45.

RENUMBERED:
2220 *allocated..*

CONDEMNED: 8/1/46.
Cut up at Darlington.

___

1243

Darlington.

To traffic 6/1909.

REPAIRS:
Dar.?/? —?/1/13.**G.**
Superheated boiler fitted.
Dar.?/? —?/1/15.**G.**
Dar.?/? —?/9/16.**G.**
Dar. 20/11/23—29/2/24.**G.**
Dar. 25/1—26/5/26.**G.**

Dar. 27/7—6/8/26.**L.**
Dar. 28/8—18/10/28.**G.**
Dar. 25/4—19/7/30.**G.**
Dar. 18/12/31—18/2/32.**G.**
Dar. 6/11—29/12/33.**G.**
Dar. 7/8—20/9/35.**G.**
Dar. 14/1—1/3/37.**L.**
Dar. 10/2—9/4/38.**G.**
Dar. 19/3—13/5/41.**N/C.**
Tender changed to G.N. type.
Dar. 7/10/41—4/11/41.**G.**
Dar. 29/9—24/10/42.**G.**
Dar. 12/6/45. *Not repaired..*

BOILERS:
D1981.
D1976 *(ex1238)* ?/1/13.
D1982 *(ex1239)* ?/1/15.
 D121 *(ex1244)* ?/9/16.
D1269 *(ex1244)* 26/5/26.
D1210 *(ex1244)* 19/7/30.
D1294 *(ex1240)* 29/12/33.
 2334 *(ex1242)* 20/9/35.
D1264 *(ex1244)* 9/4/38.
D1240 *(ex1244)* 4/11/41.

SHED:
Neville Hill

RENUMBERED:
2221 *allocated.*

CONDEMNED: 30/6/45.
Cut up at Darlington.

___

1244

Darlington.

To traffic 7/1909.

REPAIRS:
Dar.?/? —?/8/12.**G.**
Superheated boiler fitted.
Dar.?/? —?/2/16.**G.**
Dar.?/? —?/9/21.**G.**
Dar. 21/8—8/11/23.**G.**
Dar. 1—12/2/24.**L.**
Dar. 7/10/25—29/1/26.**G.**
Dar. 8/11/27—26/1/28.**G.**
Dar. 11—28/2/28.**L.**
Dar. 17/2—9/4/30.**G.**
Dar. 9—23/10/31.**N/C.**
Dar. 2/2—23/3/33.**G.**
Dar. 17/10—22/12/33.**H.**
Dar. 2/4—18/5/35.**G.**
Dar. 17/2—25/3/37.**L.**
Dar. 30/9—27/11/37.**G.**
Dar. 10/9—24/10/40.**G.**
Dar. 10—28/5/41.**N/C.**
Tender changed to G.N. type.

Dar. 4/10/44. *Not repaired.*

BOILERS:
D1982.
 D121 *(new)* ?/8/12.
D1980 *(ex1241)* ?/2/16.
D1269 *(new)* ?/9/21.
D1210 *(ex1245)* 29/1/26.
D1303 *(ex1242)* 9/4/30.
D1264 *(ex1237)* 18/5/35.
D1240 *(ex1237)* 27/11/37.
D1292 *(ex1240 & Works test boiler)* 24/10/40.

SHED:
Neville Hill.

RENUMBERED:
2222 *allocated.*

CONDEMNED: 21/10/44.
Cut up at Darlington.

___

1245

Darlington.

To traffic 8/1909.

REPAIRS:
Dar.?/? —?/3/13.**G.**
Dar.?/? —?/7/15.**G.**
Superheated boiler fitted.
Dar.?/? —?/4/19.**G.**
Dar.?/? —?/3/21.**G.**
Dar. 28/2—19/5/23.**G.**
Dar. 15/1—18/4/25.**G.**
Dar. 26/10/27—24/1/28.**G.**
Dar. 16/5—22/10/30.**G.**
Dar. 20/3—1/5/33.**G.**
Dar. 12/6—10/8/35.**G.**
Dar. 3/8—14/10/38.**G.**
Dar. 10/6—19/7/41.**L.**
Tender changed to G.N. type.
Dar. 25/8—6/9/41.**N/C.**
Dar. 3/11—11/12/42.**G.**
Dar. 11/1/46. *Not repaired.*

BOILERS:
D1983.
D1984 *(ex1246)* ?/3/13.
D1978 *(ex1237)* ?/7/15.
D1982 *(ex1245)* ?/4/19.
D1210 *(new)* ?/3/21.
 D126 *(ex1238 & spare)* 18/4/25.
D1258 *(ex1239)* 24/1/28.
D1160 *(ex1239)* 1/5/33.
D1303 *(ex1244)* 10/8/35.
D1160 *(ex1242)* 14/10/38.

SHEDS:
York.
Hull Botanic Gardens 15/6/25.
Neville Hill 22/4/31.
Starbeck 30/9/35.
Neville Hill 12/3/45.

RENUMBERED:
2223 *allocated.*

CONDEMNED: 9/2/46.
Cut up at Darlington.

___

1246

Darlington.

To traffic 8/1909.

REPAIRS:
Dar.?/? —?/3/13.**G.**
Superheated boiler fitted.
Dar.?/? —?/2/17.**G.**
Dar.?/? —?/6/21.**G.**
Dar. 14/4—14/7/23.**G.**
Dar. 31/8—4/10/23.**L.**
Dar. 25/8—10/9/24.**L.**
Dar. 28/1—27/6/26.**G.**
Dar. 18/4—21/6/28.**G.**
Dar. 3/2—18/3/31.**G.**
Dar. 8/5—2/6/31.**L.**
Dar. 9/3—27/4/33.**G.**
Dar. 6/11—12/12/33. *Tender only.*
Dar. 6/1—22/2/36.**G.**
Dar. 13/9—22/10/38.**G.**
Dar. 4—24/4/40.**N/C.**
Dar. 18/3—13/5/41.**N/C.**
Tender changed to G.N. type.
Dar. 29/6/43. *Not repaired.*

BOILERS:
D1984.
D1979 *(ex1241)* ?/3/13.
D1984 *(ex spare)* ?/2/17.
D1240 *(new)* ?/6/21.
 D126 *(ex1245)* 21/6/28.
 2329 *(new)* 18/3/31.
D1269 *(ex1239)* 22/2/36.
D1303 *(ex1245)* 22/10/38.

SHEDS:
York.
Hull Botanic Gardens 1/4/25.
Neville Hill 22/4/31.
Starbeck 30/9/35.

CONDEMNED: 17/7/43.
Cut up at Darlington.

___

WORKS CODES:- Cw - Cowlairs. Dar- Darlington. Don - Doncaster. Ghd - Gateshead. Gor - Gorton. Inv - Inverurie. Nor - Norwich. Spd - Springhead. Str - Stratford.
REPAIR CODES:- **C/H** - Casual Heavy. **C/L** - Casual Light. **G** - General. **H**- Heavy. **H/I** - Heavy Intermediate. **L** - Light. **L/I** - Light Intermediate. **N/C** - Non-Classified.

Beginning in 1929 a swan-neck standpipe for the vacuum brake was fixed to the front of the buffer beam. In 1932 No.1244 had lost its windjabber due to corrosion but it was duly restored in March 1933. Note the door between cab and tender; the instruction to fit these was issued in March 1924. York.

Not until July 1930 was a carriage heating connection provided at the front end, No.1243 being the first of the class so fitted. It was December 1938 before all the rest were equipped, No.1241 being the last. Leeds.

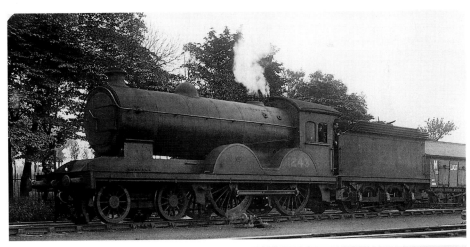

From new, until April 1941, all had the 1903 standard tender which held 5 tons of coal and 4125 gallons of water. These tenders also had pick-up apparatus but were not self-trimming. There were three rails at sides and back with a fourth rail and plating around the coal space. Darlington.

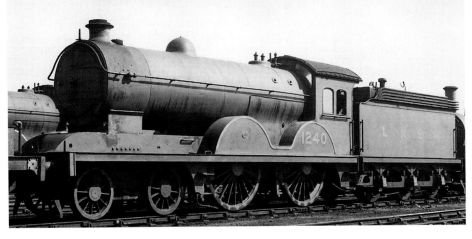

Between April and June 1941 all ten tenders were taken from these engines and were put to run with new J39 class engines that Darlington was then building. The replacement tenders were surplus Great Northern early Class B type. Darlington.

As the replacement tenders were fitted for vacuum brake, the engines were changed to that type and the Westinghouse pump and brake equipment was taken off. As sanding had been air-operated this was then changed to steam. No D21 was fitted with Group Standard buffers nor did any get sight screens on the cab. During the 1930's a drain pipe for the vacuum ejector exhaust pipe was put on to the right hand side of the smokebox.

As express passenger engines they had fully lined green with both armorials. Darlington.

The first LNER paintings had 6in. size L.&N.E.R. on the tender, and this was applied in 1923 to Nos.1241 (30th April), 1245 (19th May) and 1238 (31st May). No.1241 still had 6in. N.E.R. style on the front buffer beam but Nos.1238 and 1245 had the $4^{1}/_{2}$in. Group Standard style. On No.1242 (30th June 1923) no full points were used whilst No.1246 (14th July 1923) also lost the ampersand

During the five months when area Suffix D was used, only one D21 had it applied - No.1244 (8th November 1923). York.

In 1924 the other four engines went to the standard LNER 1924 livery straight from North Eastern. These were Nos.1243 (29th February), 1240 (22nd May), 1237 (27th June) and 1239 (28th June). York.

From June 1928 this class went into black livery with single red lining, at first with the number still on the tender; only two had this style, Nos.1243 (18th October 1928) and 1239 (16th January 1929). Doncaster.

The number was then put on the engine, centred on the rear splasher and 12in. LNER was used on the tender. The only later changes were to unlined from November 1941 and to NE only on tender from July 1942.

No.1245, here on 12th August 1935, is leaving York North shed hauling the experimental Kitson-Still locomotive to Leeds for return to its makers and owners. This D21 was ex Darlington on 10th August 1935 from a general repair and had called at York whilst returning to its home shed at Neville Hill, Leeds.

Only Nos.1240 (24th October), 1242 (3rd November) and 1245 (11th December) had just NE on tender, all applied in 1942.

Between September 1913 and June 1920 the whole class was fitted with superheaters. On the left hand side of the smokebox a steam circulating valve provided protection for the superheating elements. None of the D22's were ever fitted with the Gresley type anti-vacuum valve.

Nos.1324 and 340 had been built as 2-4-0 types of Class D but in October 1896 they had been rebuilt to 4-4-0 type. Their frames differed from those of the other thirty-five in having a concave curve at the front and a similar curve at the rear of the smokebox.

CLASS D 22

1324

Gateshead 17.86.

To traffic 11/1886.

REPAIRS:
???. ?/?—?/10/96.**G.**
Rebuilt from compound 2-4-0.
???. ?/?—?/3/98.**G.**
???. ?/?—?/8/05.**G.**
???. ?/?—?/12/17.**G.**
Superheated boiler fitted.
Ghd. ?/?—?/12/20.**G.**
Ghd. 16/2—14/5/25.**G.**
Ghd. 31/5—2/9/27.**G.**
Ghd. 13—15/9/27.**N/C.**
Ghd. 2—14/6/28.**L.**
Ghd. 21/2—19/3/29.**L.**

BOILERS:
G9.
G795 ?/3/98.
G359 ?/8/05.
D638 *(new)* ?/12/17.

SHED:
Carlisle.

CONDEMNED: 10/2/30.

18

Gateshead 14.87.

To traffic 6/1887.

REPAIRS:
???. ?/?—?/3/05.**G.**
Rebuilt from compound.
???. ?/?—?/10/16.**G.**
Superheated boiler fitted.
Ghd. ?/?—29/12/22.**G.**
Ghd. 28/1—23/4/26.**G.**

BOILERS:
G952.
G356 *(new)* ?/3/05.
D605 *(new)* ?/10/16.
G580 *(ex spare)* 29/12/22.

SHEDS:
Alnmouth.
Tweedmouth 8/3/28.
Gateshead 19/3/28.

CONDEMNED: 11/1/29.

42

Gateshead 15.87.

To traffic 6/1887.

REPAIRS:
???. ?/?—?/12/97.**G.**
???. ?/?—?/10/04.**G.**
Rebuilt from compound.
???. ?/?—?/11/08.**G.**
???. ?/?—?/9/13.**G.**
???. ?/?—?/2/15.**G.**
Superheated boiler fitted.
Dar. 19/4—17/7/23.**G.**
Dar. 11/5—31/8/25.**G.**
Dar. 1/9—26/11/27.**G.**

BOILERS:
G953.
G786 *(new)* ?/12/97.
G577 *(new)* ?/11/08.
G123 *(ex1542)* ?/9/13.
D361 *(new)* ?/2/15.
D359 *(ex777)* 17/7/23.

SHEDS:
Hull Botanic Gardens.
Scarborough 22/10/25.

CONDEMNED: 22/5/30.

115

Gateshead 16.87.

To traffic 6/1887.

REPAIRS:
???. ?/?—?/12/97.**G.**
???. ?/?—?/9/04.**G.**
Rebuilt from compound.
???. ?/?—?/3/14.**G.**
Superheated boiler fitted.
Dar. 25/9—18/12/24.**G.**
Dar. 24/5—17/8/27.**G.**
Dar. 22/5—17/7/29.**G.**
Dar. 15/12/30—11/2/31.**G.**

BOILERS:
G955.
G784 *(new)* ?/12/97.
D299 *(new)* ?/3/14.
D351 *(ex779)* 18/12/24.
D972 *(ex663)* 11/2/31.

SHEDS:
Bridlington.
Hull Botanic Gardens ?/?/25.

Starbeck 28/4/31.
Bradford (Manningham) 30/10/31.

CONDEMNED: 18/12/33.

117

Gateshead 21.87.

To traffic 11/1887.

REPAIRS:
???. ?/?—?/3/98.**G.**
???. ?/?—?/11/03.**G.**
Rebuilt from compound.
???. ?/?—?/12/07.**G.**
???. ?/?—?/9/13.**G.**
Superheated boiler fitted.
Dar. 5/9—24/11/24.**G.**
Dar. 29/9/26—8/2/27.**G.**

BOILERS:
G956.
G794 *(new)* ?/3/98.
G795 *(ex spare)* ?/12/07.
G902 *(new)* ?/9/13.

SHEDS:
Bridlington.
Hull Botanic Gardens ?/?/25.

CONDEMNED: 21/3/29.

355

Gateshead 22.87.

To traffic 11/1887.

REPAIRS:
???. ?/?—?/10/01.**G.**
Rebuilt from compound.
???. ?/?—?/9/15.**G.**
Superheated boiler fitted.
Ghd. 22/2—16/5/24.**G.**
Ghd. 25/1—9/5/27.**G.**

BOILERS:
G957.
G118 *(new)* ?/10/01.
D479 *(new)* ?/9/15.
D634 *(ex154)* 9/5/27.

SHED:
Carlisle.

CONDEMNED: 23/1/30.

514

Gateshead 23.87.

To traffic 11/1887.

REPAIRS:
???. ?/?—?/5/00.**G.**
Rebuilt from compound.
???. ?/?—?/4/08.**G.**
???. ?/?—?/3/14.**G.**
Superheated boiler fitted.
Dar. 18/10/22—29/1/23.**G.**
Dar. 29/10/24—9/2/25.**G.**
Dar. 16/11/26—17/2/27.**G.**

BOILERS:
G958.
D1553 *(new)* ?/5/00.
G794 *(ex117)* ?/4/08.
D293 *(new)* ?/3/14.
D299 *(ex115)* 9/2/25.

SHEDS:
Bridlington.
Hull Botanic Gardens ?/?/25.

CONDEMNED: 9/2/29.

663

Gateshead 24.87.

To traffic 12/1887.

REPAIRS:
???. ?/?—?/1/00.**G.**
Rebuilt from compound.
???. ?/?—?/5/11.**G.**
???. ?/?—?/10/19.**G.**
Superheated boiler fitted.
Dar. 22/5—6/8/23.**G.**
Dar. 28/9—5/10/23.**L.**
Ghd. 28/7—16/10/25.**G.**
Ghd. 26/11—2/12/25.**L.**
Ghd. 4/1—26/3/29.**G.**
Dar. 29/9—11/11/30.**G.**

BOILERS:
G959.
G800 *(new)* ?/1/00.
G901 *(new)* ?/5/11.
D972 *(new)* ?/10/19.
D959 *(ex356)* 11/11/30.

SHEDS:
Waskerley.
Gateshead ?/?/24.
Hull Botanic Gardens 11/1/29.

663 cont/.
CONDEMNED: 24/10/32.

684

Gateshead 25.87.

To traffic 12/1887.

REPAIRS:
???. ?/?—?/6/99.**G.**
???. ?/?—?/2/03.**G.**
Rebuilt from compound.
???. ?/?—?/9/13.**G.**
Superheated boiler fitted.
Dar. 15/3—22/5/24.**G.**
Dar. 19/10/25—15/1/26.**G.**
Dar. 13/2—27/4/28.**G.**

BOILERS:
G960.
G798 *(new)* ?/6/99.
G904 *(new)* ?/9/13.

SHEDS:
Bridlington.
Selby 14/5/25.
Malton 8/7/25.
Selby 28/9/25.
Saltburn 11/7/29.
Selby 25/7/29.

CONDEMNED: 17/6/30.

779

Gateshead 26.87.

To traffic 11/1887.

REPAIRS:
???. ?/?—?/10/02.**G.**
Rebuilt from compound.
???. ?/?—?/8/14.**G.**
Superheated boiler fitted.
Dar. 7/11/22—13/3/23.**G.**
Dar. 29/8—20/11/24.**G.**
Dar. 9/11/26—28/2/27.**G.**
Dar. 23/4—3/5/29.**N/C.**

BOILERS:
G961.
G134 *(new)* ?/10/02.
D351 *(new)* ?/8/14.
D961 *(ex1532)* 20/11/24.

SHED:
Scarborough.

CONDEMNED: 4/2/30.

356

Gateshead 27.87.

To traffic 12/1887.

REPAIRS:
???. ?/?—?/12/03.**G.**
Rebuilt from compound.
???. ?/?—?/3/06.**G.**
???. ?/?—?/3/20.**G.**
Superheated boiler fitted.
Dar. 21/10/24—17/1/25.**G.**
Dar. 17/8—8/9/25.**L.**
Dar. 10/11/27—10/2/28.**G.**
Dar. 21/2—7/3/29.**N/C.**
Dar. 9/9—21/10/30.**G.**

BOILERS:
G963.
G361 *(new)* ?/3/06.
D959 *(new)* ?/3/20.
D512 *(ex1536)* 21/10/30.

SHEDS:
Scarborough.
Hull Botanic Gardens 21/2/29.

RENUMBERED:
Was No.1 until 1/1/14.

CONDEMNED: 5/3/32.

230

Gateshead 28.87.

To traffic 11/1887.

REPAIRS:
???. ?/?—?/4/02.**G.**
???. ?/?—?/2/05.**G.**
New cylinders fitted.
???. ?/?—?/4/11.**G.**
???. ?/?—?/2/18.**G.**
Superheated boiler fitted.
???. ?/?—?/12/21.**G.**
Dar. 12/4—28/6/23.**G.**
Dar. 14/7—15/10/25.**G.**
Dar. 15/9—29/11/27.**G.**
Dar. 17/9—5/10/28.**N/C.**

BOILERS:
G973.
G131 *(new)* ?/4/02.
G903 *(new)* ?/4/11.
D741 *(new)* ?/2/18.
D1270 *(new)* ?/12/21.

SHEDS:
Bridlington.
Hull Botanic Gardens ?/?/25.

CONDEMNED: 7/2/30.

673

Gateshead 29.87.

To traffic 11/1887.

REPAIRS:
???. ?/?—?/11/01.**G.**
???. ?/?—?/11/05.**G.**
???. ?/?—?/2/11.**G.**
New cylinders fitted.
???. ?/?—?/2/16.**G.**
Superheated boiler fitted.
Dar. 23/11/22—28/2/23.**G.**
Dar. 20/2—14/5/24.**G.**
Dar. 18/8—14/10/25.**G.**
Dar. 22/12/25—5/1/26.**L.**
Dar. 5/10/26—2/2/27.**G.**
Dar. 29/5—30/7/29.**G.**
Dar. 20/5—15/7/31.**G.**

BOILERS:
G962.
G120 *(new)* ?/11/01.
G360 *(new)* ?/11/05.
G357 *(ex1533)* ?/2/16.
D749 *(ex1533)* 28/2/23.

SHED:
Selby.

CONDEMNED: 9/10/33.

777

Gateshead 30.87.

To traffic 11/1887.

REPAIRS:
???. ?/?—?/6/98.**G.**
???. ?/?—?/4/05.**G.**
New cylinders fitted.
???. ?/?—?/11/14.**G.**
Superheated boiler fitted.
Dar. 22/2—11/5/23.**G.**
Dar. 24/10/24—9/1/25.**G.**
Dar. 9—13/2/25.**L.**
Dar. 12/3—9/7/26.**G.**
Dar. 2/5—9/7/28.**G.**
Dar. 22/1—6/3/30.**G.**
Ghd. 13/3—11/4/32.**G.**
Dar. 17/5/35. *Not repaired.*

BOILERS:
G976.
G796 *(new)* ?/6/98.
D359 *(new)* ?/11/14.
D743 *(ex1538)* 11/5/23.
D750 *(ex1533)* 6/3/30.

SHEDS:
Hull Botanic Gardens.
Ipswich 7/1/27.

Norwich 28/3/27.
Hull Botanic Gardens 6/4/27.
Waskerley 11/7/30.

CONDEMNED: 22/5/35.

194

Gateshead 31.87.

To traffic 12/1887.

REPAIRS:
???. ?/?—?/11/01.**G.**
???. ?/?—?/7/08.**G.**
New cylinders fitted.
???. ?/?—?/12/15.**G.**
Superheated boiler fitted.
Dar. 28/8/22—23/1/23.**G.**
Dar. 21/11/24—13/2/25.**G.**
Dar. 31/3—29/6/27.**G.**
Dar. 1/11—17/12/28.**G.**

BOILERS:
G982.
G119 *(new)* ?/11/01.
D498 *(new)* ?/12/15.
D356 *(ex1532)* 17/12/28.

SHED:
Hull Botanic Gardens.

CONDEMNED: 8/4/30.

803

Gateshead 32.87.

To traffic 11/1887.

REPAIRS:
???. ?/?—?/3/01.**G.**
???. ?/?—?/6/11.**G.**
New cylinders fitted.
???. ?/?—?/1/18.**G.**
Superheated boiler fitted.
???. ?/?—?/7/22.**G.**
Ghd. 26/8—4/11/24.**G.**
Dar. 1—14/5/25.**L.**
Dar. 12/10/26—14/2/27.**G.**

BOILERS:
G977.
D1555 *(new)* ?/3/01.
D1559 *(ex1541)* ?/6/11.
D740 *(new)* ?/1/18.
D1288 *(new)* ?/7/22.

SHED:
Hull Botanic Gardens.

CONDEMNED: 6/5/29.

The frames of the other thirty-five had convex curves fore and aft of the smokebox attachment and the extension piece welded on at the front could clearly be seen. This was needed for the longer smokebox to cater for the superheater header.

At Grouping there were forty boilers available and the LNER did not build any more. All had two hand holes on the right hand side of the firebox for washout purposes.

Similarly there were two hand holes on the left hand and these were pitched further forward to give more complete coverage of the firebox crown. Botanic Gardens, June 1931.

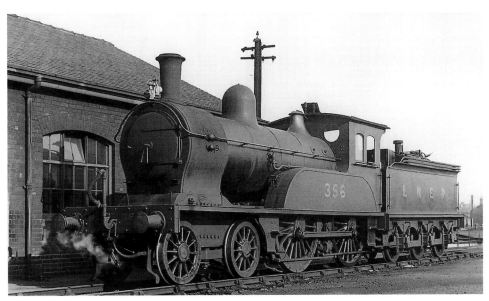

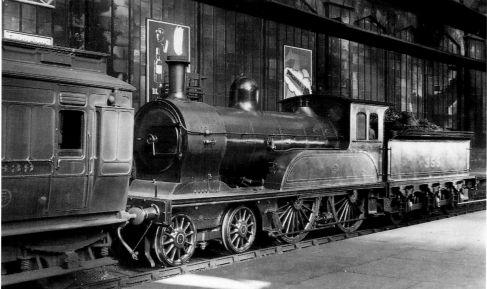

(above) Thirty of the forty boilers had Ramsbottom safety valves enclosed by the usual trumpet shaped brass cover and these were retained to withdrawal. The last of the class, No.1537, withdrawn on 15th November 1935, still had one.

(left) Five boilers built from September to December 1916 had Ross 'pop' valves and three of the five had an adapted Ramsbottom mounting so they needed a deep cover to their base.

Another batch of five boilers, built during December 1917 and January 1918, also had Ross 'pop' valves but these were mounted directly on to the firebox so only had a shallow cover.

808

Gateshead 33.87.

To traffic 12/1887.

REPAIRS:
???. ?/?—?/3/99.**G.**
???. ?/?—?/5/05.**G.**
New cylinders fitted.
???. ?/?—?/2/10.**G.**
???. ?/?—?/1/13.**G.**
???. ?/?—?/3/16.**G.**
Superheated boiler fitted.
Ghd. 2/10—8/12/24.**G.**
Ghd. 14/5—9/6/25.**L.**
Ghd. 1/11/27—31/1/28.**G.**

BOILERS:
  G978.
  G797 *(new)* ?/3/99.
  G262 *(ex1539)* ?/2/10.
  D1554 *(ex1535)* ?/1/13.
  D518 *(new)* ?/3/16.
  D531 *(ex1537)* 8/12/24.

SHEDS:
Hull Springhead.
West Hartlepool ?/?/24.
Gateshead 8/12/24.
Malton 22/7/26.
Stockton 14/10/26.

CONDEMNED: 20/2/30.

_____

1137

Gateshead 34.87.

To traffic 12/1887.

REPAIRS:
???. ?/?—?/7/02.**G.**
???. ?/?—?/12/03.**G.**
New cylinders fitted.
???. ?/?—?/1/12.**G.**
???. ?/?—?/7/19.**G.**
Superheated boiler fitted.
Dar. 8/12/22—22/3/23.**G.**
Dar. 26/11/24—28/2/25.**G.**
Dar. 22/6—27/8/25.**H.**
Dar. 18/8—11/11/27.**G.**
Dar. 27/9—16/10/28.**N/C.**

BOILERS:
  G979.
  D1561 *(new)* ?/7/02.
  G259 *(ex1537)* ?/1/12.
  D947 *(new)* ?/7/19.
  D480 *(ex340)* 22/3/23.

SHED:
Hull Botanic Gardens.

CONDEMNED: 14/11/29.

_____

85

Gateshead 35.87.

To traffic 12/1887.

REPAIRS:
???. ?/?—?/2/03.**G.**
New cylinders fitted.
???. ?/?—?/3/07.**G.**
???. ?/?—?/4/16.**G.**
Superheated boiler fitted.
Dar. 16/1—26/3/24.**G.**
Dar. 2/2—29/4/27.**G.**
Dar. 15/10—10/12/28.**G.**
Dar. 16/7—25/9/30.**G.**

BOILERS:
  G980.
  G259 *(new)* ?/2/03.
  G120 *(ex spare)* ?/3/07.
  D533 *(new)* ?/4/16.
  D361 *(ex42)* 26/3/24.
  D622 *(1546)* 25/9/30.

SHED:
Hull Botanic Gardens.

CONDEMNED: 13/10/32.

_____

96

Gateshead 36.87.

To traffic 12/1887.

REPAIRS:
???. ?/?—?/11/99.**G.**
???. ?/?—?/9/03.**G.**
New cylinders fitted.
???. ?/?—?/5/10.**G.**
???. ?/?—?/8/14.**G.**
Superheated boiler fitted.
Dar. 28/3—20/6/23.**G.**
Dar. 5/12/24—16/3/25.**G.**

BOILERS:
  G971.
  D1552 *(new)* ?/11/99.
  G797 *(ex808)* ?/5/10.
  D354 *(new)* ?/8/14.
  G903 *(ex1540)* 16/3/25.

SHED:
Hull Botanic Gardens.

CONDEMNED: 20/4/27.
After collision at Hull 14/2/27.

_____

154

Gateshead 37.87.

To traffic 12/1887.

REPAIRS:
???. ?/?—?/1/98.**G.**
???. ?/?—?/11/04.**G.**
New cylinders fitted.
???. ?/?—?/10/10.**G.**
???. ?/?—?/3/17.**G.**
Superheated boiler fitted.
Ghd. 20/12/23—31/1/24.**L.**
Ghd. 5/9—4/11/24.**G.**
Ghd. 23/11/26—16/2/27.**G.**

BOILERS:
  G981.
  G792 *(new)* ?/1/98.
  D1552 *(ex96)* ?/10/10.
  D634 *(new)* ?/3/17.
  D518 *(ex808)* 16/2/27.

SHED:
Carlisle.

CONDEMNED: 26/2/30.

_____

340

Gateshead 23.88.

To traffic 12/1888.

REPAIRS:
???. ?/?—?/10/96.**G.**
Rebuilt from compound 2-4-0.
???. ?/?—?/12/02.**G.**
???. ?/?—?/8/15.**G.**
Superheated boiler fitted.
Dar. 19/10/22—10/2/23.**G.**
Dar. 10/4—23/6/24.**G.**
Dar. 22/9—17/12/25.**G.**
Dar. 24/6—28/9/27.**G.**
Dar. 6/5—10/7/29.**G.**
Dar. 24/9—8/10/29.**N/C.**
Dar. 6/5—29/6/31.**G.**

BOILERS:
  G55.
  G260 *(new)* ?/12/02.
  D480 *(new)* ?/8/15.

D740 *(ex803)* 10/2/23.
D1271 *(ex1534)* 28/9/27.
  D605 *(ex1537)* 10/7/29.

SHED:
Hull Botanic Gardens.

CONDEMNED: 9/12/33.

_____

1532

Gateshead 44.90.

To traffic 12/1890.

REPAIRS:
???. ?/?—?/1/02.**G.**
???. ?/?—?/9/05.**G.**
Rebuilt from compound.
???. ?/?—?/6/20.**G.**
Superheated boiler fitted.
Dar. 20/5—25/8/24.**G.**
Dar. 29/9/26—26/1/27.**G.**
Dar. 17/4—14/6/28.**G.**

BOILERS:
G270.
G121 *(new)* ?/1/02.
D961 *(new)* ?/6/20.
D356 *(ex1535)* 25/8/24.
D479 *(ex355)* 14/6/28.

SHEDS:
Selby.
Hull Botanic Gardens 13/5/25.

CONDEMNED: 30/4/30.

_____

1533

Gateshead 45.90.

To traffic 12/1890.

REPAIRS:
???. ?/?—?/7/05.**G.**
Rebuilt from compound.
???. ?/?—?/4/15.**G.**
???. ?/?—?/4/18.**G.**
Superheated boiler fitted.
???. ?/?—?/11/22.**G.**
Dar. 5/11/23—14/1/24.**G.**
Dar. 15/6—20/10/26.**G.**
Dar. 19/3—25/5/28.**G.**
Dar. 29/10—21/12/29.**G.**

BOILERS:
G271.
G357 *(new)* ?/7/05.

_____

WORKS CODES:- Cw - Cowlairs. Dar- Darlington. Don - Doncaster. Ghd - Gateshead. Gor - Gorton. Inv - Inverurie. Nor - Norwich. Spd - Springhead. Str - Stratford.
REPAIR CODES:- **C/H** - Casual Heavy. **C/L** - Casual Light. **G** - General. **H**- Heavy. **H/I** - Heavy Intermediate. **L** - Light. **L/I** - Light Intermediate. **N/C** - Non-Classified.

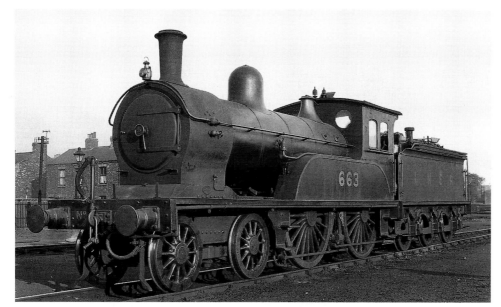

Only one of the class, No.663, was fitted with Group Standard buffers and coupling hook, in March 1929.

(left) On the fastening of smokebox doors there was no pattern which could be identified. The wheel and handle type were as common as the two handle type. Scarborough.

(below) In fact it was possible to see both types used by the same engine, No.777 having changed to two handles for its last years in service. Darlington, June 1935.

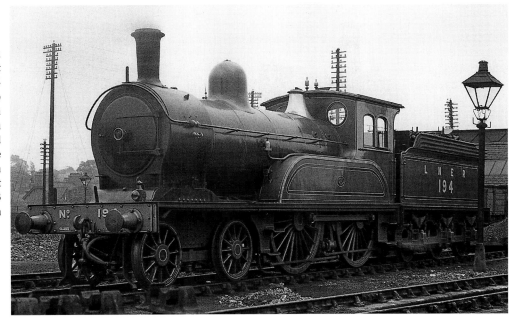

In February 1925 Darlington added two footsteps to the front plate of the smokebox on Nos.194 and 514 to aid access to the top lamp iron. At least another seven got steps but some Darlington maintained engines never had them fitted. No.1542 (*see* page 111) was shopped at Darlington in February 1931 and still did not have them fitted, whereas No.663 (*see* page 105, centre) had them put on in November 1930.

(above) The five engines which were maintained by Gateshead, Nos.18, 154, 355, 808 and 1324, never had these steps fitted.

Raven fog signalling apparatus was fitted and the striker can be seen between the bogie and leading coupled wheel. All except No.1537 would retain it to withdrawal, that one being ex works on 22nd November 1933 the last of the class to be repaired.

1533 cont/.
G125 *(ex1545)* ?/4/15.
D749 *(new)* ?/4/18.
D750 *(ex1534)* ?/11/22.
D525 *(ex1545)* 21/12/29.

SHED:
Starbeck.

CONDEMNED: 5/9/31.

————————————

1534

Gateshead 46.90.

To traffic 12/1890.

REPAIRS:
???. ?/?—?/6/03.**G.**
???. ?/?—?/12/04.**G.**
Rebuilt from compound.
???. ?/?—?/4/18.**G.**
Superheated boiler fitted.
???. ?/?—?/12/21.**G.**
Dar. 27/2—12/5/23.**G.**
Dar. 22/5—18/8/24.**G.**
Dar. 28/2—23/5/27.**G.**
Dar. 11/6—13/7/28.**H.**

BOILERS:
 G272.
 G261 *(new)* ?/6/03.
 D750 *(new)* ?/4/18.
 D1271 *(new)* ?/12/21.
 D533 *(ex1535)* 23/5/27.

SHEDS:
Hull Botanic Gardens.
Selby 12/3/25.

CONDEMNED: 10/10/29.

————————————

1535

Gateshead 47.90.

To traffic 12/1890.

REPAIRS:
???. ?/?—?/1/00.**G.**
???. ?/?—?/2/05.**G.**
Rebuilt from compound.
???. ?/?—?/2/12.**G.**
???. ?/?—?/9/14.**G.**
Superheated boiler fitted.
Dar. 3/3—12/6/24.**G.**
Dar. 25/1—30/4/26.**G.**
Dar. 2/7—31/8/28.**G.**
Lined Black.
Dar. 21/4—23/6/31.**G.**

BOILERS:
G273.
D1554 *(new)* ?/1/00.
D1561 *(ex1137)* ?/2/12.
 D356 *(new)* ?/9/14.
 D533 *(ex85)* 12/6/24.
 D947 *(ex1539)* 30/4/26.

SHED:
Selby.

CONDEMNED: 27/7/33.

————————————

1536

Gateshead 48.90.

To traffic 12/1890.

REPAIRS:
???. ?/?—?/3/01.**G.**
???. ?/?—?/11/04.**G.**
Rebuilt from compound.
???. ?/?—?/1/14.**G.**
Superheated boiler fitted.
Dar. 21/2—13/5/24.**G.**
Dar. 4/9—27/11/25.**G.**
Dar. 31/8—18/11/27.**G.**
Dar. 14/3—6/5/29.**G.**
Dar. 28/7—12/9/30.**H.**

BOILERS:
 G274.
D1558 *(new)* ?/3/01.
 G577 *(ex42)* ?/1/14.
 D512 *(ex1544)* 27/11/25.
 D961 *(ex779)* 12/9/30.

SHEDS:
Bridlington.
Hull Botanic Gardens ?/?/25.

CONDEMNED: 4/9/31.

————————————

1537

Gateshead 49.90.

To traffic 12/1890.

REPAIRS:
???. ?/?—?/1/05.**G.**
Rebuilt from compound.
???. ?/?—?/5/08.**G.**
???. ?/?—?/11/11.**G.**
???. ?/?—?/4/16.**G.**
Superheated boiler fitted.
Ghd. 28/12/23—14/3/24.**G.**
Dar. 10/3—27/7/26.**G.**
Dar. 27/12/28—19/2/29.**G.**
Dar. 24/3—30/4/31.**G.**
Dar. 3/10—22/11/33.**G.**
Dar. 14/11/35. *Not repaired.*

BOILERS:
G275.
 G259 *(ex85)* ?/5/08.
D1555 *(ex803)* ?/11/11.
 D531 *(new)* ?/4/16.
 D605 *(ex18)* 14/3/24.
 D498 *(ex194)* 19/2/29.
D1270 *(ex230)* 30/4/31.

SHEDS:
Selby.
Scarborough 14/5/25.
Selby 6/7/25.

CONDEMNED: 15/11/35.

————————————

1538

Gateshead 50.90.

To traffic 12/1890.

REPAIRS:
???. ?/?—?/5/01.**G.**
Rebuilt from compound.
???. ?/?—?/3/11.**G.**
???. ?/?—?/6/18.**G.**
Superheated boiler fitted.
Dar. 13/11/22—10/1/23.**G.**
Dar. 8/9—11/12/25.**G.**
Dar. 6/3—5/5/28.**G.**
Dar. 25/3—18/5/31.**G.**

BOILERS:
G276.
D1557 *(new)* ?/5/01.
D1553 *(ex spare)* ?/3/11.
 D743 *(new)* ?/6/18.
 D741 *(ex230)* 10/1/23.

SHEDS:
Hull Springhead.
Scarborough ?/?/24.

CONDEMNED: 23/6/33.

————————————

1539

Gateshead 51.90.

To traffic 12/1890.

REPAIRS:
???. ?/?—?/3/04.**G.**
Rebuilt from compound.
???. ?/?—?/12/09.**G.**
???. ?/?—?/12/13.**G.**
Superheated boiler fitted.
Dar. 21/12/23—28/2/24.**G.**
Dar. 18/9—30/12/25.**G.**
Dar. 17—25/11/27.**L.**
Dar. 9/8—8/10/28.**G.**

BOILERS:
G277.
 G262 *(new)* ?/3/04.
 G786 *(ex42 & spare)* ?/12/09.
 G905 *(new)* ?/12/13.
 D947 *(ex1137)* 28/2/24.
 D293 *(ex514)* 30/12/25.

SHEDS:
Bridlington.
Hull Botanic Gardens ?/?/25.

CONDEMNED: 10/2/30.

————————————

1540

Gateshead 52.90.

To traffic 12/1890.

REPAIRS:
???. ?/?—?/2/02.**G.**
???. ?/?—?/7/05.**G.**
Rebuilt from compound.
???. ?/?—?/7/18.**G.**
Superheated boiler fitted.
Dar. 2/11/22—15/3/23.**G.**
Dar. 3/10—16/12/24.**G.**
Dar. 22/12/25—31/3/26.**G.**
Dar. 27/5—15/6/26.**L.**
Dar. 30/1—30/4/28.**G.**

BOILERS:
G278.
G122 *(new)* ?/2/02.
G903 *(ex230)* ?/7/18.
G905 *(ex1539)* 16/12/24.

SHEDS:
Hull Botanic Gardens.
Cambridge 6/1/27.
Hull Botanic Gardens 28/3/27.

CONDEMNED: 16/10/29.

————————————

1541

Gateshead 53.90.

To traffic 12/1890.

REPAIRS:
???. ?/?—?/6/01.**G.**
???. ?/?—?/5/05.**G.**
Rebuilt from compound.
???. ?/?—?/5/11.**G.**
???. ?/?—?/2/20.**G.**
Superheated boiler fitted.
Dar. 18/2—30/4/24.**G.**
Dar. 11/12/25—12/3/26.**G.**
Dar. 16/3—25/5/28.**G.**
Dar. 27/1—28/3/30.**G.**
Dar. 10/5—21/6/32.**G.**

(right) **The usual whistles were two bell-shape types, fitted above the cab roof, the larger one on the driver's side.**

(below) **On No.42 the whistle positions were reversed but this seems to have been an isolated example.**

(above) **No.1542 was another one with a difference because its larger bell shape had been changed to an organ pipe. Har-**

The Worsdell chimney on this class did not usually have a windjabber.

One five, Nos.18, 154, 355, 1324 and 1538 had a chimney with a windjabber. The three Carlisle shedded engines, and No.18 were all maintained by Gateshead, but in its LNER days No.1538 went to Darlington for repairs. Note original style of parallel case buffers still fitted. Carlisle London Road.

The normal buffers were the later type with taper shank. Note the driving wheels have springs of laminated type which were used on the twenty-two built in 1886-1888.

1541 cont/.
Dar. 3—24/2/33.**H.**

BOILERS:
G279.
D1559 *(new)* ?/6/01.
 G131 *(ex230)* ?/5/11.
 D960 *(new)* ?/2/20.

SHEDS:
Scarborough.
Starbeck 9/10/25.

CONDEMNED: 18/9/34.
Into Dar. 21/9/34 for cut up.

———————————————

1542

Gateshead 54.90.

To traffic 12/1890.

REPAIRS:
???. ?/?—?/1/02.**G.**
???. ?/?—?/6/05.**G.**
Rebuilt from compound.
???. ?/?—?/5/13.**G.**
???. ?/?—?/4/20.**G.**
Superheated boiler fitted.
Dar. 11/10/22—17/1/23.**G.**
Dar. 26/1—6/2/23.**N/C.**
Dar. 11/3—26/6/25.**G.**
Dar. 26/1—31/3/28.**G.**
Dar. 6/1—19/2/31.**G.**

BOILERS:
G300.
G123 *(new)* ?/1/02.
G262 *(ex808)* ?/5/13.
G901 *(ex663)* ?/4/20.
D740 *(ex340)* 31/3/28.

SHEDS:
Scarborough.
Stockton 22/2/30.

CONDEMNED: 14/7/33.

1543

Gateshead 55.90.

To traffic 12/1890.

REPAIRS:
???. ?/?—?/9/04.**G.**
???. ?/?—?/10/05.**G.**
Rebuilt from compound.
???. ?/?—?/1/17.**G.**
Superheated boiler fitted.
Dar. 12/10/23—9/1/24.**G.**
Dar. 14/3—9/7/25.**G.**
Dar. 26/4—30/7/27.**G.**
Dar. 1/11/28—4/1/29.**G.**
Dar. 25/7—29/9/30.**G.**

BOILERS:
G301.
G263 *(new)* ?/9/04.
D630 *(new)* ?/1/17.

SHED:
Hull Botanic Gardens.

CONDEMNED: 24/8/32.

———————————————

1544

Gateshead 56.90.

To traffic 12/1890.

REPAIRS:
???. ?/?—?/9/01.**G.**
???. ?/?—?/3/05.**G.**
Rebuilt from compound.
???. ?/?—?/2/16.**G.**
Superheated boiler fitted.
Dar. 21/11/22—15/3/23.**G.**
Dar. 4/5—11/8/25.**G.**
Dar. 14/6—16/8/28.**G.**

BOILERS:
G302.
D1560 *(new)* ?/9/01.

D512 *(new)* ?/2/16.
D354 *(ex96)* 11/8/25.

SHEDS:
Selby.
Ipswich 24/12/26.
Norwich 25/3/27.
Selby 2/4/27.

CONDEMNED: 7/8/29.

———————————————

1545

Gateshead 57.90.

To traffic 4/1891.

REPAIRS:
???. ?/?—?/4/02.**G.**
???. ?/?—?/11/05.**G.**
Rebuilt from compound.
???. ?/?—?/3/14.**G.**
???. ?/?—?/3/16.**G.**
Superheated boiler fitted.
Dar. 9/11/22—23/2/23.**G.**
Dar. 30/12/24—15/4/25.**G.**
Dar. 16/4—1/6/26.**L.**
Dar. 4/8—31/10/27.**G.**
Dar. 23/11—8/12/27.**L.**
Dar. 27/11/28—15/1/29.**L.**
Dar. 20/9—22/11/29.**G.**

BOILERS:
G303.
G125 *(new)* ?/4/02.
D1558 *(ex1536)* ?/3/14.
D525 *(new)* ?/3/16.
D1271 *(ex340)* 22/11/29.

SHED:
Starbeck.

CONDEMNED: 8/12/31.

———————————————

1546

Gateshead 58.90.

To traffic 4/1891.

REPAIRS:
???. ?/?—?/4/01.**G.**
Rebuilt from compound.
???. ?/?—?/2/10.**G.**
???. ?/?—?/12/16.**G.**
Superheated boiler fitted.
Ghd. 3/3—17/5/24.**G.**
Ghd. 7/2—1/6/27.**G.**
Dar. 4/2—8/4/30.**G.**
Dar. 29/5—11/6/30.**N/C.**
Dar. 5/5—16/6/32.**G.**
Dar. 15/1/35. *Not repaired.*

BOILERS:
 G304.
D1556 *(new)* ?/4/01.
 G580 *(new)* ?/2/10.
 D622 *(new)* ?/12/16.
 D743 *(ex777)* 8/4/30.

SHEDS:
Gateshead.
Tweedmouth 19/3/28.
Hull Botanic Gardens 20/3/29.

CONDEMNED: 24/1/35.

———————————————

(below) **The fifteen engines built in 1890/1891, Nos.1532 to 1546, had Helical springs and later Nos.85, 154 and 194 changed to that type.**

Tenders were all standard 5 tons and 3038 gallons capacity and originally had just two coal rails. At least eight - those attached to Nos.335, 356, 514, 663, 779, 1324, 1538 and 1546 remained that way except for plating behind.

The tenders with at least twenty-two engines, Nos. 18, 42, 85, 96, 115, 154, 194, 230, 340, 673, 684, 777, 808, 1533, 1535, 1536, 1537, 1539, 1541, 1542, 1543 and 1545, had a third rail added and also a fourth just round the coal space.

From building all the class were fitted with Westinghouse brake for engine and for train working, and most had the front connection below the buffer mean. Except for five, Nos.42, 115, 356, 1540, 1543 they were also recorded as having a carriage heating connection at the front end.

(above) **The last fifteen were also fitted with vacuum ejector for train brakes and four of the earlier engines had this added. Nos.1324 and 340 got it in October 1896 and Nos.777 and 808 in June 1899. Castle Howard.**

(right) **By early LNER days, eight at least, Nos.18, 154, 355, 514, 779, 1324, 1538, 1541 had all been fitted with a short standpipe for the Westinghouse brake, the front end vacuum connection remaining below the buffer beam.**

After the Unification of Brakes Programme began in June 1928, nine of the eighteen Westinghouse only engines had a vacuum ejector added. Between October 1928 and August 1929 these were Nos.115 (July 1929), 779 (May 1929), 663 (March 1929), 356 (March 1929), 230 (October 1928), 673 (July 1929), 1137 (October 1928), 85 (December 1928) and 194 (December 1928). The other nine were withdrawn still as Westinghouse only. From 1928 a tall swan-neck vacuum standpipe was put on at the front end. Doncaster shed.

At Grouping all had North Eastern fully lined green passenger livery. Benton Quarry.

Ex Darlington on 10th February 1923, No.340 engine retained NER style including large brass number plates, but the tender had N.E.R. and the engine number.

(below) Only two, No. 777 out on 11th May 1923 and No. 1534 out on 12th May 1923 got L. & N.E.R. but there were two in June 1923 with L&NER sans full points, Nos. 96 (20th) and 230 (28th). The ampersand was then discarded, and before the area suffix D was introduced, two got just LNER above the number in 1923 - Nos.42 (17th July) and 663 (6th August).

During the five months use of the suffix, two acquired it. Nos.1543 (9th January 1924) and 1533 (14th January 1924). The latter did not go to works again until June 1926 and here seems to have had the suffix obliterated leaving the number off-centre. York.

The remainder went direct to the LNER style, the last being No.18 on 23rd April 1926 because it was ex works from its previous painting just two days before the Grouping. All thirty-seven duly got this style.

(below) **Black became standard from early June 1928 but still with number on the tender, and nine were so treated. Nos. 777 (9th July 1928), 1534 (13th July 1928), 1544 (16th August 1928), 1535 (31st August 1928), 1539 (8th October 1928), 85 (10th December 1928), 194 (17th December 1928), 1543 (4th January 1929) and 1537 (19th February 1929). From March 1929 (No.663) to November 1933 (1537) eighteen had the number moved to the splasher.**

(above) **From January 1913 to March 1916 all the D23's were superheated and had a steam circulating valve for element protection. At Grouping they were in NER green lined livery.**

(left) **The boilers had two hand holes on the left hand side of the firebox for washout purposes.**

On the right hand side the two hand holes were nearer to the cab. A North Eastern designed mechanical lubricator served the cylinders and valves with oil boxes on the front of the splasher for the journals of the coupled wheels.

CLASS D 23

557

Darlington 31.

To traffic 11/1887.

REPAIRS:
???. ?/?—?/12/00.**G.**
Rebuilt from 2-4-0.
???. ?/?—?/2/04.**G.**
???. ?/?—?/1/13.**G.**
Superheated boiler fitted.
Dar. 29/9/22—31/1/23.**G.**
Dar. 15/12/24—27/2/25.**G.**
Dar. 29/12/26—28/3/27.**G.**
Dar. 9/11/28—3/1/29.**G.**

BOILERS:
D572.
D1585 *(new)* ?/12/00.
D1727 *(new)* ?/2/04.
D161 *(new)* ?/1/13.
D307 *(ex274)* 3/1/29.

SHEDS:
Hull Botanic Gardens.
Darlington 9/2/28.

CONDEMNED: 3/1/31.

_____

678

Darlington 32.

To traffic 11/1887.

REPAIRS:
???. ?/?—?/12/99.**G.**
???. ?/?—?/7/02.**G.**
Rebuilt from 2-4-0.
???. ?/?—?/11/07.**G.**
???. ?/?—?/1/12.**G.**
???. ?/?—?/1/14.**G.**
Superheated boiler fitted.
Dar. 22/6—29/8/23.**G.**
Dar. 7/3—25/8/25.**G.**
Dar. 4/4—12/7/27.**G.**
Dar. 14/11—12/12/28.**N/C.**
Dar. 26/4—4/7/29.**G.**
Dar. 24/2—9/4/31.**G.**

BOILERS:
D567.
D1319 *(new)* ?/12/99.
D1320 *(ex222)* ?/11/07.
D1564 *(ex23)* ?/1/12.
D170 *(new)* ?/1/14.
D390 *(exJ24 1825)* 9/4/31.

SHEDS:
Starbeck.
Darlington 8/2/28.
Waskerley 29/7/29.
Kirkby Stephen 11/7/30.

CONDEMNED: 1/12/33.

_____

675

Darlington 33.

To traffic 12/1887.

REPAIRS:
???. ?/?—?/10/98.**G.**
???. ?/?—?/5/04.**G.**
Rebuilt from 2-4-0.
???. ?/?—?/7/09.**G.**
???. ?/?—?/3/14.**G.**
Superheated boiler fitted.
Dar. 31/12/23—5/3/24.**G.**
Dar. 19/11/25—27/2/26.**G.**
Dar. 24/10/27—21/1/28.**G.**
Dar. 17/10—11/11/29.**N/C.**

BOILERS:
D573.
D1314 *(new)* ?/10/98.
D1570 *(new)* ?/7/09.
D191 *(new)* ?/3/14.
D308 *(ex223)* 5/3/24.

SHEDS:
Hull Botanic Gardens.
Barnard Castle ?/2/25.
Darlington ?/?/29.
Barnard Castle 29/1/30.

CONDEMNED: 26/3/30.

_____

676

Darlington 34.

To traffic 12/1887.

REPAIRS:
???. ?/?—?/9/00.**G.**
???. ?/?—?/5/04.**G.**
Rebuilt from 2-4-0.
???. ?/?—?/4/14.**G.**
Superheated boiler fitted.
???. ?/?—?/7/22.**G.**
Dar. 9/1—27/4/23.**G.**
Dar. 21/6—2/10/24.**G.**
Dar. 27—31/7/25.**L.**
Dar. 5/8—29/9/25.**G.**

Dar. 6/7—4/8/26.**L.**
Dar. 16/2—23/4/28.**G.**

BOILERS:
D574.
D1321 *(new)* ?/9/00.
D302 *(new)* ?/4/14.
D301 *(ex217 & spare)* ?/7/22.
D761 *(exJ22 571)* 29/9/25.

SHEDS:
Hull Botanic Gardens.
Barnard Castle ?/2/25.

CONDEMNED: 27/1/30.

_____

677

Darlington 35.

To traffic 12/1887.

REPAIRS:
???. ?/?—?/5/02.**G.**
Rebuilt from 2-4-0.
???. ?/?—?/11/13.**G.**
Superheated boiler fitted.
???. ?/?—?/8/16.**G.**
Dar. 27/3—17/5/23.**G.**
Dar. 7/11/24—30/1/25.**G.**
Dar. 7/2—25/6/27.**G.**
Dar. 24/1—19/3/29.**G.**
Dar. 14/7—26/9/30.**G.**
Dar. 31/3—17/4/31.**L.**

BOILERS:
D575.
G174 *(new)* ?/5/02.
D165 *(new)* ?/11/13.
D177 *(ex372)* ?/8/16.
D174 *(ex472)* 17/5/23.
D191 *(ex222)* 25/6/27.
D174 *(ex1120)* 26/9/30.

SHEDS:
Hull Botanic Gardens.
Kirkby Stephen 3/1/29.

CONDEMNED: 1/12/33.

_____

679

Darlington 36.

To traffic 12/1887.

REPAIRS:
???. ?/?—?/9/98.**G.**

???. ?/?—?/5/03.**G.**
Rebuilt from 2-4-0.
???. ?/?—?/6/07.**G.**
???. ?/?—?/7/13.**G.**
Superheated boiler fitted.
Dar. 13/11/22—10/3/23.**G.**
Dar. 19/6—17/9/24.**G.**
Dar. 27—31/7/25.**L.**
Dar. 2/3—22/4/26.**H.**
Dar. 5/10/26—15/3/27.**H.**
Dar. 6/11—20/12/28.**G.**

BOILERS:
D576.
D1313 *(new)* ?/9/98.
D1312 *(ex1120)* ?/6/07.
D163 *(new)* ?/7/13.
D302 *(ex222)* 17/9/24.
D301 *(ex676)* 22/4/26.

SHEDS:
Hull Botanic Gardens.
Darlington 19/6/24.

CONDEMNED: 3/1/31.

_____

274

Darlington 37.

To traffic 12/1887.

REPAIRS:
???. ?/?—?/1/99.**G.**
???. ?/?—?/7/04.**G.**
Rebuilt from 2-4-0.
???. ?/?—?/10/06.**G.**
???. ?/?—?/3/16.**G.**
Superheated boiler fitted.
Dar. 3/9—9/11/23.**G.**
Dar. 25/11/25—22/2/26.**G.**
Dar. 11/5—28/6/28.**G.**
Dar. 25/3—8/5/29.**H.**
After collision.

BOILERS:
D570.
D1316 *(new)* ?/1/99.
D1562 *(ex472 & spare)* ?/10/06.
D311 *(new)* ?/3/16.
D307 *(ex214)* 9/11/23.
D309 *(ex521)* 28/6/28.

SHEDS:
Starbeck.
Darlington 8/2/28.
Barnard Castle 20/3/30.
Darlington 18/12/30.

(above) **No.337 was the only one to have a windjabber fitted. Note it has a circulating valve, none acquiring a Gresley anti-vacuum valve. Most were fitted with Raven fog signalling apparatus; the striker can be seen just behind the rear bogie wheel. Worsdell chimney without windjabber was the standard fitting and all carried Ramsbottom safety valves throughout. Darlington shed.**

(left) **Around the time of superheating, seven engines, Nos.214, 222, 337, 472, 521, 679 and 1120 were fitted with new frames. These were Raven pattern with a level top edge and a convex curve at the front end.**

The others had frames which were deeper only in the area adjacent to the smokebox. Barnard Castle.

Superheating required a longer smokebox and a corresponding extension piece was welded to the front end of the frames.

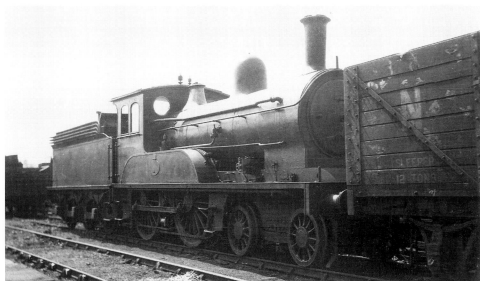

(right) The normal whistle gear was two bell shaped above the cab roof, the larger being on the right hand side - the driver's side. Darlington.

(below) Three were observed with the driver's whistle changed to an organ pipe, Nos.217, 223 and 676. Normal buffers were taper shank type, but some had a collar on them (*see* opposite, bottom). Darlington.

274 cont/.

CONDEMNED: 22/12/30.

23

Darlington 38.

To traffic 12/1887.

REPAIRS:
???. ?/?—?/4/01.**G.**
Rebuilt from 2-4-0.
???. ?/?—?/2/04.**G.**
???. ?/?—?/10/11.**G.**
???. ?/?—?/2/13.**G.**
Superheated boiler fitted.
???. ?/?—?/4/17.**G.**
Dar. 6/10/23—7/1/24.**G.**
Ghd. 5/10/25—6/1/26.**G.**
Ghd. 28/9/27—9/1/28.**G.**
Ghd. 25/7—16/8/28.**L.**

BOILERS:
 D568.
D1600 *(new)* ?/4/01.
D1564 *(new)* ?/2/04.
D1701 *(ex901 2-4-0 905)* ?/10/11.
 D169 *(new)*?/2/13.
 D165 *(ex677)* ?/4/17.

SHEDS:
Hull Botanic Gardens.
Tweedmouth 2/2/25.
Waskerley ?/3/26.

CONDEMNED: 7/8/29.

258

Darlington 39.

To traffic 4/1888.

REPAIRS:
???. ?/?—?/3/02.**G.**
Rebuilt from 2-4-0.
???. ?/?—?/5/07.**G.**
???. ?/?—?/5/14.**G.**
Superheated boiler fitted.
Dar. 12/12/22—12/4/23.**G.**
Dar. 10/12/24—20/4/25.**G.**
Ghd. 30/3—2/6/27.**G.**
Ghd. 6/3—10/5/29.**G.**

BOILERS:
 D569.
D1694 *(new)* ?/3/02.
D1317 *(ex337)* ?/5/07.
 D304 *(new)* ?/5/14.

SHEDS:
Hull Botanic Gardens.
Duns 16/5(4?)/25.
Tweedmouth ?/3/26.
Starbeck 15/5/29.

CONDEMNED: 27/11/31.

328

Darlington 40.

To traffic 4/1888.

REPAIRS:
???. ?/?—?/6/99.**G.**
???. ?/?—?/8/04.**G.**
Rebuilt from 2-4-0.
???. ?/?—?/8/06.**G.**
???. ?/?—?/6/14.**G.**
Superheated boiler fitted.
Dar. 7/5—19/7/24.**G.**
Dar. 6/10/26—25/4/27.**G.**
Dar. 13/5—20/7/29.**G.**
Dar. 9/8—11/9/29.**N/C.**

BOILERS:
 D571.
D1318 *(new)* ?/6/99.
D1315 *(ex214 & spare)* ?/8/06.
 D303 *(new)* ?/6/14.

SHED:
Bradford (Manningham).

CONDEMNED: 26/10/31.

222

Darlington 51.

To traffic 6/1888.

REPAIRS:
???. ?/?—?/4/00.**G.**
???. ?/?—?/8/01.**G.**
Rebuilt from 2-4-0.
???. ?/?—?/3/07.**G.**
???. ?/?—?/7/12.**G.**
???. ?/?—?/9/14.**G.**
Superheated boiler fitted.
???. ?/?—?/11/22.**G.**
Dar. 24/5—13/8/24.**G.**
Dar. 16/12/26—9/3/27.**G.**
Dar. 12/12/28—8/2/29.**G.**

BOILERS:
 D625.
D1320 *(new)* ?/4/00.

D1316 *(ex274)* ?/3/07.
D105 *(new)* ?/7/12.
D305 *(new)* ?/9/14.
D302 *(ex676)* ?/11/22.
D191 *(ex675)* 13/8/24.
D302 *(ex679)* 9/3/27.

SHEDS:
Hull Botanic Gardens.
Barnard Castle 23/2/25.

CONDEMNED: 16/12/30.

223

Darlington 52.

To traffic 6/1888.

REPAIRS:
???. ?/?—?/6/01.**G.**
Rebuilt from 2-4-0.
???. ?/?—?/9/14.**G.**
Superheated boiler fitted.
Dar. 10/10—21/12/23.**G.**
Ghd. 31/12/25—1/4/26.**G.**
Ghd. 14/12/28—22/2/29.**G.**
Dar. 15/5—5/6/29.**N/C.**
Dar. 17/2—27/3/31.**G.**

BOILERS:
 D626.
D1682 *(new)* ?/6/01.
D308 *(new)* ?/9/14.
D311 *(ex274)* 21/12/23.
D317 *(ex521)* 27/3/31.

SHEDS:
Hull Botanic Gardens.
Duns 2/2/25.
Tweedmouth ?/3/26.
Duns 8/12/27.
Kirkby Stephen 22/2/29.
Darlington 8/4/29.
Barnard Castle 18/12/30.

CONDEMNED: 20/4/33.

337

Darlington 53.

To traffic 6/1888.

REPAIRS:
???. ?/?—?/2/99.**G.**
???. ?/?—?/8/04.**G.**
Rebuilt from 2-4-0.
???. ?/?—?/11/06.**G.**

???. ?/?—?/2/14.**G.**
Superheated boiler fitted.
Dar. 14/8—24/10/24.**G.**
Dar. 12/1—31/3/27.**G.**
Dar. 14/11—10/12/28.**N/C.**
Dar. 16/1—26/3/29.**G.**
Dar. 13—17/5/29.**N/C.**
Dar. 28/1—19/3/31.**G.**
Dar. 18/3—25/4/32.**L.**

BOILERS:
 D627.
D1317 *(new)* ?/2/99.
D1569 *(new)* ?/11/06.
D173 *(new)* ?/2/14.
D163 *(ex679)* 24/10/24.
D191 *(ex677)* 19/3/31.

SHEDS:
Hull Botanic Gardens.
Darlington ?/2/25
Barnard Castle 15/6/31.

CONDEMNED: 16/8/33.

521

Darlington 54.

To traffic 6/1888.

REPAIRS:
???. ?/?—?/2/01.**G.**
Rebuilt from 2-4-0.
???. ?/?—?/7/05.**G.**
???. ?/?—?/11/14.**G.**
Superheated boiler fitted.
Dar. 11/6/22—16/2/23.**G.**
Dar. 20/2—30/6/25.**G.**
Dar. 26/3—31/5/28.**G.**
Dar. 22/8—16/9/29.**N/C.**

BOILERS:
 D628.
D1596 *(new)* ?/2/01.
D1563 *(ex372)* ?/7/05.
D309 *(new)* ?/11/14.
 D317 *(ex1120)* 31/5/28.

SHEDS:
Hull Botanic Gardens.
Darlington 28/5/27.

CONDEMNED: 16/12/30.

WORKS CODES:- Cw - Cowlairs. Dar- Darlington. Don - Doncaster. Ghd - Gateshead. Gor - Gorton. Inv - Inverurie. Nor - Norwich. Spd - Springhead. Str - Stratford.
REPAIR CODES:- **C/H** - Casual Heavy. **C/L** - Casual Light. **G** - General. **H**- Heavy. **H/I** - Heavy Intermediate. **L** - Light. **L/I** - Light Intermediate. **N/C** - Non-Classified.

In February 1929 No.223 left the Berwickshire lines where it had worked for four years to run in the Darlington district. In May 1929 it was called into works specially to be fitted with Raven fog signalling apparatus. It was fitted in March 1931 with Group Standard buffers and coupling hook. Croft Spa.

The only other to get Group Standard buffers and hook was No.258, fitted in May 1929. For smokebox door fastening this one retained the wheel and handle, Nos.23, 223 and 677 being fitted similarly.

By Grouping, most had been changed to two handles for fastening the smokebox door. Note the taper shank buffers with a collar on them.

When rebuilt to 4-4-0 type, the tender water capacity was increased from 2651 to 3038 gallons by the addition of a well tank. By 1917 the original two coal rails had been augmented by a third with a fourth around the coal space and all twenty tenders were so altered. Note the standpipes for both brake types. Newcastle, 1929.

Until October 1928 all the D23's had only Westinghouse brake for engine and for train working with the front end connection below the buffer beam.

1120

Darlington 55.

To traffic 6/1888.

REPAIRS:
???. ?/?—?/4/97.**G.**
???. ?/?—?/12/02.**G.**
Rebuilt from 2-4-0.
???. ?/?—?/1/07.**G.**
???. ?/?—?/10/15.**G.**
Superheated boiler fitted.
Dar. 6/12/22—26/3/23.**G.**
Dar. 15/1—20/4/25.**G.**
Dar. 4/7—12/10/27.**G.**
Dar. 12/8—17/10/29.**G.**
Dar. 17/12/29—14/1/30.**L.**
Dar. 26/4—13/6/32.**G.**
Dar. 28/7—12/10/33.**G.**
Dar. 14/5/35. *Not repaired.*

BOILERS:
D629.
D1312 *(new)* ?/4/97.
D1318 *(ex328)* ?/1/07.
D317 *(new)* ?/10/15.
D174 *(ex677)* 12/10/27.
D550 *(exJ24 1846)* 17/10/29.

SHEDS:
Starbeck.
Hull Botanic Gardens 20/10/25.
Starbeck 11/1/29.
Bradford (Manningham) 18/12/33.

CONDEMNED: 18/5/35.

214

Darlington 56.

To traffic 10/1888.

REPAIRS:
???. ?/?—?/1/99.**G.**
???. ?/?—?/5/03.**G.**
Rebuilt from 2-4-0.
???. ?/?—?/4/05.**G.**
???. ?/?—?/8/09.**G.**
???. ?/?—?/9/14.**G.**
Superheated boiler fitted.

Although withdrawn in November 1930, No.472 had been provided with lifting holes in the front end of its frames. These were not normally put in prior to 1932. No.1120 and 337 were the only other D23's noted with them, the latter acquiring them on 25th April 1932.

Dar. 4/6—29/8/23.**G.**
Dar. 2/3—30/6/27.**G.**

BOILERS:
D680.
D1315 *(new)* ?/1/99.
D1237 *(ex'13' 0-6-0 554)* ?/4/05.
D1686 *(ex217 & spare)* ?/8/09.
D307 *(new)* ?/9/14.
D177 *(ex677)* 29/8/23.

SHEDS:
Malton.
Hull Botanic Gardens 3/4/25.
Malton 18/5/25.

CONDEMNED: 22/5/30.

217

Darlington 57.

To traffic 10/1888.

REPAIRS:
???. ?/?—?/9/01.**G.**
Rebuilt from 2-4-0.
???. ?/?—?/10/07.**G.**
???. ?/?—?/4/14.**G.**
Superheated boiler fitted.
???. ?/?—?/4/20.**G.**
Dar. 7/12/22—29/3/23.**G.**
Dar. 7/2—26/5/25.**G.**
Dar. 21/5—9/8/27.**G.**
Dar. 19/4—21/6/29.**G.**

BOILERS:
D631.
D1686 *(new)* ?/9/01.
D1694 *(ex258)* ?/10/07.
D301 *(new)* ?/4/14.
D169 *(ex23 & spare)* ?/4/20.

SHEDS:
Scarborough.
Malton ?/?/24.
York ?/?/24.
Middleton in Teesdale 14/5/25.
Barnard Castle 18/12/30.
Middleton in Teesdale 15/6/31.

CONDEMNED: 8/8/31.

372

Darlington 58.

To traffic 10/1888.

REPAIRS:
???. ?/?—?/8/01.**G.**
???. ?/?—?/6/03.**G.**
Rebuilt from 2-4-0.
???. ?/?—?/4/05.**G.**
???. ?/?—?/4/13.**G.**
Superheated boiler fitted.
???. ?/?—?/3/16.**G.**
Dar. 8/10—30/12/24.**G.**
Dar. 1/9—26/11/26.**G.**
Dar. 9/7—14/9/28.**G.**
Dar. 14/2—14/3/29.**N/C.**

BOILERS:
D632.
D1563 *(new)* ?/8/01.
D1568 *(new)* ?/4/05.
D177 *(new)* ?/4/13.
D1569 *(ex337 & spare)* ?/3/16.
D166 *(ex1107)* 30/12/24.

SHED:
Darlington.

CONDEMNED: 22/12/30.

472

Darlington 59.

To traffic 11/1888.

REPAIRS:
???. ?/?—?/12/00.**G.**
???. ?/?—?/6/03.G.
Rebuilt from 2-4-0.
???. ?/?—?/3/05.**G.**
???. ?/?—?/9/13.**G.**
Superheated boiler fitted.
Dar. 3/2—24/3/23.**G.**
Dar. 20/11/25—23/2/26.**G.**

Dar. 13/6—16/8/28.**G.**
Dar. 3—23/5/29.**N/C.**
Dar. 13/11—9/12/29.**L.**

BOILERS:
D633.
D1562 *(new)* ?/12/00.
D1567 *(new)* ?/3/05.
D174 *(new)* ?/9/13.
D305 *(ex222)* 24/3/23.

SHEDS:
Scarborough.
Neville Hill ?/?/24.
Darlington ?/?/28.

CONDEMNED: 25/11/30.

1107

Darlington 60.

To traffic 11/1888.

REPAIRS:
???. ?/?—?/12/01.**G.**
Rebuilt from 2-4-0.
???. ?/?—?/2/13.**G.**
Superheated boiler fitted.
Dar. 8/1—1/2/23.**L.**
Dar. 7/7—18/9/23.**G.**
Dar. 22/9—11/12/24.**G.**
Dar. 6/1—30/3/27.**G.**
Dar. 14/8—10/10/28.**G.**

BOILERS:
D634.
D1691 *(new)* ?/12/01.
D166 *(new)* ?/2/13.
D173 *(ex337)* 11/12/24.

SHEDS:
Scarborough.
Hull Botanic Gardens 29/8/24.
Kirkby Stephen 28/12/28.

CONDEMNED: ?/6/30.

125

From October 1928 to November 1929 all except three, Nos.23, 214 and 676 had a vacuum ejector added, and with it a tall swan-neck stand pipe fixed to the front of the buffer beam. There was usually a carriage heating connection at the front end.

Until they lost their North Eastern identity, they had green livery, the last to retain it being No.521 which went to works on 20th February 1925. With coupled wheels only 6ft 1¼in. diameter, D23 class was below the limit for LNER green livery and so went straight to black with single red lining.

Whilst the area suffix was being applied, four D23's got it: Nos.1107D (18th September 1923), 274D (9th November 1923), 223D (21st December 1923) and 23D (7th January 1924).

(above) **In July and August 1923, between dropping the ampersand and the introduction of the suffix, just LNER and the number was used, and on 29th August 1923 Nos.214 and 678 were ex works in that style.**

(right) **From February 1924, LNER and number on the tender was standard until March 1929 and all twenty went into that style.**

(below) **The final livery was with the number centred on the combined splasher and 12in. LNER on the tender, but only nine engines: Nos.217, 223, 258, 274, 328, 337, 677, 678 and 1120 survived to get it. Darlington, May 1933.**

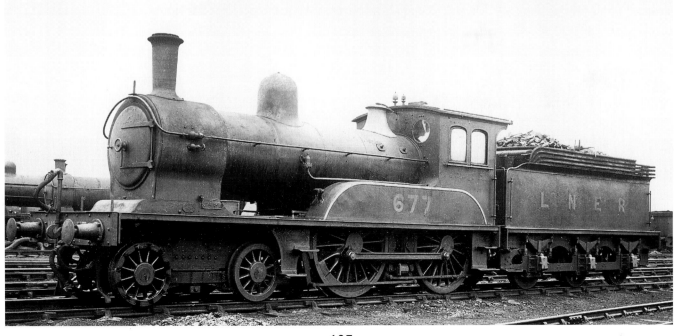

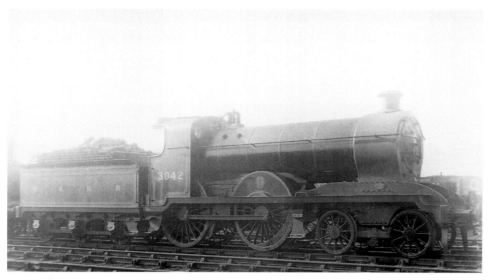

(left) **During 1922 these five engines were renumbered into NER stock by adding three thousand to their H&BR numbers, although still on original livery with one exception. Springhead, June 1923.**

(below) **Ex Springhead works on 9th November 1922, No.3038 was the only one of the five to acquire North Eastern green livery. Although it got the armorial transfers, the number remained on the cab in H&BR size transfers and no cast number plate was fitted. Springhead, June 1923.**

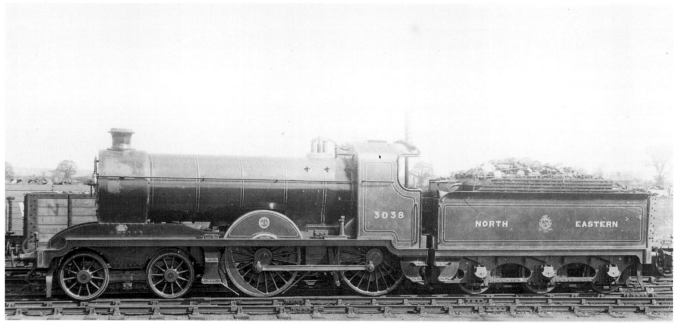

Until 1929 the original domeless boilers were retained. On the right hand side of the firebox were three hand holes for washing out purposes. These boilers had internal exhaust pipe for the vacuum ejector. For a while, the H&BR smokebox door was retained. This was flush fitting and whilst it had two handles for fastening the lower part also had three clips to help resist buckling from hot ash accumulation. Springhead (store).

CLASS D 24

3033/2425

Kitson 4700.

To traffic 12/1910.

REPAIRS:
Spd. ?/?—?/10/23.**G**.
Dar. 8/7—31/10/25.**G**.
Dar. 21/12/26—22/3/27.**G**.
Dar. 5/8—28/9/29.**G**.

BOILERS:
H&B 33.
2101 *(new)* 28/9/29.

SHEDS:
Hull Springhead.
Hull Botanic Gardens 13/7/24.
Selby 17/4/31.

RENUMBERED:
2425 *on* 30/5/24.

CONDEMNED: 14/8/33.

3035/2426

Kitson 4701.

To traffic 12/1910.

REPAIRS:
Spd. ?/?—?/9/23.**G**.
Dar. 24/10/24—30/1/25.**G**.
Dar. 16/12—18/3/27.**G**.
Dar. 28/4—27/5/27.**L**.

Dar. 12/4—3/7/30.**G**.
Dar. 10/8—4/10/33.**G**.

BOILERS:
H&B 35.
2356 *(new)* 3/7/30.

SHEDS:
Hull Springhead.
Hull Botanic Gardens 13/7/24.

RENUMBERED:
2426 *on* 26/5/24.

CONDEMNED: 28/12/33.

3038/2427

Kitson 4702.

To traffic 12/1910.

REPAIRS:
Spd. ?/?—9/11/22.**G**.
Dar. 10/10/24—24/1/25.**G**.
Dar. 9/7—23/11/26.**G**.
Dar. 12/4—7/7/30.**G**.

BOILERS:
H&B 38.
2361 *(new)* 7/7/30.

SHEDS:
Hull Springhead.
Hull Botanic Gardens 13/7/24.
Selby 17/4/31.

RENUMBERED:
2427 *on* 23/4/24.

CONDEMNED: 4/1/34.

3041/2428

Kitson 4703.

To traffic 12/1910.

REPAIRS:
Spd. ?/?—?/3/22.**?**.
Spd. ?/?—31/5/23.**G**.
Dar. 4/8—31/12/24.**G**.
Dar. 19/10/26—15/2/27.**G**.
Dar. 3/11/27—24/1/28.**G**.
Dar. 18/2—15/4/30.**G**.

BOILERS:
H&B 41.
2348 *(new)* 15/4/30.

SHEDS:
Hull Springhead.
Hull Botanic Gardens 13/7/24.

RENUMBERED:
2428 *on* 12/6/24.

CONDEMNED: 12/12/33.

3042/2429

Kitson 4704.

To traffic 12/1910.

REPAIRS:
Spd. ?/?—?/5/22.**?**.
Spd. ?/?—26/4/23.**G**.
Dar. 6/3—29/7/25.**G**.
Dar. 22/12/25—30/4/26.**G**.
Dar. 16/12/26—28/2/27.**L**.
Dar. 9/10—27/11/29.**G**.

BOILERS:
H&B 42.
2226 *(new)* 27/11/29.

SHEDS:
Hull Springhead.
Hull Botanic Gardens 13/7/24.

RENUMBERED:
2429 *on* 11/7/24.

CONDEMNED: 21/9/34.

On the left hand side of the boiler there were also three hand holes but these were set nearer to the cab to give better coverage of the firebox crown when washing out. Note that there was a vacuum brake standpipe until into the middle 1920's when Darlington removed it in line with their own practice at that time.

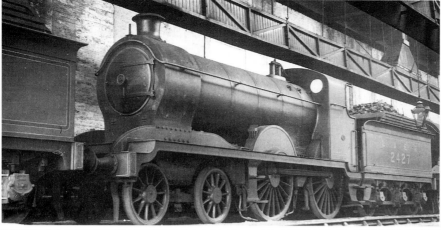

When Springhead works closed in August 1924, the subsequent repairs were done at Darlington. Nos.2425 (31st October 1925) and 2427 (24th January 1925) had their smokebox door changed to the NER type with a wheel and a handle for fastening. The lamp iron was moved from the door and fixed to the top of the front plate of the smokebox. Note that the steam sanding to both sides of driving wheels had superseded the gravity type shown in the photograph on page 128, centre.

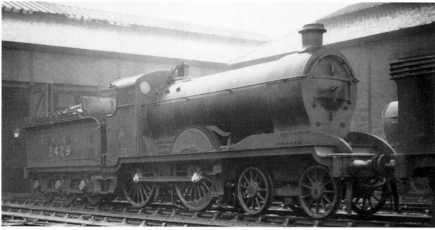

At their first Darlington visit, Nos.2425, 2426 and 2429 were fitted with windjabbers on their H&B chimney. No.2429 retained its flush fitting smokebox door but lost its vacuum brake standpipe and at that July 1925 repair did not have a ventilator fitted on the roof of the cab.

Nos.2427 and 2428 did not have a windjabber put on. At this period, Nos.2426 and 2428 were the only ones fitted with a ventilator on the cab roof; these dated from 1922/1923.

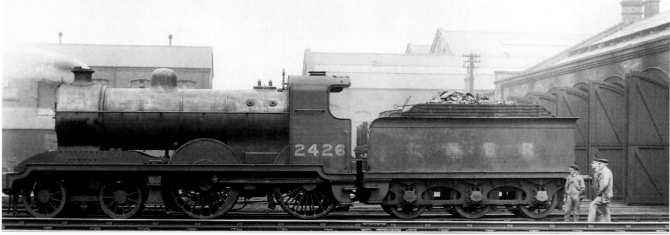

Between September 1929 and July 1930 all five D24's were changed to domed boilers of Darlington design. These boilers had Ross 'pop' safety valves instead of the open Ramsbottom type, and only two hand holes on the left hand side. A slightly shorter chimney of Class C7 pattern was used and all five engines got a windjabber. Springhead.

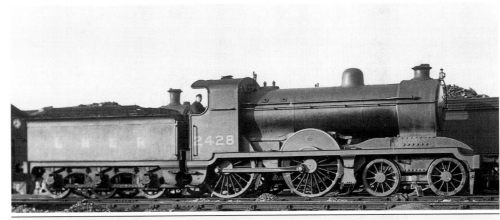

On the right hand side there was still three hand holes on a pitch overlapping those on the opposite side. The vacuum ejector exhaust pipe was now fitted externally.

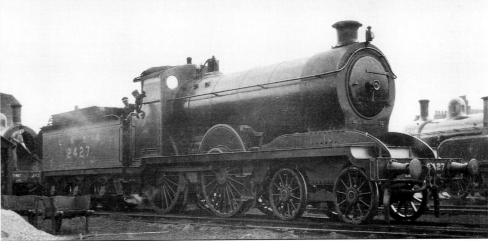

The Hull & Barnsley whistle was a single bell shaped type on the firebox, between the safety valves and the cab front plate.

(below) Darlington changed the whistle type to an organ pipe but not all of these were done at the first Darlington visit, the same mounting continued to be used. Darlington.

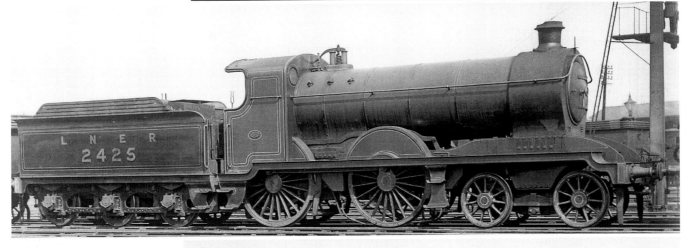

(right) At the reboilering, all the class got NER style twin whistles, organ pipe on the driver's side and bell shape on the fireman's. They were still mounted in front of the cab but were now well above cab roof.

(left) The change to a domed boiler was accompanied by a change to a large diameter smokebox door, and on the front plate of the box a footstep was fitted on each side to give easier access to the lamp iron. Springhead works.

(below) When No.2429 was re-boilered in November 1929, its cab roof had a ventilator fitted but Nos.2425 and 2427 were never so equipped.

(left) The original buffers remained unaltered. They had a circular flange and the taper shank had a substantial collar at the forward end.

(below) The tender had three open coal rails until late H&BR days when a fourth was added but they were only plated behind the rails after they went to Darlington. All five had and kept Iracier axleboxes. Botanic Gardens shed, 6th May 1933.

All the class kept their Hull & Barnsley buffers but two engines were recorded as changing to North Eastern Railway coupling hook - these were Nos.2426 and 2428. Hull (Paragon).

When taken over by the North Eastern, some engines retained their Hull & Barnsley livery and the addition of 3000 to their number was the first change (*see* page 128, top).

The first LNER paintings were done by Springhead works. Green lined livery being applied to No.3041, which was out on 31st May 1923, when L.&N.E.R. was put on.

In September 1923 No.3035 was out of Springhead works in green and whilst they had dropped the ampersand they still put the full points on, resulting in one of the very rare cases of L.N.E.R. On 26th May 1924 the number was changed to 2426 by patching. Springhead, June 1923.

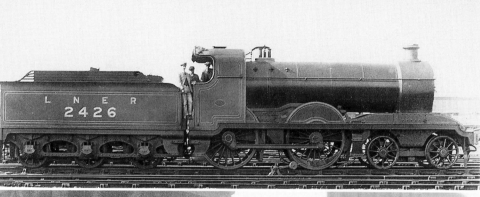

Darlington then took over all the repairs of the class and all five engines got this standard style. No.2428 (31st December 1924), 2427 (24th January 1925), 2426 (30th January 1925), 2429 (29th July 1925) and 2425 (31st October 1925).

Although listed to go into black livery from June 1928, none did so whilst the number was still being put on the tender or indeed whilst they still had a domeless boiler. The number was put on the cab and 12in. LNER on the tender when they were re-boilered. No.2425 (28th September 1929), 2429 (27th November 1929), 2428 (15th April 1930), 2426 (3rd July 1930) and 2427 (7th July 1930). Cudworth shed, October 1931.

This was their final livery as they were withdrawn between 14th August 1933 and 21st September 1934. Note that the last one No.2429 arrived at Darlington, in 1934, still with a wheel on the smokebox door and carrying the re-railing jack.